POLICY & SOCIAL WORK PRACTICE

SAGE was founded in 1965 by Sara Miller McCune to support the dissemination of usable knowledge by publishing innovative and high-quality research and teaching content. Today, we publish more than 850 journals, including those of more than 300 learned societies, more than 800 new books per year, and a growing range of library products including archives, data, case studies, reports, and video. SAGE remains majority-owned by our founder, and after Sara's lifetime will become owned by a charitable trust that secures our continued independence.

Los Angeles | London | New Delhi | Singapore | Washington DC

POLICY & SOCIAL WORK PRACTICE

EDITED BY
TONY EVANS & FRANK KEATING

Los Angeles | London | New Delhi
Singapore | Washington DC

Los Angeles | London | New Delhi
Singapore | Washington DC

SAGE Publications Ltd
1 Oliver's Yard
55 City Road
London EC1Y 1SP

SAGE Publications Inc.
2455 Teller Road
Thousand Oaks, California 91320

SAGE Publications India Pvt Ltd
B 1/I 1 Mohan Cooperative Industrial Area
Mathura Road
New Delhi 110 044

SAGE Publications Asia-Pacific Pte Ltd
3 Church Street
#10-04 Samsung Hub
Singapore 049483

Editor: Kate Wharton
Production editor: Katie Forsythe
Copyeditor: Jane Fricker
Indexer: Linda Haylock
Marketing manager: Camille Richmond
Cover design: Lisa Harper-Wells
Typeset by: C&M Digitals (P) Ltd, Chennai, India
Printed and bound by CPI Group (UK) Ltd,
Croydon, CR0 4YY

Library of Congress Control Number: 2015938783

British Library Cataloguing in Publication data

A catalogue record for this book is available from
the British Library

ISBN 978-1-84860-697-5
ISBN 978-1-84860-698-2 (pbk)

At SAGE we take sustainability seriously. Most of our products are printed in the UK using FSC papers and boards.
When we print overseas we ensure sustainable papers are used as measured by the Egmont grading system.
We undertake an annual audit to monitor our sustainability.

Contents

About the Editors and Contributors

Tony Evans is a registered social worker and has practiced as a forensic mental health social worker. He is Professor of Social Work at the University of London and Head of the Department of Social Work at Royal Holloway, University of London. His research explores the intersection of policy, professional practice and ethics. His published work has focused on the analysis of professional discretion in the context of managerialised public services, moral economies of practice, professional expertise and judgement.

Frank Keating is a Senior Lecturer in Health and Social Care at the Department of Social Work at Royal Holloway, University of London, where he is Director of Research and Graduate studies. His main research interests are ethnicity, gender and mental health, particularly focusing on African and Caribbean communities. He is a strong advocate for racial equality in mental health services through his writing, teaching and public speaking.

Maria Brent is a Senior Lecturer at Kingston University and St George's, University of London, specialising in adult social care. Maria qualified as a social worker in 1996, and has worked in local authority frontline services for 15 years, working with adults and having a specialist interest in learning disabilities and neuro rehab. Maria progressed into a dual role in adults' workforce development, where she had a lead in supporting social workers develop their knowledge and skills in relation to safeguarding adults and personalisation whilst also working part time as a Teaching Fellow at Royal Holloway, University of London. Maria is a qualified Practice Teacher and Best Interest Assessor and is currently in the process of undertaking a Professional Doctorate with her doctoral thesis exploring social workers' experiences of working with adults who self-neglect.

Stefan Brown is a Lecturer in Social Work at Royal Holloway, University of London. He teaches on the MSc course in Social Work, specialising in mental health. His interests and teaching are mental health policy, mental capacity and social policy. Stefan is also a registered social worker and has worked primarily in mental health settings as a forensic mental health social worker, an approved mental health professional and a Best Interests Assessor. Stefan is currently undertaking a PhD exploring mental capacity and marginalised groups.

Donna Chung is Professor of Social Work at Curtin University. Her work in the area of gendered violence has spanned over two decades and includes research, programme evaluation and providing policy advice to governments. Current areas of research include the impact of domestic violence on women's employment, mental health, housing and homelessness, programmes for male perpetrators of domestic violence and preventing sexualised violence against young women from culturally diverse communities.

Anna Gupta is a Senior Lecturer in Social Work at Royal Holloway, University of London. Anna teaches on the qualifying, post-qualifying and doctorate programmes at the Department of Social Work. She is also a registered social worker with extensive experience of working in the family courts. Her research interests include critical social work practice, decision-making in the child protection and family court systems, and children looked after. She is currently involved in an ESRC funded research seminar series on unaccompanied and separated children seeking asylum, and a project working with families who live in poverty and have experience of the child protection system.

Mark Hardy is Lecturer in Social Work at the University of York. He is author (with Tony Evans) of *Evidence and Knowledge for Practice* (Polity Press, 2010) and *Governing Risk: Care and Control in Contemporary Social Work* (Palgrave Macmillan, 2015). He is associate editor of the journal *Qualitative Social Work* and with Ian Shaw (York) and Jeanne Marsh (Chicago) has recently edited the Sage Major Work in *Social Work Research*. Currently, he is editing two collections: *Mental Health Social Work: The Art and Science of Practice* (with Martin Webber, Routledge); and *Social Work: Developing Professional Practice* (with Jonathan Parker, Palgrave). His practice experience entailed work with young and adult offenders and in forensic mental health, and he retains research interests in both of these areas.

Rick Hood is a Senior Lecturer in Social Work at Kingston University and St George's, University of London. He qualified as a social worker in 2007 and has mainly specialised in statutory work with children and families. Before becoming a social worker, Rick was employed in the voluntary sector and ran a youth project in Camberwell, South London. His doctoral research explored complexity and interprofessional working in children's services, and he has also contributed to research into integrated health and social care teams and personalisation in adult services. He is currently working on an evaluation of Caring Dads, a group intervention programme for fathers, and a study of performance measures in child protection services.

Hannah Jobling is a Lecturer in Social Work at the University of York. Until fairly recently, she worked as practitioner in the youth justice field. Since joining academia, she has researched and written on mental health policy and practice, social work with young people, the policy–practice relationship, ethics in everyday practice and critical realism.

Fabian Kessl is Professor of Social Work at the University of Duisburg-Essen. His research interests are in the welfare transformation of social work and social policy. Fabian (and Tony Evans) have recently edited a special issue of the *European Journal of Social Work* on 'Travelling Knowledge in Social Work'.

Alix Walton is a registered social worker with experience in both children and families and adult services. Alix now specialises in social work education and training and has worked in local authority workforce development, and in further and higher education. Alix currently works as a Senior Lecturer on Post-Qualifying Social Work Programmes at Royal Holloway, University of London, and as a freelance trainer and consultant.

Introduction: Policy and Social Work

Tony Evans

Introduction

An underlying theme of this book is a sense that the relationship between social policy and social work does not appear 'out of the blue' – it has a history, and this history has a continuing relationship with the way policy concerns are understood, the policy roles social work can take on, and social work's evaluation of current policy for practice – positive, negative or at various critical points in-between.

In this introductory chapter, I want to provide an overview of the local history of social work and social policy as a way of exploring the interaction between the concerns and operation of social policy and the role and opportunities for social work practice. A sense of this history is important because it offers resources to explore and question contemporary arrangements.

The history of social work over the last century and a half, reflects an ambivalence in the relationship of social work and policy. At times, social work has identified with prevailing policy to make welfare work; at other times, it has actively challenged the limitations and contradictions of policy – speaking truth to power.

At base, social policy can be seen as the organised response of society to problems of poverty, inequality and vulnerability. The nature and extent of this response is not fixed but changes, reflecting the different concerns and priorities in politics and wider society. Social policy is in the DNA of social work. It profoundly influenced the development of social work in the 19th century, and changed the nature of social work during the 20th century; and it continues to be a significant influence on contemporary social work in moves to redefine and retrench welfare service.

Social policy and the emergence of social work

The emergence of social work in Britain is associated with two approaches to social problems in the second half of the 19th century, which reflected different responses to the 1834 Poor Law – the cornerstone of 19th-century social policy. These approaches were represented by the Charities Organisation Society (COS) and its casework method, focusing on the responsibility of individuals; and the Settlement Movement, focusing on communities and collective action (Skehill 2010).

The 1834 Poor Law in England and Wales reflected a new welfare mindset – a mix of free-market economics, individual responsibility and minimal support. Welfare under the Poor Law was limited to those in pressing need and set at a level that would discourage dependency and encourage self-reliance (Fraser 1984). However, as the century progressed there was a significant growth in philanthropy in the face of the breakdown of traditional community networks, growing urbanisation and widespread poverty. To some, the piecemeal growth of charitable welfare seemed to undermine the Poor Law's promotion of hard work and self-reliance. The COS was established in 1869 to bring order to chaos, by coordinating the work of charities and introducing an organised method of casework with individuals and their families, offering practical and moral assistance, and distinguishing those in 'exceptional' need from those who they saw as taking advantage of charitable generosity (Fraser 1984). The goal of casework was to offer focused and disciplined instruction which, in the words of Octavia Hill, one of the founders of the COS, 'has little to do with outward gifts, and much to do with human sympathy, little with the dispensing hand, much with the helping one' (Whelan 2001: 14).

The Settlement Movement developed in the 1880s in the same context of Victorian poverty as the COS, but viewed the conditions of urban poverty quite differently. The Settlement Movement sought to use culture, education and social action to improve the conditions of communities degraded and disfigured by poverty (Thane 1996). However, through this work many settlements such as Toynbee Hall, in East London, also engaged with the material hardship they saw people facing in their daily lives, and sought 'to enquire into the condition of the poor and to consider and advance plans calculated to promote their welfare' (Till 2013). This commitment to social action can be seen in the story of one settlement worker, Ada Slater, who first became involved in the West London mission, then moved to work for the Settlement Movement in South London, and through this work became involved in women's rights and active in a local political campaign for improved housing and living conditions in inner city London (Spartacus Education).

While the origins of social work lay outside the state, the COS and Settlement Movement were both concerned with the role of state in social policy. However, they disagreed about how social work should manage the grey areas where individual needs and private problems pushed up against public concerns and policy issues.

The sociologist C. Wright Mills (1959) distinguished between seeing social concerns as private problems and public issues – and understanding this distinction can help us understand the different ideas of social work and social policy the COS and Settlement Movement represented (and how these differences have continued to resonate in social work). Private problems are the individual stress and distress of people within their particular milieu: people who often find themselves overwhelmed by their day-to-day struggles and situations. Public issues are those problems that are shared, although they are also likely to give rise to individual distress; they reflect broader social issues, which need to be addressed at collective and individual levels (Mills 1959). In Mills' terms, the COS viewed poverty as a private problem, an individual tragedy or personal failing requiring individual support or guidance; whereas the Settlement Movement saw poverty as a public issue, a reflection of social disadvantage amenable to social and political action.

Social work and social policy in the developing welfare state

The COS's commitment to organised charity and antipathy to public provision of welfare was increasingly out of sympathy with society, as local and national government took on greater responsibility for welfare services in the first half of the 20th century (Timms 1983). In the context of the developing welfare state, social work as a profession became increasingly involved in and identified with public social services. During the first decades of the 20th century, the Poor Law was subject to piecemeal reform. In 1929, its administration was transferred to local government. The Poor Law was finally abolished in 1948 and as part of wider welfare reforms new children's, health and welfare departments were established in local authorities. Social casework became increasingly influential in these departments (Forder 1969). This also meant that the relationship between social work and social policy became more intense and integrated. This process culminated in several developments in the late 1960s and early 1970s, when social work was finally established as a unified profession (British Association of Social Workers), with professional training regulated by a single body (the Central Council for Education and Training in Social Work) and with most social workers now working in a single local government department (Social Work Department in Scotland from 1968 and Social Services Department in England and Wales from 1970). Furthermore, these departments were characterised by a culture in which professional staff were afforded significant freedom not just in administering policy, but also in interpreting and adapting it to local circumstances (Harris 1998; Pithouse 1998).

The relationship between policy and professional practice within the welfare state tended to reflect underlying assumptions in the wider social and political environment. The welfare state was established in the context of optimism about welfare; public officials were seen as deserving deference, and their expertise was idealised as the judgement of the wise (Stedman Jones 2012). In this context, the role of professionals tended to be seen positively as translating general policy into particular provision (Marshall and Rees 1985). Policy was seen as sketchy, requiring professional staff to create and develop a workable policy in practice. This approach to policy can be characterised as a 'bottom-up' approach; an approach which started from the assumption that policy is complex, fragmented and a challenge to implementers, who had to make sense of it and make it sensible (Barret and Fudge 1981).

However, alongside these developments, voices were also calling into question the effectiveness of social policies and the active role of welfare professionals, including social workers. On the one side, critics challenged assumptions that welfare policy was working – pointing to the persistence of basic problems such as poverty (e.g. Townsend 1962). Questions were also asked about the concerns and priorities of social policy – whose interests did they serve? Whose needs were being ignored? The work of feminist critics, for instance, linked individual problems of care and domestic violence with wider social issues of systematic gender inequalities and violence (see Chapter 9). Anti-racist theorists identified systematic discrimination against Black communities and their exclusion from many of the benefits of the welfare state (see Chapter 7). These developments also problematised social work's relationship with policy, seeing social work as a profession working in the interest of ruling elites – with movements such as Case Con in the 1970s criticising social workers for blaming the victims of poverty and prejudice rather than challenging underlying problems of structural inequality and disadvantage. Another set of concerns focused on the power of welfare professionals in making decisions about the provision of welfare. Disabilities campaigners, for instance, accused professionals of acting as gatekeepers, limiting access to social rights and preventing service users from having cash to control their services (Oliver 1999). Another set of critics, from the New Right, painted a picture of the welfare state and its bureaucracy as wasteful and unresponsive, and characterised professionals in the welfare state as self-serving, out-of-control empire-builders creating need and dependency rather than encouraging self-reliance and independence from the state (Stedman-Jones 2012).

Social work, social policy and welfare retrenchment

Following the election of Margaret Thatcher's radical Conservative government in 1979, it was the last of these critical views, the New Right, that came to influence public policy and to characterise the experience of social work, the welfare state and social policy. In the following decade, government policy, under the influence of neo-liberal ideas, reflected a fundamental distrust of state action and welfare professionals, and a preference for market solutions (Alaszewski and Manthorpe 1990). Over this period, too, the relationship between welfare professionals and social policy was reframed in the terms of a managerial discourse, and the notion that professionals, alongside other employees, should have their work specified, directed and closely monitored by business-minded managers became the organising principle of public services (Harris 1998).

An early result of this change was a shift in social work's relationship with policy. Policy was increasingly presented as specific instructions that should be followed, and professional freedom increasingly seen as a problem. This approach is captured in the business idea of the relationship between the employer and employee as 'principal and agent', where policy-makers and senior mangers are principals, employing frontline professionals, such as social workers, as their agents to implement their policy instructions (Ulhoi 2007). Policy is understood as top-down instructions that frontline workers need to know and should follow and put into effect; and frontline worker practice should be measured and monitored to ensure compliance with the policy blueprint (Hogwood and Gunn 1984). The result was that policy became an ever-extending series of guideline and performance targets – in the early 2000s, for instance, the Performance Assessment Framework, which measured the performance of social services departments, involved 50 detailed indicators covering areas across children's and adults' services, such as quality of services, 'effectiveness of service delivery and outcomes', cost and efficiency and national priorities (DH 2003).

More recently, however, there seems to have been another shift in broader political attitudes, away from top-down control, and management bureaucracy and targets have come to be treated with more scepticism. The Munro Review, commissioned by the Conservative–Liberal Coalition government, argues that 'the extent of prescription has not been helpful. ... As the system's dependency on rules and prescription has grown, there has been insufficient freedom and confidence in exercising professional judgement' (Munro 2011: para. 8.17).

However, what is striking about the promotion of professional judgement in the report is the limited consideration of resources to provide services (Evans 2013). The relationship between policy and practice is once more changing, with a return to policy endorsement of professional discretion; though less concerned with the promotion of social rights and more focused on the promotion of efficiency and effectiveness, to obtain more for less within constrained resources (Evans 2015). This new chapter in the relationship between social policy and social work seems less a return to the 1970s and active policy development on the frontline and more a shift even further back into the history of social work to the COS with a new **entrepreneurial** twist.

This change needs to be understood within the broader context of the retrenchment of welfare. Whelan, for instance, from the right-leaning think-tank Civitas, has argued that, in providing help to people in need, what is required are: 'the services of a friendly visitor trained in the COS approach, capable of assessing character, motivation and the relative significance of the behavioural and structural causes of welfare dependency in particular cases' (Whelan 2001: 104). However, this is a particular approach to understanding the nature and the role of social work, the profession can also look back to the constructive and critical approach to social policy associated with the Settlement Movement as another, equally important aspect of the relationship between social work and social policy in an age of austerity.

Chapter outlines

In the chapters that follow, the authors examine different aspects of social policy and social work and consider the room for constructive and critical approaches to practice and policy.

The first section of the book looks at social work as a profession constructed by policy and professional discretion as an approach to policy work. **Mark Hardy** looks at the historical context of professional discretion in social work and contemporary debates about the extent and role of discretion in social work practice. Discretion is a problem because, while it can give professionals the freedom to respond to unexpected situations creatively, it also relies on the skills and commitments of individuals. Professionals can get things wrong and can pursue their own agenda regardless of others' interests. In the first part of the chapter, Mark looks at the ways in which particular approaches to knowledge, decision-making and judgement have influenced how both professionals and policy-makers understand their discretion (and not necessarily in the same way), and how the tension and shifts in these ideas have played a central role in the way the function and role of social work and social worker discretion have changed and shifted. The point here is that there have been – and it is likely there will always be – disputes about discretion, because this is closely connected to the flexibility and creativity of professional practice, and the potential to exert arbitrary authority. In the past 25 years, a particular combination of man-agement power, business practices and evidence-based practice has raised questions in the profession and among policy-makers about the continuation of discretion and its role and purpose. Hardy argues that discretion persists, but that it has changed and continues to change, as it always had to. He suggests that, as professionals, we have to recognise that this is not necessarily a good or bad thing, but that its value needs to be assessed in particular settings of use.

Starting with the Seebohm reforms in England and Wales (which were greatly influenced by the Kilbrandon report and the establishment of unified social work departments in Scotland), **Alix Walton** traces the fragmented and fractured developments and sea changes in social work education over the past 40 years. Taking an overview of these developments, the chapter identifies key debates that have underpinned these changes and continue to resonate in contemporary debates: What is the role of social work? Should social workers be educated or trained? What should the relationship be between theoretical and research knowledge and practical placement experience? What is the balance between generic social work skills and knowledge and specialist expertise, and what should be the emphasis between each at different stages of social workers' professional (qualifying and post-qualifying) career? How can continuing professional development be properly supported? She also links these questions to the priorities and concerns of different groups involved in social work education and training.

The next section considers substantive areas of policy, primarily within the con-text of social work in England. **Rick Hood's** chapter reviews policy in children's services, placing current policy in the context of developments over the last century. He points out that, while there have been dramatic moves and shifts in policy and provision, often associated with tragic events, these changes need to be understood in the broader and changing context of the way children are seen within the family and the ambivalent relationship between the families and the state; and shifting concerns about neglect and abuse, prevention and protection, etc. Children have emerged from the family as the focus of services and as bearers of their own rights, while families have been cast in an ambivalent role – idealised as the foundation of children's wellbeing, while also liable to be the subject of suspicion and investigation. The policy response has also changed and shifted over time focusing on protec-tion while at times striving to engage with a more preventative role, looking at the broader context of the lives of children and families in need. In the second part of the chapter, Rick considers the impact of New Labour's *Every Child Matters* policy and its future in a changed fiscal and political climate – of financial austerity and an ideological shift back to narrower child protection concerns.

Anna Gupta's chapter looks at children who come into the care of the state and explores the ways in which changing ideas of the relationship between children, families and the state have influenced policy. Policy structures state intervention in private family life and establishes a framework within which children's needs for stability, security, identity, belonging and resilience are balanced. This chapter traces the development of services for looked after children and considers the historical, social, political and economic forces that shape the thresholds for compulsory state intervention. The final part of the chapter reviews different approaches to substitute care – residential care, care by extended family and friends and long-term adoption – and considers evidence and debates about their use. Anna argues that a sensitive care system that aspires to engage with children's basic rights should ensure that a range of services is available to respond to the diverse needs of children who need care and their families.

Maria Brent examines personalisation, which is presented as a sea change from the care management introduced from America in the 1990s. She outlines the development of personalisation as a movement within social care and presents the arguments of both the advocates and critics of personalisation in social care. The policy is promoted in terms of empowering service users to be consumers, with cash to spend on care, driving the quality of services up through market competition; and the ability of service users to co-produce the services they want. However, critics point out that many advocates of personalisation embrace neoliberal ideas about the primacy of markets and the loaded rhetoric of 'the nanny state'. These critics point out that, while some service users seem to value the policy, there are others who are at best sceptical of the claims of empowerment and choice. Critics also point out that the policy tends to cast service users not as citizens but as consumers, and that consumers of care may have some rights, but they also have responsibilities to strive to be independent and to be resourceful – and as austerity bites, personalisation increasingly emphasises the need for consumers to be entrepreneurial in meeting their own care needs. Maria points out that the values of empowerment and partnership are long-standing principles underpinning good social practice, and that the challenge of personalisation is to promote these goals with service users as citizens.

Stefan Brown looks at the policy context for working with people whose capacity is impaired. He outlines the current legal framework – the Mental Capacity Act 2005 – and considers its relationship with different approaches to understand capacity. Throughout his chapter, Stefan argues that the legal framework can be understood in a dynamic relationship with the broader social and political context, which is also reflected in the tensions and contradictions inherent in policy and practice. He explores the dynamics of capacity by considering how closely the idea is related to the notions of paternalism and autonomy. Contemporary approaches to capacity have moved away from paternalism and are now largely shaped by ideas of autonomy, but elements of paternalism persist in policy and professional practice. He also argues that the elision of capacity and individual autonomy is also linked to neoliberal assumptions about decision-making as an atomised process entailing individual responsibility and a calculating approach. He contrasts this with more collective approaches to welfare and to social rights as the cornerstone of involving all service users as far as is possible in supported and respectful decision-making.

Frank Keating's chapter explores the relationship between race, ethnicity and policy to provide an analysis of social welfare and racialisation. This is explored through a combination of Critical Race Theory, which sees racism as endemic in a society dominated by White power, and a recognition that inequalities such as racism do not exist in isolation but often intersect with other dimensions of identity and inequality such as gender, age and sexuality. In this chapter, Frank clarifies key concepts such as 'race' and argues for a nuanced understanding that shifts away from pseudoscientific certainty and recognises the ways in which racialised categorisations can be used to marginalise groups within policy. The main body of the chapter argues for the value of exploring social policy and racism along three axes: ideas of race, attitudes to immigration (and its relationship to a putative 'British' identity) and approaches to racial equality. A key issue throughout the chapter is the way in which racism can be embedded in institutional practices and assumptions and the struggles that have arisen in unmasking and challenging these.

The final section of the book considers social work and social policy in their international context. **Tony Evans and Fabian Kessl** look at the challenges of comparing social work in different countries. They argue that the close connections between policy and social work practice means that we should not assume that social work is the same across policy regimes. Rather, because social policy frames the focus of social work in different ways in different countries, it is difficult to understand social work away from its particular policy context. However, international comparison is valuable not only as a source of learning from other settings but also because comparison can help us identify and explore assumptions about social work and social policy in our own country of practice. Regime Theory – which focuses on the welfare state and the labour market – is a common framework in comparing social work internationally. Evans and Kessl argue that, in understanding social work, this needs to be augmented by a wider conception of social policy that recognises the role of welfare as also playing a significant role in supporting and regulating care.

Donna Chung explores the recognition of domestic violence over the last 40 years. This chapter explores the development of policy-makers' understanding of domestic violence and its impact on victims; and their approaches to perpetrators in both the UK and Australia, which is explored in three key areas – the law, housing and homelessness, and partnership working and service coordination. Law reform at first focused on recognising domestic violence as a criminal offence. This in turn raised questions about legal enforcement, and alongside this has been the development of civil law remedies to enable victims to remain safe at home. Property and power are closely linked and policies in both countries have initially focused on refuges for victims as safe places away from abuse; but increasingly the concern has become the removal of the abuser and support for victims to remain at home. Alongside these developments, there has also been increasing emphasis on the need for agencies to work together and coordinate their support for victims. Policies in both countries continue to develop in the light of continuing challenges, including the recognition of the diversity of victims such as: women with disabilities, where care needs and vulnerability intersect; mid-age women whose responses to domestic violence may be coloured by family pressures; and older women where the experience of domestic violence needs to be factored into discussions of vulnerability, abuse and protection.

Hannah Jobling looks at community treatment orders (CTOs) in mental health – the idea that people can be required to have treatment while in the community – to explore processes of international policy transfer. She locates the origin of the community treatment orders in America as a response to concerns of patients' rights, providing an alternative to forcible hospital admissions. However, over time, an initially restricted idea of community treatment expanded to include a wider and potentially more coercive approach, with lower criteria applying to its use and a focus on risk and prevention. She identifies a range of common factors that have contributed to the widespread adoption of CTOs such as: the deinstitutionalisation of mental health care; a growing concern about community safety and risk; dominant ideologies of individual responsibility; and the predominance of neurobiology and emphasis on drugs as the solution in mental health. While these common factors have influenced the widespread adoption of community treatment orders, there is also evidence of selective take-up of elements of the original policy when CTOs have been transferred to other countries. These elements have also had to be adapted to fit existing provision – resulting in significant differences in CTOs in different countries. Jobling offers a framework to analyse these differences in terms of: approaches to the ability of service users to make informed decisions about treatment; the role of risk assessment in decision-making; the balance of compulsion and a reciprocal responsibility to provide services; and the extent of discretion operating in decision-making.

A critical appreciation of social policy is central to effective social work practice. The following chapters explore the relationship between the profession of social work as a profession and social policy, the policy frameworks in a range of areas of practice, and insights from international comparisons of policy and practice. Overall, these chapters offer a constructive and critical approach to working with social policy in an era of welfare retrenchment.

References

Alaszewski, A. and Manthorpe, J. (1990) 'Literature review: the new right and the professions', *British Journal of Social Work*, 20: 237–251.

Barret, S. and Fudge, C. (eds) (1981) *Policy and Action*. London: Methuen.

Department of Health (DH) (2003) *Social Services Performance Assessment Framework Indicators 2002–2003*. London: Department of Health. Available at: http://webarchive. nationalarchives.gov.uk/20130107105354/www.dh.gov.uk/prod_consum_dh/groups/dh_ digitalassets/@dh/@en/documents/digitalasset/dh_4081361.pdf

Evans, T. (2013) 'Organisational rules and discretion in adult social work', *British Journal of Social Work*, 43 (4): 739–758. First published online 7 March 2012.

Evans, T. (2015) 'Street-level bureaucracy, management and the corrupted world of service', *European Journal of Social Work*, in press.

Forder, A. (ed.) (1969) *Penelope Hall's Social Services of England and Wales*. London: Routledge and Kegan Paul.

Fraser, D. (1984) *The Evolution of the British Welfare State*. London: Macmillan.

Harris, J. (1998) *Managing State Social Work*. Aldershot: Ashgate.

Hogwood, B. and Gunn, L. (1984) *Policy Analysis for the Real World*. Oxford: Oxford University Press.

Marshall, T. and Rees, A. (1985) *Social Policy*. London: Hutchinson.

Mills, C. Wright (1959) *The Sociological Imagination*. New York: Oxford University Press.

Munro, E. (2011) *The Munro Review of Child Protection: Final Report: A Child-Centred System*. London: Department of Education.

Oliver, M. (1999) *The Disability Movement and the Professions*. Available at: http://disability-studies.leeds.ac.uk/files/library/Oliver-The-Disability-Movement-and-the-Professions.pdf

Pithouse, A. (1998) *Social Work: The Social Organisation of an Invisible Trade*. Aldershot: Ashgate.

Skehill, C. (2010) *History of Social Work in the United Kingdom*. Oxford: Bibliographies Online Research Guides.

Spartacus Education. Available at: http://spartacus-educational.com/PRsalterAD.htm

Stedman-Jones, D. (2012) *Masters of the Universe*. Princeton, NJ: Princeton University Press.

Thane, P. (1996) *The Foundations of the Welfare State*. London: Longman.

Till, J. (2013) *Icons of Toynbee Hall: Samuel Barnet*. London: Toynbee Hall. Available at: www.toynbeehall.org.uk/data/files/About_Toynbee_Hall/Barnett_low_res.pdf

Timms, N. (1983) *Social Work Values: An Enquiry*. London: Routledge, Kegan and Paul.

Townsend, P. (1962) 'The meaning of poverty', *British Journal of Sociology*, 13(3): 210–27.

Ulhoi, J. (2007) 'Revisiting the principal-agent theory of agency: comments on the firm level and the cross-national embeddedness thesis', *Journal of Organizational Behaviour*, 28: 75–80.

Whelan, R. (2001) *Helping the Poor. Friendly Visiting, Dole Charities and Dole Queues*. London: Civitas.

1

Discretion in the History and Development of Social Work

Mark Hardy

Autonomous decision-making is often cited as a defining trait of professionalism and so discretion – to utilise one's knowledge, skills and values as a basis for decision-making – is central to what it is to 'be' a professional social worker. Given recent concerns about the quality of social work practice, there have been developments which have sought to constrain discretion in practice. This is on the basis that practitioner discretion is implicated in poor decision-making, and so needs to be constrained if the quality of outcomes in social work are to be improved. In this chapter, I revisit particular 'moments' in the history of social work to illustrate how discretion had been utilised in practice over time. I explore how developments within social policy have shaped the nature and purpose of social work, focusing on the way in which changing ideas about the state's responsibility for citizens' social welfare have given rise to shifts in the degree of discretion that practitioners have employed. Key developments include the alternative 'visions' of social work embodied within the practice of the Charities Organisation Society and the Settlement Movement; the development of the traditional casework model; the establishment of social services departments in the 1970s; the impact of critiques of state social work in the late 20th century; developments in social work under New Labour's modernisation agenda; as well as ideas within Coalition government policies for social work. Each of these developments entails a particular assemblage of approaches to knowledge, decisions and judgements, whether objective or subjective, clinical or structured, professional or proceduralised. What becomes apparent when we investigate discretion from a historical perspective is that its extent and function fluctuates over time, depending on how central social work is to wider agendas within social policy and politics more generally. Conventional narratives, which portray recent trends in social policy as threatening the professionalism of practitioners, therefore seem to overstate both the 'death of discretion' but also the extent to which discretion can or ought to be a defining trait of the particular varieties of bureau-professionalism which characterise much of contemporary social work.

The role that social work plays as a mechanism via which wider policy objectives might be achieved means that there is a link between politics, policy and practice. Although it would be a mistake to assume that social work determines its own parameters, equally practice cannot be straightforwardly taken as subordinate to policy. This understanding of the policy–practice relationship disturbs the conventional narrative regarding what it is to 'be' a professional, but for good reasons. First, it highlights that the critique of the 'top-down', hierarchical model whereby policy-makers and managers determine priorities 'on high', with little thought for the 'realities' within the 'swampy lowlands' (Schon 1983) of practice, generally disregards that policy-makers at times need distance from practice to determine policy aims. It is axiomatic that within a democratic society, however imperfect, stakeholders other than practitioners should have some input in determining what social work is for and how it should be undertaken. Second, there is also a 'dark side' to discretion, and so, potentially, to social work too. Thus, although discretion is necessary within social work, it is not always beneficial. This is because by its nature, social work entails the use of authority and dispersal of resources on behalf of the state. Social workers utilise this authority to make key decisions regarding the wellbeing of the individual but also the wider community. The exercise of authority is dependent on two related elements – power and legitimacy. Power always has the potential to disempower, and so to retain legitimacy it demands some degree of accountability. This cannot be meaningfully achieved unless mechanisms exist to restrict the operation of professional discretion. Although critics of social work often overstate the extent to which practitioners use discretion in ways which are mistaken or oppressive, it is nevertheless important for the state to intervene to constrain the ways in which practitioners utilise the power that is vested within their role. As we shall see, whether such intervention is itself legitimate or effective is another matter.

Enduring debates in social work

Social work is a broad church, encompassing a wide variety of specialist 'domains' brought together by a shared understanding of social problems and the attendant need to intervene to alleviate their impact, whether at the level of the individual or the collective. However, social work is actually a highly contested subject. There is a lack of consensus regarding both how social work should be *understood* and *undertaken*. This reflects disagreement about the underlying function of social work, and is evident in various controversies which have characterised its history and development. First, there are disagreements regarding the nature and objectives of practice (the 'what is social work?' debate). A central theme here is the nature of the relationship between the individual and the state. There is also a lack of consensus regarding whether practice should be individualised or 'social', whether the problems social workers address represent the consequence of social factors, individual functioning or some combination of the two. Relatedly, there is disagreement about whether these aims are best achieved via voluntary engagement or compulsion and the extent to which social work should be seen as a form of 'care', primarily concerned with individual wellbeing, or a form of 'control', contributing to the maintenance of social order. My primary concern here is to illuminate the lack of consensus which characterises these ongoing controversies, and their implications for discussions regarding the role of professional discretion in social work. In this chapter, I review how these enduring debates relate to contemporaneous approaches to thinking about and doing social work, and make some tentative suggestions regarding the ways in which the shifting parameters of professional discretion influence practice and practitioners.

The origins of social work

While the protection of the vulnerable, caring for those in distress and seeking to alleviate need are arguably fundamental to the nature of collective life (Clarke 2004), social work as an organised activity is often traced to 19th-century developments associated with the increasing rate of urbanisation resulting from the industrial revolution. Poverty in the countryside meant that expanding towns and cities attracted large numbers away from rural areas with the potential of a wage. Conditions in many urban areas were poor and so many people lived in overcrowded, insanitary conditions which were not conducive to health and wellbeing (Pierson 2011). At the same time, the informal communal support which characterised traditional rural living was absent in many areas of urban life, as long-established relations of kith and kin could not be straightforwardly replicated in these newly established urban centres. Consequently, forms of informal reliance diminished. For the urban poor, reliance on charitable giving, or the workhouse, came to represent necessary alternatives to homelessness and starvation.

Although at this time there was some consensus that 'something' *ought* to be done about these issues, there was also divergence regarding what *should* be done, depending on underlying assumptions concerning individual responsibility. On the one hand, particularly in a context where religious influence held considerable sway, there was concern that many of the poor were simply idle (idleness being one of the 'seven deadly sins') and that they should not be rewarded for their idleness via material assistance, as this would merely encourage dependency. On the other hand, experience and observation suggested that destitution mirrored economic and class arrangements, and that the wider social environment impacted on individual behaviour. Different varieties of intervention therefore emerged which reflected underlying beliefs concerning the 'causes' of the issues they were seeking to remedy.

The original casework method which has been so significant in the heritage of social work can be traced to political debates and associated developments at this time. Over the course of the 19th century, various philanthropically funded charitable bodies developed which sought to remedy the ills associated with poverty. However, the rationale for the organisation and provision of assistance was somewhat haphazard. The Charities Organisation Society (COS) was established in 1869 so as to offer a mechanism via which this could be organised. A distinction was drawn between those individuals who were deemed wilfully poor and those whose position reflected circumstances beyond their control – the 'undeserving' and the 'deserving'. Only the deserving would be provided with assistance, which was geared towards the development of habits that would strengthen the capacity for work, while the undeserving were left with residual Poor Law provision. Independence and hard work were the means via which the poor could escape poverty, within the context of strong commitments to the stable family unit as the bedrock of society. In order to be able to make a distinction between the 'deserving' and 'undeserving', COS case workers undertook an 'investigation', in which both moral character and material circumstances were considered. Rather than seeking to understand the interplay between wider social factors and individual situations, the emphasis here was on individualised characteristics (Cree 2002). Case workers were required to establish how likely to benefit from support and assistance an individual might be – in essence, whether intervention would encourage independence or merely perpetuate dependency. Where deserving, forms of assistance might be via a financial loan or alternatively officers would provide advice and support, particularly regarding employment possibilities. By undertaking such investigations, COS officers were laying the basis for a form of discretionary practice – assessment – which would be significant throughout social work's history. From the outset, then, it is apparent that expertise in role and task in social work is dependent on the appropriate and effective exercise of discretion. Crucially, in categorising status, COS practitioners instrumentalised moral judgements on an individualised basis.

While the COS favoured charitable giving, alternative approaches emphasised the potential that state intervention had for the alleviation of suffering. Close links were established with sociology and social policy and the practice of those 'varieties' of social work informed by collectivist assumptions. The Settlement Movement is the principal example of this 'practical socialism' (Wilson et al. 2008). The rationale underpinning this approach was that the actual causes of social problems lay beyond the motivation and temperament of the individual concerned. It was therefore theorised that if these issues were to be addressed, social circumstances would have to change. One means of achieving this end would be for educated volunteers to live ('settle') within afflicted communities, as a focal point for collective local action to develop. Here, then, we see the origins of community work, which has been a strand of social work ever since. In determining which communities to settle, the work of early social reformers such as the Fabians, including the Webbs, was significant (Offer 2006), enabling developing understanding of socio-economic indicators and demographic characteristics to be incorporated into decision-making.

These two exemplars represent different approaches to dealing with social problems. Crudely, while the COS accepted society as it was, and sought to change the individual, the Settlement Movement was concerned with improving the lot of individuals via social change. These two approaches – individualism and social reform – have vied for prominence throughout the history of social work. Each equates to a 'vision' of the nature and function of social work and how it should be undertaken.

Welfare in policy and practice

Distinctions between individualism and social reform should not be overstated. Some theorists recognised the advantages of integrating aspects of supposedly competing approaches, pointing to the need for 'psychosocial' approaches to practice.

Mary Richmond's (1917) work on the skills required to work with individuals and families has come to be regarded as a defining influence on the development of social work theory and method, both in the United States and Europe. She saw no necessary contradiction in combining the idealist motivation of social activists with the applied investigation of COS case workers. Indeed, in her insistence that it is the intersection between society and the individual that represents the foci of social work practice, the need for forms of practice which might facilitate both individual and environmental adjustment was highlighted. The model which she developed conceived of such change as following a gradual and progressive process and comprising a number of related components – investigation, case formulation (diagnosis), planning, identification of resources and intervention – basic elements of a process which arguably still characterises the majority of social work practice. Although undertaken within particular institutional structures, it was for practitioners to determine, on the basis of their skills and beliefs, who to work with, and how. Again, the exercise of professional discretion assumes key significance in the achievement of potential outcomes.

Richmond, then, laid the foundations for broadly 'therapeutic' approaches, and practice with its roots in psychological theory came to the fore. Theories originally derived from both psychology and psychiatry were influential in social work from the 1920s to the 1960s. Social problems came to be seen as underlain by the psychological needs of the person concerned (Rose 1998). Freudian ideas about the role of the unconscious mind, conflicts in the interaction between id, ego and superego and the impact of past experiences on current behaviour, offered both answers and, potentially, remedies. The emphasis on early relationships added weight to models of practice which emphasised the potential of a positive relationship between client and practitioner to counteract the effects of less than ideal precursors. Central to this was the notion of a therapeutic relationship as a 'safe space' in which clients were able to talk about issues and problems which were concerning them. By articulating their thoughts and feelings, they could be enabled to make links between past experiences and current actions, gaining insight into how assumptions and patterns established in early life impacted unconsciously in the 'here and now' via symptomatic behaviour. The practitioner's role was to facilitate expression of, and reflection upon, emotions and anxieties, and to offer their own interpretations, so as to enable clients to develop insight. Only then could attempts to limit the effects of damaged and disturbed previous experiences be successfully undertaken. Crucially, interpretation, though sometimes contemporaneously badged as 'scientific', was clearly a subjective rather than objective activity. At this time there was no doubt that the worker's role was as 'expert' in diagnosis and treatment, based on theoretical knowledge, experience and clinical skills. Discretion to make judgements regarding the nature of the presenting problem, its roots, prognosis and treatment was central, and one of the main rationales driving the expansion of education, training and professionalisation. Even later, when psychoanalytic models were challenged by the rise of behavioural approaches due to a lack of evidence of effectiveness, the emphasis on discretion in case formulation as the manifestation of practitioner expertise remained to the fore.

Between the 1930s and 1950s, the influence of both the COS and the Settlement Movement declined as 'therapy' became institutionalised, and statutory provision expanded. Services which had previously been provided voluntarily, funded by charitable provision, were increasingly incorporated into state provision, not least in post-Second World War welfare. As Cree puts it, while the general welfare state would address issues of poverty, disadvantage and inequality, 'the task of social work would be to pick up the small number of people who fell through the welfare net' (2002: 272). Thus, in 1948, local authorities assumed responsibility for what have come to be seen as 'prime' social work tasks: children's departments, welfare departments for the elderly, handicapped and homeless; and health departments for the physically disabled. Certainly by the end of the 1950s, most social workers were employed by statutory agencies of one sort or another.

Although theoretical allegiances to psychological approaches were by now well integrated with casework, practice in the early years of 'welfare' encompassed much more than simply the application of psychological principles in practice. Indeed, given the centrality of social perspectives to the expansion of the welfare state, it would have been paradoxical had it not. In particular, Biestek's (1961) account of casework as an ethical and practical activity was arguably more influential than the psychological pioneers. He privileged the relationship between practitioner and client as the essence of casework, and the practice manifestation of social work's essential values: acceptance, non-judgementalism, individualisation and respect for the individual, the purposeful expression of feelings and a controlled emotional involvement, confidentiality and self-determination. Although psycho-therapeutic approaches remained influential, their dominance was challenged by developing debates in the social sciences regarding the relationship between individual agency and social structure, which informed the development of 'the social nature of the work, as distinct from rescuing or treating the individual' (Cree 2003: 90). Welfarism, then, came to represent a vehicle for the achievement of what Parton (1994: 21) specifies as 'ameliorative, integrative and redistributive' aims. These were grounded in a commitment to social justice and social progress, which would be achieved through state activity in which 'improvements could be made in the lives of individuals and families via judicious professional interventions'.

A secure base for social work

Despite increased status and to some extent a shared sense of identity, it was not until the early 1970s that social work in England and Wales 'unified', following the recommendations of the Seebohm Committee Report (1968) that integrated local authority social services departments be established, and generic training and qualifications introduced. These recommendations were accepted by the government and put into effect by the Local Authority Social Services Act 1970. It was envisaged that 'the new generic, professional departments would spearhead the development of community-based alternatives to … incarceration … in asylums, hospitals, institutions and prisons' (Cree 2003: 87). The disparate training arrangements, whereby ordinarily child care officers, hospital and psychiatric social workers and probation officers undertook specialised but separate training courses of variable quality, were to be replaced by a standardised and regulated qualification framework.

Systems theory offered promise as a unifying theoretical framework which might lend itself to the task of enabling social workers to fulfil their responsibilities within these newly established social service departments. In a post-Seebohm context, practitioners would deal with all clients, on the basis that the skills, knowledge and values required to deal with diverse groupings were transferable. Systems theory relied heavily on the assessment expertise of the practitioner. Family members were seen as being involved in constant processes of reciprocal, interactive communication which impacts in complex fashion. Each individual was conceived of as a system, as was the family as a whole, as well as 'subsets' within the family, most notably, but not exclusively, parents and children. Other, external systems were also interacted with, impacted upon and had effect. Rather than assuming that a client was behaving in a particular manner because this was some manifestation of individualised character or temperament, problematic situations or actions were seen as developing out of the interaction between various 'sub-systems' within a wider system. Because of the complexity of these interactions, it was rare that a single cause could be identified and so multiple perspectives needed to be accommodated, and it was the practitioner's role to formulate, specify and intervene to address these.

Systems theory took seriously the diversity of social work and sought to develop a unified theory of practice in which complexity and interaction are acknowledged as key, and so different approaches to practice – psychological, 'social', community-based – were required if problems were to be appropriately and effectively responded to. Indeed, the sheer complexity of interaction between systems and their various component members necessitated such expertise (Payne 2002). Making these links was clearly not straightforward and arguably as a consequence neither systems theory as an integrated model for practice, nor generic social work more generally delivered on their promise. Gradual recognition of genericism's limitations led to a shift towards specialisation, a process which was formalised via subsequent developments in the 1980s and 1990s, such as the introduction of the approved social worker role in mental health, and a split between adult and children's services. Nevertheless, this post-Seebohm period arguably represented the high water mark for what Howe (1996) refers to as 'bureau professionals' of state social work. What was gained was an organisational and occupational base for social work which 'guaranteed social work its service-user base and its continuing legitimacy' (Cree 2002: 282). Conversely, 'it also restricted the kind of activity that social workers could be involved in, and *the autonomy and discretion that social workers could exercise*' (Cree 2002: 283, italics added). This was especially the case in relation to the mandate for social reform which was seen by some as having been sacrificed in return for enhanced professional status. The discretion of social workers to highlight and address social rather than individual factors was limited. In its quest for professional status, something of the positive, facilitative relationship between social worker and client that Biestek envisaged had been lost. Instead, social workers represented '"the iron fist in the velvet glove", the acceptable face of state repression … agents of social control' (Horner 2003: 90).

A radical revival

Within each of these perspectives, whether social, psychological or psycho-social, there was a presumption that social work intervention was 'a good thing', with potential benefits for either the service user or society. Such beliefs, however, were not unanimous. The radical critique of social work, in which practice is conceived of as an oppressive arm of the state maintaining rather than challenging the status quo, became especially influential from the mid-1970s onwards. Radical theorists challenged social work's preferred self-identity as a 'caring' or 'helping' profession. Instead, social work was represented as a means via which the state controlled disadvantaged and disempowered sections of society, better to preserve and protect the interests of capital. The roots of 'radical' social work lie in those 'versions' of early social work which argued that problems in communities were indicative of social disadvantage, and that their resolution lay not in individualised treatment but rather in wholesale social reform. Key factors included the realisation that despite the promises inherent within the welfare state, poverty remained a grim reality for many people, not least children. There was also growing recognition that the reality of institutional care was often far removed from the ideal, that abuse occurred within supposedly caring environments, and acknowledgement that against such a backdrop it was hard to substantiate the claim that social work was a 'caring' profession. Structural analysis had been out of favour during the decades in which psychological approaches to practice were dominant, but became increasingly evident once more during the 1970s and 1980s. Perhaps surprisingly, this critique, with its roots in critical sociology, became influential *within* social work, reflecting concerns that the individualising tendencies of dominant psychological models pathologised clients. The influence of individualised approaches in social work was challenged, not least on the basis that they positioned practitioners as 'agents of social control', seeking to control recalcitrant sections of society in order to perpetuate the unjust capitalist social and economic order. Marxist theory became important once more, with radical non-intervention, material assistance and community-based activism the preferred means of challenging the conservative hegemony and the pervasive effects of labelling. If practice was to be truly effective it must address the structural disadvantages experienced by the majority of clients, either immediately via the provision of material assistance, in the mid-term by changing the distribution of resources within society, or via a long-term political strategy which would fundamentally alter the constitution of society.

Towards neoliberal hegemony

At the same time that the radical left critique of social work became influential, criticism from the 'New Right' also impacted on social work. Certainly by the late 1970s, with the election of right-wing administrations in Britain, there was a notable shift away from assuming that state intervention across the public sector was in itself likely to lead to positive change without attention also being paid to the role of the free and responsible individual. This reflected scepticism regarding the viability and ethics of the welfare consensus and relatedly, the theory and practice of state social work, not least the emphasis in radical analysis on the effects of structural disadvantage on individual's capabilities, opportunities and behaviour. Critics regarded the welfare state, with its emphasis on state-mandated collective action as standing in opposition to the rights and responsibilities of the individual to be free to live their life, for better or worse, according to the choices they deemed appropriate. Concerns were expressed about the extent to which, at a practical level, the welfare 'safety net' encouraged dependency and stifled initiative, and at a philosophical level, that the enduring tension between the rights of the individual and the power of the state, between freedom and equality, were unbalanced. The balance between the individual and the state had tipped too far towards the latter, and reversal via retrenchment was required.

The influence of neoliberal ideology within the institutions and practices of government impacted on both policy and practice. Various initiatives are associated with this neoliberal worldview and the associated rise of the 'new public management' across the public sector. These include the purchaser–provider split, whereby the alleged 'monopoly' role that social services played in the provision of services was challenged by compulsory competitive tendering. The assumption was that there was scope for improvement of the quality and efficiency of services and that competition represented the best available mechanism to enable this to occur. There was also an associated shift in culture whereby the ethos and practices of business made inroads into an arena which had thus far been relatively immune to such developments (Harris 2003). Thus managerialism impacted at various levels, and in enduring ways. The financial constraints within which social work had always operated became more explicit as social workers became care managers (Sheppard 1995) operating within internal markets with fixed budgets available for the provision of services irrespective – at least according to critical commentators – of actual need experienced by service users. Managerialism was also associated with the development of an 'audit culture' in social work, whereby the decisions and actions of practitioners are subject to routine procedural oversight and ratification in the name of accountability, leading to concern that professional autonomy and discretion had been eroded (Munro 2004). Social work also arguably became more receptive to perspectives which were more congruent with 'New Right' principles than had previously been the case. Thus, certainly by the early 1980s, when traditional casework was facing criticism from both radical and conservative theorists, there was space for the emergence of behavioural approaches, which claimed to be more effective and cheaper. Many critics regarded the efficacy of such approaches as overstated and ethically suspect, but claims of rationalism, responsibility, applicability, effectiveness and efficiency ensured that the cognitive model rose to prominence as a means of enhancing the legitimacy of social work practice.

'New' Labour

This was a challenge that the 'New' Labour government, elected in 1997, vigorously responded to. The government set about 'reforming the strategic direction for social work, together with the structures of social work regulation, with the stated aims of modernising the social services and improving the status of, and confidence in, the social work profession' (Horner 2003: 108). The aim was to enhance effectiveness and consistency by improving the organisation and coordination of services, with professionals having clarity regarding roles and responsibilities. This agenda was to be taken forward via 'raising quality standards through the regulation of three inter-connected systems: the service system, the staff system and the training system' (2003: 110). There was an emphasis on inter-agency practice to ensure that areas of risk or need outside the expertise of one profession could be addressed by another. Further integration followed, with health in relation to adult care and education in relation to work with children and families, via legislation such as the Health and Social Care Act 2001 and the establishment of the Department for Children, Schools and Families within government after 2004. The aim was to improve communication between professionals who had traditionally operated within separate arenas and thus arguably not communicated adequately, and so reduce failings and improve outcomes.

Various criticisms have been levelled at such changes, at various levels. Some see social work and managerialism as inherently incompatible; others see changes in the nature of practice as detrimental to the traditional relationship between practitioner and service user. More broadly, inter-agency and inter-professional practice is seen as a threat to social work's core identity, challenging the distinctiveness of what social workers do, and the neoliberal agenda of government, emphasising individual responsibility, is seen as at odds with the ethic of welfare. In sum, managerialism and associated changes are thought to have altered the nature and objectives of social work, and so its traditional identity is under threat. For critics, there is a bitter irony that these initiatives, with their emphasis on 'better quality services', seek to achieve improvement via processes which cumulatively limit the discretion of social workers to formulate and implement solutions in a particular 'case' on the basis of their hard earned skills, knowledge and experience. According to Rogowski (2013) this amounts to ideologically motivated deprofessionalisation.

Evidence-based practice

Many of the trends evident within the implementation of new public management within social work – the emphasis on effectiveness, the prioritisation of objectivity in practitioner judgement and decision-making, the need for systems of accountability – are mirrored in the emphasis on 'evidence-based' policy and practice. This developed independently of government. The Cochrane Collaboration, for example, was first established as a database of systematic reviews in health but expanded under Labour's programme of 'modernising governance' and an emphasis on 'what works'. While it is hard to argue against the idea that policy and practice should be based on good evidence, the idea of evidence-based practice (EBP) is controversial in social work, and for good reasons (Evans and Hardy 2010). At heart, debates concerning the merits and appropriateness of EBP reflect differing presumptions regarding how best to understand and undertake social work. On the one hand, some regard EBP as the single best possible means of practitioners to better achieve their objectives by basing practice on knowledge generated from particular methodological strategies, including randomised control trials, systematic reviews and meta-analysis, according to hierarchical principles. The assumption is that practice is consequently more likely to be effective, which will be beneficial for service users and also enhance the standing of the profession. Others, however, regard EBP as itself a threat to professionalism, because in its implementation it entails limits on practitioner freedom to decide what is going on in a particular case and how to respond. In its attempt to offer proscribed guidance regarding how practitioners should respond in particular social work scenarios, there is little recognition that many of the decisions which practitioners must make occur in conditions of inherent uncertainty and so will, by definition, need to be made on the basis of professional discretion.

Consequently, the principal obstacles to the achievement of EBP, according to its advocates, are practitioners themselves, with their commitment to humanistic forms of practice which, rightly or wrongly, are regarded as antithetical to the more empirical approaches entailed by EBP. Sheldon et al. regard 'the curse of Carl Rogers' (2005: 18) as promoting the view that 'science' undermines the humanistic, relationship based 'art' of social work (England 1986). Additionally, the organisational culture of social work agencies privileges custom and practice ahead of 'considered action informed by robust research' (Sheldon and Macdonald 2009: 71). From the opposite perspective, critics characterise EBP as a mechanism via which social work is utilised to achieve wider neoliberal policy objectives which are distant from its heritage, strengths and values. Mono-therapeuticism, associated with the prioritisation of interventions which perform well in outcome studies, limits discretion in case formulation and intervention and so marginalises many of the theories and methods associated with 'social' approaches to practice. An emphasis on consistency and standardisation is associated with a tendency towards bureaucratisation and managerialism, because in their application, if not their principles (see Sackett et al. 1996), evidence-based approaches downplay the value attached to clinical skills and experience as a basis for practice in favour of forms of technical proceduralism. EBP also seeks to categorise the varied circumstances and experiences of service users into relatively precise classifications which do not reflect their diversity. This occurs because the discretion of practitioners to deviate from guidelines is limited by structures of accountability which promote rigid rather than flexible application. Consequently, social problems are decontextualised and there is a failure to acknowledge that effective change is dependent upon social context and relationships, neither of which lend themselves to proceduralisation.

The impact of risk on professional discretion

Concerns about risk also feed into the emphasis within policy on standardisation of practice via the reduction of practitioner discretion. Fawcett and Karbon (2005) argue that 'scientific' reforms, particularly EBP and actuarialism, are driven by a belief that service failures result from poor decision-making by practitioners, and that the limiting of practitioner discretion represents a means of minimising risk. Such issues rose to the fore in social work from the mid-1980s onwards, since when in light of particularly high profile 'service failures', political and public concerns about the ability of social workers have been prevalent. Originally, this was in relation to child care, with particular cases – Maria Colwell, and later Victoria Climbié – having significant effect (Parton 2006). Subsequently, the focus fell on mental health, with notable cases such as those of Jason Roberts and Christopher Clunis assuming iconic status (Warner 2006). There have also been concerns directed at community care following abuse of professional power in work with vulnerable adults (Butler and Drakeford 2003). These failings, and attendant scrutiny of practice quality, have led to a variety of developments which generally shift the basis for decision-making away from informal knowledge sources to seemingly more objective criteria. Professional decision-making appears, then, to increasingly occur on the basis of empirical evidence from risk assessment schedules and 'evidence-based' guidelines implemented in accordance with proscriptive managerial and policy directives on how to respond to high risk cases.

Risk triggers particular kinds of organisational response, which impact at the level of practice. The nature and focus of the services that are offered by agencies become increasingly focused on the identification and management of risk. Practitioners' responsibilities are 'not so much for the cure or reform of clients … but for their administration according to the logic of risk minimisation' (Rose 1996: 349), and their attentions directed accordingly. Judgements are made on the basis of cumulative banks of data drawn from the experiences of similarly categorised individuals rather than the particular details of a case as interpreted on the basis of individual professional discretion. Actuarialism contributes to risk-averse organisational cultures and thus to precautionary judgements and decisions. Risk practices are therefore seen as part of the apparatus via which a governmental commitment to welfare provision is displaced (Culpitt 1999). In line with the priority attached to individualism and responsibility within neoliberal thought, service users are deemed to have contributed to their own misfortune by virtue of 'individual failing and moral ineptitude' (Lavalette 2011: 1). Being 'a risk' or 'at risk' is a manifestation of either a failure to fulfil one's responsibility to function capably within society, or a moral lapse indicative of a flawed identity which – tautologically – comes to be seen as a risk indicator. In policies and procedures, risk is conceived of as an 'artefact' rather than a subjectively 'constructed' phenomenon and so 'social' models give way to 'administrative' approaches (Parton 1996). By limiting discretion, the architects of the neoliberal project are better able to ensure that approaches which more closely accord with neoliberal understandings of freedom (Rose 2000) predominate.

Is discretion constrained?

This is a powerful critique. It does seem that cumulatively, managerialism, EBP and risk have combined to limit the discretion that practitioners have to decide for themselves, on the basis of their professional knowledge, skills and experience, how best to intervene. 'Scientific' developments – the use of actuarial tools, the emphasis on empiricism, the insistence that practice be based on objective knowledge rather than subjective expertise – are taken as distancing practice from its ideal, a broadly humanistic form of 'artistic' person-centred casework in which expert practitioners have discretion to engage in creative practices which are necessarily highly individualised, reflecting the relationship they have with a particular service user and their unique circumstances and lived experience. This, at least, is the 'critical consensus'. However, although this critique is substantive and influential, it is important to retain a degree of scepticism regarding its comprehensiveness and applicability across the various domains of social work. There are a number of perspectives which, at the very least, complicate the all-encompassing nature of the dominant narrative that discretion has been unnecessarily curtailed.

There are two related debates that we need to disentangle when considering the role of discretion in social work, the first empirical, the second normative. With regard to the first, it is not actually clear whether or not practitioner discretion is actually increasingly constrained. One of the main reasons that concerns are expressed within government and management regarding practitioner discretion is that it provides an explanation for 'failures' of government policy *separate from* the failings of politicians or policy-makers. But the policy response to policy failure is itself potentially subject to implementation failure, and so efforts to constrain discretion may not succeed. Contrary to the suggestion that discretion has been curtailed, Evans (2010) suggests that in some settings practitioners certainly do retain and exercise discretion, albeit reconfigured in light of changes in the context and purposes of practice over time. Similarly, Taylor and Kelly (2006) query the extent to which procedural constraints actually limit the need for professionals to grapple with ethical dilemmas in the public sector more generally. Wallander and Molander (2014) suggest that even within highly proceduralised environments, space exists for differential approaches to reasoning and judgement among professionals, while Carson et al. (2015) highlight the ways in which top-down contractual relations between state and third sector organisations nevertheless leave space for discretion as a means of navigating complexity. Clearly, then, proliferation of policy should not be confused with the actual substantive and meaningful restriction on discretion. Even where policy does constrain, the mechanism for constraint can open up novel discretionary spaces where the nature of the decision may have changed but still requires practitioners to exercise judgement.

Points for reflection

Think about your own experience as trainee professional on placement.

- How much discretion did you have to decide for yourself how to intervene in the cases you were allocated?
- Was the amount of discretion you had more or less than you had hoped for?
- How did the discretion you had differ from that of qualified colleagues you worked alongside, and why?
- If you were a qualified social worker, with more discretion than a social work student, what would you have done differently in the work you undertook with service users? Try to think of specific examples.

Should discretion be constrained?

There is also the related but distinct normative issue to consider –should practitioners continue to exercise discretion? On the one hand, there *are* problems associated with the exercise of professional discretion, which problematise the simplistic assertions that discretion is necessarily 'a good thing', but also that it is so fundamental to professionalism that it must always, whatever the circumstances, remain unconstrained. The notion that discretion should be curtailed because practitioner judgements are (perceived to be) inaccurate is dependent on the assumption that professional decision-making contains inherent potential for poor practice. Here, practitioner discretion undermines the quality of social work. If we accept this at face value, then sometimes efforts to curtail discretion represent necessary adjustments following recognition of previous failings. Relatedly, discretion potentially enables practice which is oppressive, and – in extreme cases – abusive. The disproportionate numbers of Black service users in secure mental health settings is a good example of how discretion in practitioner judgement can facilitate unjust practices. Concerns of a similar nature also manifest in a more widespread tendency towards defensive or precautionary practice. However, while critics of 'the rise of risk' argue that defensive practice results from the logic of actuarialism, actually it is better understood as a function of the operation of practitioner discretion in a context in which fear of blame plays a significant role (Hardy 2015).

The *benefits* of discretion

Issues such as these – bias in practitioner judgements and overly precautionary practice – are of course concerning and need to be addressed, and policy initiatives to limit the discretion for practitioners to act on what, to all intents and purposes, equates to unjustified bias, would be broadly welcomed, at least in principle. But if *negative* experiences and outcomes in social work can be attributed to the failings of discretionary practice, then by the same token, *positive* experiences of social work can also be attributed to the appropriate and effective use of discretion. Although critics of social work routinely suggest that social workers make poor decisions, this is on the basis of perceptions gained from extreme or iconic cases, which are few and far between and unrepresentative of day-to-day practice. Although we cannot generalise to say how accurate social work decision-making is across domains, agencies or cases, we do know, for example, that the number of child deaths per annum remain about constant or are in decline (Corby 2006) and that international reviews indicate high levels of satisfaction with social welfare services. These facts are hardly suggestive of incompetence unless competence is equated with infallibility, and suggests that concerns about the quality of practitioner judgement, if not unwarranted, then certainly overstated.

Irrespective of the reality of discretionary practice, questions about whether it should be constrained or continue tend to be framed in dichotomous terms. It is true to say that social work organisations could not function without some degree of practitioner discretion. What Evans and Harris (2004: 892) refer to as 'freedom of movement to deal with uncertainty' represents a necessary prerequisite for practice in situations in which uncertainty is ubiquitous but practitioners nevertheless need to make judgements and act. It is increasingly clear that, whatever its merits, the goal and practicality of EBP are open to challenge. Cartwright and Hardie (2012: 161) sum up the key problematic as follows: 'they attempt to impose structured, rule-based procedures, where success depends on the process we call thinking or deliberating, which cannot be replaced by such procedures'. Sheldon et al. (2004) correctly question the extent to which organisational cultures within social work lend themselves to empirically based practice. However, while they might argue this culture is problematic, others regard it as a necessary reflection of the sorts of issues which social workers must grapple with and the dilemmas and decisions which flow from these (Munro 2008). Hence the appropriate approach to decision-making – artistic, intuitive and informal versus analytic, objective and systematic – in a particular social work scenario remains contentious (Fish and Hardy 2015; Kahneman 2011). As a result there is now much more emphasis on 'research minded' practice, wherein practitioners engage with and critically appraise research findings and incorporate these into decision-making, in ways that inform and guide rather than dictate or proscribe. With regard to risk, meanwhile, the notion that the logic of actuarialism constrains practitioner discretion is increasingly recognised as an overstated claim. But it is clearly also the case that, in some situations, procedur-alisation is necessary and does have advantages. For example, it might go some way to ensuring objective knowledge counters defensive practice, or limit the potential for partisanship of the sort which manifests in the so-called 'rule of optimism' (Dingwall et al. 1983). Consequently, it is clear that the issue is not whether social work prac-tice ought to be based on either practitioner discretion or procedural practice, but in which situations and circumstances practitioners might differentially draw upon proceduralised knowledge as opposed to relying on professional judgement. Mapping such a model is potentially a 'very big' job, and inclination to engage in it, either in particular agencies or more generally, will to some extent depend on whether or not one is particularly convinced that the quality of social work decision-making is in any case actually a cause for concern.

The 'golden age' of discretion?

Examining social work historically raises another significant issue for contemporary debates regarding discretion, namely whether or not there ever was a 'golden age' in which practitioners had true, unfettered discretion. This assumption generally underpins the 'curtailment' perspective. Arguably, a 'rose-tinted prism' is used to compare contemporary arrangements with an idealised period in which practice was unencumbered by the preoccupations and pressures of the present. This is apparent in the suggestion that increasingly, legal and policy developments inhibit the ability of practitioners to act upon their traditional commitment to social justice. Traditional ethical priorities are undermined within generalised organisational con-texts in which the inability of practitioners to develop and exercise discretion enhances the potential for 'administrative evil' through the mundanity of policy and procedure (Preston-Shoot 2011). In mental health, for example, there is a tendency to compare social work as it is currently perceived – bureaucratic, non-therapeutic, statutory, risk-driven – with some alternative mode of practice in which clinical discretion was privileged (Cooper 2002; Nathan and Webber 2010) and which is generally taken to inhibit workers' abilities to practise in user-centred ways. Critics thus lament the shift 'from therapy to administration' (Sawyer 2005), and the missed potential of the (radical) 'road not taken' (Ferguson 2008).

It is important to problematise this tendency for counterposing past and present. It is clear from contemporaneous literature and historical research that the belief that ongoing developments represent a threat to transcendental aspects of practice was also apparent among earlier generations of social workers. Indeed, there does seem to be a tendency in social work to 'nostalgically yearn for a bygone "golden" past' (Garrett 2009: 152) in which concerns regarding the welfare of the individual are perceived as having been untrammelled by issues of accountability, evidence or risk. But such nostalgia disregards the widely acknowledged limits of traditional approaches, including the sociological critique of therapy, the radical critique of individualised practice, the inconsistency inherent within informal, wholly subjective assessment, and the many injustices which have arisen on the basis of clinical approaches to decision-making – the very problems which policy initiatives over the decades have sought to ameliorate via shifts in the formulation of practitioner discretion.

Perhaps surprisingly, the election of a 'Con-Dem' coalition government in 2010 coincided with a 'loosening of the shackles' that social work operates within, apparently intended to enable practitioners to better engage in 'frontline' practice. In this way, they tapped into the *zeitgeist*, at least as it applies in social work, in various ways. First, following the Munro Report (2011), there was recognition that the quality of professional practice was likely to be diminished where bureaucratic requirements minimised time available for face-to-face contact with service users. Second, theoretically, there has been a resurgence of interest in broadly 'relationship-based' approaches to practice (e.g. Ruch 2005; Wilson et al. 2008) which reiterate the centrality of the interaction between service user and worker as the bedrock for sound social work. Finally, politically, the Coalition government has explicitly rejected aspects of the 'top-down' statism which critics argue characterised 'New' Labour. At least initially, these shifts were broadly welcomed as challenging the hold that managerialism has had on the public sector since the 1970s, and heralding a return to 'traditional' methods, with increased scope for professional discretion in making judgements. However, questions are emerging about the extent to which in practice such developments have actually addressed the issues highlighted here. For example, although enhanced discretion might hold intuitive appeal, it also entails enhanced responsibility and accountability. Given the current context for practice, in which practitioners fear the consequences of being judged to have made an inaccurate decision, it seem unlikely that reforms will meaningfully reduce fear of blame and its contribution to risk-averse decision-making. Unless expectations of infallibility are countered, and blaming tendencies within organisations diminish, neither relationship-based approaches nor enhanced discretion will reduce the pressure for practitioners to make the 'right' decision. Paradoxically, they may well accentuate it (Hood 2011).

Conclusion

It does appear that many of the issues and tensions which characterise contemporary debates regarding discretion are enduring rather than novel. This makes it difficult for the impartial observer to determine to what extent perceived 'threats' to professionalism reflect substantive concerns based on fundamental changes, or a possibly intrinsic tendency to highlight the negative potential of any new initiative on the basis of an idealised perception of either what practice entailed in the past, or more fundamentally, the nature of social work itself. Either way, it is notable that advocacy of the merits of professionalism is often utilised as a basis for what is perceived to be resistance to politicisation. Managerialism, evidence-based practice and risk have all been criticised as attempts to undermine the professional in pursuit of particular ideological aims. As historical analysis demonstrates, however, it is a mistake to construe the work of social workers in non-political terms. Fundamentally, the nature of social work as a politically designated (and funded) activity means that discretion is always subject to some degree of restriction. This is because as a profession its aims are 'set' elsewhere, and via the resources made available to it and the policy priorities it sets, government can and does legitimately seeks to shape objectives, methods and outcomes. It is crucially important to recognise that the nature and function of social work is to a significant extent determined at political rather than practitioner level. Politics reflects, and interacts with, social, economic and cultural debates, which play out in public sector organisations. It should not therefore be either surprising or problematic that 'political' issues – risk, trust, legitimacy – are evident within the practice arena. Historically, social work has routinely been drawn upon to contribute to the resolution of what Rose and Miller (1992) refer to as 'problematics of government', whether conceived of as social order issues associated with poverty, mental health problems requiring therapeutic intervention, individual issues symptomatic of wider social dysfunction, or manifestations of individual failures to take responsibility.

Arguably, such an analysis allows only a limited view of the nature of professional social work, and relegates professional social workers to the role of 'bureau functionaries'. However, the bureau professionalism which characterises contemporary social work is arguably distinct from earlier and different manifestations in its history and development, and thus the requirements on practitioners less straightforward than the standardised model of professionalism allows for. However, and significantly, this does not mean that the skills and knowledge which practitioners require to fulfil their roles are in some way 'lesser' than those which characterise – for example – medicine or law. They are, however, different, as are the objectives of social work and the circumstances and situations in which social workers intervene (see Cheragi-Sohi and Calnan [2013] for a similar discussion in relation to the emergence of new forms of professionalism in medicine). In this, they reflect the enduringly contested nature of the issues and problems that social work intervenes in, and the lack of consensus regarding the causes or cures of social problems.

I began this chapter by highlighting the link between politics, policy and practice. Although the judgements and decisions of professionals ought to be free from political interference, social work is nevertheless a politically defined activity, a recognition which has implications. In particular, the centrality accorded to autonomy and discretion as defining characteristics in a transcendental formulation of professionalism seems misplaced. This does not, however, mean that social work is necessarily weakened as a consequence. Rather, it demonstrates why government should be more understanding, sympathetic and supportive of its own 'operatives'. After all, they routinely often find themselves in the same 'damned if you do, damned if you don't' position as elected politicians. Rather than focusing on whether or not policy and practice have been followed to the letter, politicians and policy-makers should acknowledge that like political decision-making, the judgements that practitioners must make have an inherent potential for inaccuracy. And just like the decisions politicians make, there is a need for a system of checks and balances to ensure that the way in which practitioners undertake decision-making is fair and proportionate. Thus, it is perfectly appropriate for professionals and others to take issue with the particular ways in which policy-makers might seek to set parameters around the function and methods of professional discretion. It is less convincing, however, to argue that they should not have the discretion to do so at all.

References

Biestek, F. (1961) *The Casework Relationship*. London: Allen and Unwin.

Butler, I. and Drakeford, M. (2003) *Social Policy, Social Welfare and Scandal: How British Public Policy is Made*. Basingstoke: Palgrave Macmillan.

Carson, E., Chung, D. and Evans, T. (2015) 'Complexities of discretion in social services in the third sector', *European Journal of Social Work*, 18 (2): 167–184.

Cartwright, N. and Hardie, J. (2012) *Evidence-based Policy: A Practical Guide to Doing it Better*. Oxford: Oxford University Press.

Cheragi-Sohi, S. and Calnan, M. (2013) 'Discretion or discretions? Delineating professional discretion: the case of English medical practice', *Social Science and Medicine*, 96 (November): 52–59.

Clarke, J. (2004) 'Dissolving the public realm: the logics and limits of neo-liberalism', *Journal of Social Policy*, 33 (1): 27–48.

Cooper, A. (2002) 'Keeping our heads: preserving therapeutic values in a time of change', *Journal of Social Work Practice*, 6: 7–13.

Corby, B. (2006) *Child Abuse: Towards a Knowledge Base*. Maidenhead: Open University Press.

Cree, V. (2002) 'Social work and society', in M. Davies (ed.), *The Blackwell Companion to Social Work* (2nd edition). Oxford: Blackwell.

Cree, V. (2003) 'The changing nature of social work', in R. Adams, L. Dominelli, and M. Payne (eds), *Social Work: Themes, Issues and Critical Debates* (2nd edn). Basingstoke: Palgrave Macmillan.

Culpitt, I. (1999) *Social Policy and Risk*. London: Sage.

Dingwall, R., Eekalaar, J. and Murray, T.C. (1983) *The Protection of Children: State, Intervention and Family Life*. Oxford: Blackwell.

England, H. (1986) *Social Work as Art – Making Sense for Good Practice*. London: Allen and Unwin.

Evans, T. (2010) *Professional Discretion in Welfare Services*. Aldershot: Ashgate.

Evans, T. and Hardy, M. (2010) *Evidence and Knowledge for Practice*. Cambridge: Polity Press.

Evans, T. and Harris, J. (2004) 'Street-level bureaucracy, social work and the (exaggerated) death of discretion', *British Journal of Social Work*, 34: 871–895.

Fawcett, B. and Karbon, K. (2005) *Contemporary Mental Health: Theory, Policy and Practice*. London: Routledge.

Ferguson, I. (2008) *Reclaiming Social Work: Challenging Neo-liberalism and Promoting Social Justice*. London: Sage.

Fish, S. and Hardy, M. (forthcoming 2015) 'Complex issues, complex solutions: Applying complexity theory in social work practice', *Nordic Social Work Research* (Special issue on 'Social work and sociology').

Garrett, P.M. (2009) *Transforming Children's Services: Social Work, Neo-Liberalism and the 'Modern' World*. Maidenhead: Open University Press.

Hardy, M. (2015) *Governing Risk: Care and Control in Contemporary Social Work*. Basingstoke: Palgrave Macmillan.

Harris, J. (2003) *The Social Work Business*. Abingdon: Routledge.

Hood, C. (2011) *The Blame Game: Spin, Bureaucracy and Self Preservation in Government*. Woodstock: Princeton University Press.

Horner, W. (2003) *What is Social Work?* Exeter: Learning Matters.

Howe, D. (1996) 'Surface and depth in social work practice', in N. Parton (ed.) *Social Theory, Social Change and Social Work*. London: Routledge.

Kahneman, D. (2011) *Thinking Fast and Slow*. London: Allen Lane.

Lavalette, M. (ed.) (2011) *Radical Social Work Today*. Bristol: Policy Press.

Munro, E. (2004) 'The impact of audit on social work practice', *British Journal of Social Work*, 34: 1075–1095.

Munro, E. (2008) *Effective Child Protection* (2nd edn). London: Sage.

Munro, E. (2011) *The Munro Review of Child Protection: Final Report. A Child-centered System*. London: Department for Education.

Nathan, J. and Webber, M. (2010) 'Mental health social work and the bureau-medicalisation of mental health care: Identity in a changing world ', *Journal of Social Work Practice*, 24 (1): 15–28.

Offer, J. (2006) *An Intellectual History of British Social Policy: Idealism versus Non-Idealism*. Bristol: Polity Press.

Parton, N. (1994) '"Problematics of government", (post) modernity and social work', *British Journal of Social Work*, 24: 9–32.

Parton, N. (1996) 'Social work, risk and the 'blaming system', in N. Parton (ed.), *Social Theory, Social Change and Social Work*. London: Routledge.

Parton, N. (2006) *Safeguarding Childhood: Early Intervention and Surveillance in Late Modern Society*. Basingstoke: Palgrave Macmillan.

Payne, M. (2002) 'The politics of systems theory within social work', *Journal of Social Work*, 2: 269–292.

Pierson, J. (2011) *Understanding Social Work: History and Context*. Maidenhead: Open University Press.

Preston-Shoot, M. (2011) 'On administrative evil-doing within social work policy and services: law, ethics and practice', *European Journal of Social Work*, 14 (2): 177–194.

Richmond, M. (1917) *Social Diagnosis*. New York: Russell Sage Foundation.

Rogowski, S. (2013) *Critical Social Work with Children and Families*. Bristol: Policy Press.

Rose, N. (1996) 'The death of the social? Reconfiguring the territory of government', *Economy and Society*, 25: 327–356.

Rose, N. (1998) 'Governing risky individuals: the role of psychiatry in new regimes of control', *Psychiatry, Psychology and Law*, 5: 177–195.

Rose, N. (2000) 'Government and control', *British Journal of Criminology*, 40: 321–339.

Rose, N. and Miller, P. (1992) 'Political power beyond the state: problematics of government', *British Journal of Sociology*, 43: 173–205.

Ruch, G. (2005) 'Relationship-based and reflective practice in contemporary child care social work', *Child and Family Social Work*, 10 (2): 111–123.

Sackett, D., Rosenberg, W., Muir Gray, J., Haynes, R. and Richardson, W. (1996) 'Evidence-based medicine: What it is and what it isn't', *British Medical Journal*, 312: 71–72.

Sawyer, A.M. (2005) 'From therapy to administration: Deinstitutionalisation and the ascendancy of psychiatric "risk thinking"', *Health Sociology Review*, 14: 283–296.

Schon, D. (1983) *The Reflective Practitioner: How Professionals Think in Action*. New York: Basic Books.

Seebohm Report (1968) *Report of the Committee on Local Authority and Allied Personal Social Services*, Cmnd 3703. London: HMSO.

Sheldon, B., Ellis, A., Mooseley, A. and Tierney, S. (2004) *Evidence-Based Social Care – An Update of Prospects and Problems.* Centre for Evidence-Based Social Care: University of Exeter.

Sheldon, B. and Macdonald, G. (2009) *A Textbook of Social Work.* London: Routledge.

Sheldon, B., Chilvers, R., Ellis, A, Moseley, A. and Tierney, S. (2005) 'A pre-post empirical study of obstacles to, and opportunities for, evidence-based practice in social care', in A. Bilson (ed.), *Evidence-Based Practice in Social Work.* London: Whiting and Birch.

Sheppard, M. (1995) *Care Management and the New Social Work: A Critical Analysis.* London: Whiting and Birch.

Taylor, I. and Kelly, J. (2006) 'Professionals, discretion and public sector reform in the UK: re-visiting Lipsky', *International Journal of Public Sector Management*, 19 (7): 629–642.

Wallander, L. and Molander, A. (2014) 'Disentangling professional discretion: a conceptual and methodological approach', *Professions and Professionalism*. Available at: http://dx.doi.org/10.7577/pp.808 (accessed 29 July 2015).

Warner, J. (2006) 'Inquiry reports as active texts and their function in relation to professional practice in mental health', *Health, Risk and Society*, 8: 223–237.

Wilson, K., Ruch, G., Lymbery, M. and Cooper, A. (2008) *Social Work: An Introduction to Contemporary Practice.* Harlow: Pearson Longman Education.

2

Social Work Education and Training as a Policy Issue

Alix Walton

Within the UK, social work forms part of the state welfare apparatus and is therefore affected by changing political and economic climates and welfare ideologies. Social work education and training in turn is inextricably linked to such shifting contexts and policy. This chapter focuses on key developments and debates in social work education and training in the UK. Three phases of development are considered before exploring the current context through the lens of ongoing debates, tensions and binaries affecting social work education to date. The chapter focuses on social work rather than the wider social care workforce. In addition, although some developments and debates refer to the UK as a whole, the chapter is guilty of an England-centric focus (with apologies to colleagues in other countries). Despite their importance, within this chapter it is only possible to give limited consideration to: the role of service users and carers in social work education; approaches to teaching and learning; post-qualifying education and training and inter-professional education and training.

Post-Seebohm

The Committee on Local Authority and Allied Personal Social Services, chaired by Frederic Seebohm, was established by the Labour government in 1965 with a remit to recommend changes needed to secure an effective family service (Dickens 2011). The publication of the Seebohm Report in 1968 signalled a significant phase in the development of contemporary social work and social work education. The central recommendation of the report was the establishment of a new department within local authorities providing a unified community-based and family-orientated service. The Local Authority Social Services Act 1970 was the vehicle for the introduction of social services departments in local authorities which were established over the next two years (Dickens 2011). These departments became the workplace for the majority of social workers for the foreseeable future.

The Local Authority Social Services Act 1970 also legislated for the introduction of the Central Council for Education and Training in Social Work (CCETSW), replacing the Council for Training in Social Work and a number of other bodies responsible for varying aspects of social work education (Stevenson 1976a). CCETSW developed the first national social work qualification, the Certificate of Qualification in Social Work (CQSW) which was launched in 1972. The CQSW was a generic qualification as recommended within the Seebohm Report, although the report had also acknowledged the need for specialisation within the course (Seebohm 1968). Although the CQSW saw the formation of one national, generic qualification for social workers, there were actually four routes and academic levels to the award. These routes were non-graduate (two years), undergraduate (normally four years as part of degree in social sciences), post-graduate diploma (one year) and Masters (two years). The range of routes and academic levels leading to the new social work qualification was perhaps expedient given the rise in demand for social workers, primarily from the new social services departments (Stevenson 1976b), but as a consequence quantity of places on social work programmes took priority over consistency in structure and academic level (Lyons 1999). However, this variety in programmes also offered the possibility of entry to the profession by a wide range of applicants, including some who may otherwise have been lost to the profession (Stevenson 1976a). A differing interpretation is that the failure to provide a single, more coherent, route to qualification was due to CCETSW's desire to avoid conflict with the established social work programmes and their institutions (Lyons 1999). It can also be seen as illustrative of the uncertainty about the academic status of social work within the educational institutions and the profession itself (Green 2006; Parsloe 2001) and increasingly through the 1970s, by employers (Jones 1996).

A further major development for social work in this period was the establishment of the British Association of Social Workers (BASW) in 1970, through the merger of seven separate associations (Dickens 2011). Although the establishment of a professional body for social work was seen as (another) reason for optimism within the profession during this period, it was not without its challenges. One of the first challenges was a debate about whether membership should be closed: restricted to those who held a social work qualification, or open to unqualified social workers who at this point formed the majority of basic grade field social workers (Sackville 2013). The recent development of a national social work qualification was a factor in this debate but the significant numbers of social workers who remained without a qualification perhaps played the most significant role in securing an open membership.

This initial phase in the development of contemporary social work and social work education is commonly described using terms such as unified and unification (Dickens 2011; Harris et al. 2008; Lyons 1999). This is exemplified through the establishment of unified social services departments, a unifying social work education and training body and qualification and a unifying professional body. However, simply identifying this as a period of unification also serves to mask the divisions, tensions and debates which existed within social work education and the wider policy context.

One area of tension which became apparent very early in CCETSW's existence related to the influence of employers (Jones 1996; Lyons 1999). Indeed, in their second annual report CCETSW (1975) noted that employers were seeking to influence social work education and pressing the value of practical training (Jones 1996). It is perhaps unsurprising then that 1975 also saw CCETSW launch a second qualification, the Certificate in Social Service (CSS). The CSS was a qualification primarily for staff working in residential and day care and was delivered on a work release basis. Webb (1996) argues that the CSS was also noteworthy because of the requirement for employers to be involved in decisions about the nature and content of the courses in order for courses to secure CCETSW approval. Alongside these developments the 'civil war' (Copper 2012: 149) between psychoanalytic casework and radical social work was a feature of the period. This served to distract some of the attention and energies of the academy and profession, as well as increasing employers' concerns about the 'type' of social workers emerging from courses and whether they would perform the job as employers required. These 'difficult years for the social-work academy' (Jones 1996: 201) weakened their ability to resist the growing influence of employers over social work education.

This period in social work education can therefore be encapsulated as one containing some considerable achievements and unification but also a period of substantial challenge which ultimately resulted in social work education entering the 1980s with 'its confidence shaken and resources depleted' (Lyons 1999: 13) and with some questions regarding its survival (Brewer and Lait 1980). The next 18 years of Conservative government from 1979 to 1997 set the context for the next phase of social work education to be explored in this chapter.

Three years or two?

In terms of social work education, this phase is perhaps best characterised by the fight for, and failure to achieve, a three-year social work qualification. CCETSW made the case for a three-year qualification on the basis of the length of time required to ensure social workers possessed the breadth and depth of knowledge and skills to practise effectively (Lymbery 2009; Lyons 1999). This argument was made in the context of ongoing concerns from employers about the relevance of the social work qualification and their demands for more emphasis on skills training. Social work education was also receiving criticism in child death inquiries (Blom-Cooper 1985) as well as needing to accommodate changes in new legislation and in the way social services were being organised and delivered. To strengthen their argument for a three year qualification CCETSW also drew attention to European Directives and norms in respect of the duration and academic level of professional training (Lyons 1999). However, in 1989 the government rejected CCETSW's proposal, arguing that the funding required would be better used to support in-service training and the establishment of National Vocational Qualifications (NVQs) (Moriarty 2011). CCETSW quickly proposed the creation of a two-year qualification (CCETSW 1989). Although the speed of the new proposal impacted negatively on CCETSW's credibility (Lymbery et al. 2000) it was endorsed by government and resulted in the development of the Diploma in Social Work (DipSW) as the new national qualification for social work. Paper 30 (CCETSW 1989) underpinned the DipSW, specifying the knowledge, values and skills needed to achieve competence in social work practice including the requirement for a specialist orientation in the second year (Cutmore and Walton 1997). The DipSW was to be delivered at the minimum academic level of Diploma in Higher Education (DipHE), although courses at degree and post-graduate level were still permitted. The DipSW was introduced in 1990 and by 1994 all intakes to social work programmes were to the DipSW.

Parsloe (1990: 20) described the failure to win the argument for a three-year qual-ification as 'a blow to the standing of British social work and social work education', while Webb (1996: 187) refers to CCETSW as having 'revenged itself' on the univer-sities via the DipSW. Views about the reasons for failure differ but alongside political interests, employer influence is generally cited as the most significant. Commentators advancing this view argue that the influence of employers can be seen through the use of the CSS as the model or 'Trojan horse' (Webb 1996: 181) for the new DipSW rather than the CQSW (Lyons 1999; Rogowski 2010; Webb 1996). Like the CSS, the establishment of formal partnerships between colleges and employer organisations was a requirement of the DipSW. Additionally, in 1989, CCETSW confirmed the parity of the CSS with the CQSW, something which had never been an intention (Rogowski 2010).

Another criticism of the DipSW related to the introduction of a competence-based approach (Orme et al. 2009; Preston-Shoot 2004) or what has been termed the 'NVQisation' of social work education (Carey 2007), which was seen as reductionist and mechanistic: a 'tick-box' approach. This approach was viewed as employer-led and by some commentators as a statement of anti-intellectualism, posing a threat to the development of critical thinking, use of critical theories and other aspects of academic learning (Green 2006; Jones 1999; Preston-Shoot 2004; Rogowski 2010). A number of strengths of a competence-based approach have been noted, including clear standards against which assessment takes place, the emphasis on performance and observation within assessment and the empowerment of candidates within the process (Kelly and Horder 2001; Weinstein 1998). However, the overwhelming response from the social work academy has been damning.

A further source of debate and critique was CCETSW's statements within Paper 30 (1989, 1991) about its commitment to anti-racism within the social work education curriculum, particularly its reference to the 'endemic racism' within British society. While achieving the inclusion of these commitments and statements was seen as significant and hard-fought progress (Williams 1997), at the same time CCETSW found itself under serious attack. On one side, CCETSW was criticised by those who saw the statements as 'superficially radical' (Rogowski 2010: 120), failing to address structural concepts sufficiently and weakened by the parallel commitment to a compe-tence-based approach. On the other, CCETSW faced a sustained attack from a more powerful group of politicians, employers and media who labelled their approach as 'politically correct' (Collins et al. 2000; Phillips 1993; Pinker 1993). This criticism of CCETSW paved the way for further reform of social work and the beginnings of the dominance of the discourse of 'common sense' initiated by Virginia Bottomley, then Secretary of State for Health and formerly a social worker (Green 2006; Walker 2002). CCETSW was restructured, with a reduction in the size of the Council and the abolition of the Black Perspectives Committee, and in 1995 a revised Paper 30 was issued containing greatly diluted statements regarding racism and anti-racist practice (Keating 2000). Although this retreat from anti-racist initiatives (Williams 1997) was met with concern, it was also met with a more optimistic call for the development of a more coherent, integrated model of oppression (Keating 2000).

New Labour

The advent of the 'New Labour' government in 1997 and its modernising agenda (DH 1998) signalled the beginning of another phase of substantial changes in the arena of social work education. Within the broader modernising framework of increased regulation, inspection and managerialism (Welbourne 2011) the new government emphasised the development of training arrangements to support the delivery of a competent and confident workforce (DH 1998) and built on this further in its subsequent report *Options for Excellence* that outlined the long-term vision for the workforce (DfES and DH 2006). These initial positive signals for social work were balanced with clear messages of concern about the quality of social work practice, education and their supporting infrastructure. Reviews of social work education were announced, as was the closure of CCETSW (Orme 2001).

By 2001, the Department of Health had announced the introduction of a three-year undergraduate degree as the new minimum qualification in social work, starting in September 2003. This remained a generic qualification, despite the separation of children's and adults' social care services within Local Authorities. The degree was to be regulated by CCETSW's replacement in England, the General Social Care Council (GSCC), and was accompanied by a recruitment campaign and financial support. In addition, specific funds were made available to support the requirement to involve service users and carers in all aspects of the new programmes. Lymbery (2009: 903) notes that the introduction of a social work degree 'appeared to herald a bright future for the development of social work and its education', after all a graduate entry profession had been a long sought after goal for many. Nevertheless, caution was voiced in some quarters. The degree was to be underpinned by National Occupational Standards (TOPSS 2002) and therefore remained an essentially competence-based approach. There were concerns regarding the government's lack of clarity about the future place of social work in welfare provision and thus the purpose of the new structures of regulation, education and training (Orme 2001). The continuation of the regulatory and managerial policies of the right was also cause for concern (Orme 2001; Rogowski 2010). For example, the government's drive to raise standards through regulatory mechanisms can be inferred from the change in language from CCETSW 'advisors' to GSCC 'inspectors' (Bellinger 2010). Furthermore, Ferguson and Woodward (2009: 153) believe that the social work degree simply reinforced the government's view of social work as a failing profession and 'of practitioners and educators as people who cannot be trusted'. Meanwhile, the influence of employers remained strong. Indeed, the Department of Health (2002) foreword to the degree requirements specifically refers to the importance of placement opportunities in ensuring 'that tomorrow's social workers are properly trained to do their job' (2002: i). The government support of employers is also demonstrated through their encouragement of 'flexible and attractive training routes into social work, including work-based training' (HM Treasury 2003: 11). These were commonly termed 'employment-based' or 'grow your own' routes to social work qualification and attracted substantial ring-fenced government funding from 2005 to 2007, through the National Training Strategy Grant (Harris et al. 2008).

In relation to practice placements, the demise of CCETSW had also seen the end of Approved Agency status, however the increased requirement of 200 days in placement maintained the pressure on supply of placements. The Practice Learning Taskforce was established by government in 2002 on a time-limited basis to work to address the ongoing problems regarding quantity and quality of placements. In addition, a performance indicator for practice learning was introduced for local authorities in 2003. Despite finding favour with the sector (Lymbery 2009), the performance indicator was discontinued in 2008. This timing coincided with the introduction of a revised post-qualifying (PQ) framework for social work education and training (GSCC 2005) and the end of the Practice Teaching Award which was announced in 2007, with final awards being completed in 2008. The revised PQ framework was designed to build on the new social work qualification, with practice education being embedded into the revised PQ awards. However, the impact of this was commonly significantly less teaching in this area and confusion about changes in the language of, and requirements for, the former practice teaching role (Bellinger 2010).

Debates, tensions and binaries

The current phase of social work education finds itself in the aftermath of the recommendations of a Social Work Task Force commissioned by the previous Labour government (Social Work Task Force 2009); a review of child protection commissioned by the Secretary of State for Education under the Coalition government (Munro 2011); further criticism of post-qualifying training (Rixon and Ward 2012); separate reviews of children and families and adult social work education (Croisdale-Appelby 2014; Narey 2014); and the response to all of these by the current government and a myriad of stakeholders, including the recently appointed Chief Social Workers for Children and Families and Adults (DfE and DH 2013). An initial response by the new Conservative government was the announcement of a Child Protection Taskforce 'focusing on transforming social work and children's services and improving inspection' (Prime Minister's Office, 2015). It is in the context of this heady mix that the debates, tensions and binaries which continue to affect social work education will now be considered. Although specific areas are considered in turn, they are in reality closely interwoven, impacting on and influencing each other.

The first area relates to the purpose, roles and tasks of social work. One could argue that in order to reach a consensus about the design and content of social work education there first needs to be a consensus about the purpose, roles and tasks of social work itself. After all, if we do not know what social work is, how can we educate for it? This has been an area of ongoing debate (GSCC 2007; Jones, 1996; Jones 2014; Stevenson 1976b), epitomised by the work of the Barclay Committee established in 1980 to clarify the roles and tasks of social workers in England and Wales (Rogowski 2010), but which instead produced one majority and two minority reports setting out the diverging views of committee members (Lymbery 2005). It is noteworthy that the Social Work Task Force (Social Work Task Force 2009) chose only to develop a 'public description of social work' and to refer to its implications for the roles and tasks of social workers rather than attempt to specify these in more detail. In addition, the Centre for Workforce Intelligence refers merely to the fact that 'social worker' is a protected title in law (CfWI 2011). This is perhaps unsurprising since, as Stevenson (1979) points out, it is much easier to locate deficiencies in social work education than to resolve the question of what social work is all about. Moreover, Welbourne (2011: 406) highlights the paradoxical position of UK social work being 'ideologically committed to partnership and empowerment but structurally enmeshed' with state apparatus and a role contributing to the maintenance of the social order. And so, achieving a consensus regarding purpose, roles and tasks seems unlikely; however, in the meantime social workers continue to need to qualify. It may be more realistic therefore to strive for agreement at least in terms of key curriculum areas or broad content of initial social work education, or to acknowledge that the purposes of social work will vary depending on role and employing organisation and to develop a mixed model of education accordingly.

The differing use of the terms 'education' and 'training' illuminates a second area of debate and tension. Within this chapter, the term education has been used as an umbrella term referring to initial qualification and post-qualifying awards, as well as broader continuing professional development activity. In some social work literature, the terms education and training are used interchangeably or as a single phrase where distinction between the terms is not clear, while elsewhere 'education' is used to refer to activity resulting in qualification or generally associated with the involvement of Higher Education Institutions (HEIs) and 'training' is used to indicate other professional development activity particularly activity which is 'in-house' and employer driven. Underpinning this latter usage there may also be an inference that education is something more comprehensive, academic and extending whereas training is more specific and bounded (Malloch et al. 2011). It is from these inferences that the second core debate emerges: the extent to which social workers should be 'educated' for a profession or 'trained' to fulfil agency functions; agency referring predominantly in this context to local authorities.

Davies (1981) refers to the tension between education and training when conceding that there is a need to 'accommodate the real world of agency practice' but not at the cost of isolation from mainstream academia or local authority control over course content. The introduction of the DipSW in 1990, and particularly the adoption of a competence-based approach, as well as the increase in number of placement days was interpreted by some as a shift towards an emphasis on training (Preston-Shoot 2004; Rogowski 2010; Webb 1996). And while the introduction of the social work degree in 2003 (DH, 2002) represented an extended university education, there was also an increase in the number of days in practice placement and retention of a competence-based approach. In addition, the expansion of employer-based routes to qualification (whether termed 'Grow Your Own', 'Employment Based' or 'Step-Up' programmes) which emphasise being work-based rather than campus-based, and generally choose to use the term 'trainees' rather than students, can also be viewed as a shift in emphasis towards a 'training' model of social work qualification. 'Frontline' is the latest addition to such work-based programmes (DfE 2013). Debates surrounding its development have also signalled the return by some to the criticism of campus-based programmes for delivering social workers 'filled with "idealistic" left-wing dogma' (Paton 2013) rather than the practical skills required to 'do the job'. It is interesting to note the use of the terms education and training within Frontline documentation which initially describes the design of the programme as a blend of 'university education and on-the-job-training' (MacAlister 2012: 19) but later chooses to refer to 'intense practical and academic training' (Frontline 2013).

Linked to debates regarding education and training are questions about the proportion of time social work students should spend in practice placement settings. The introduction of the Degree in Social Work in 2007 saw a rise in the number of placement days from a minimum of 130 to 200 days. However, by 2009, the Social Work Task Force had recommended a reduction to 170 days. The rationale for this was to allow programmes more time to deliver important elements of the curriculum, to ensure a sharper focus on what the placement is meant to achieve in terms of the student's learning and development and to enable all students to have better quality placements (Social Work Task Force 2009). These changes illustrate the difficulty in balancing education for social work with direct practice experience. Although placements are arguably the aspect of the qualification where employers can exert most influence over the development of social work students, there have been ongoing problems regarding the quantity and quality of placements, particularly in the statutory sector. Employer-based schemes have had the advantage of guaranteeing placements within their own organisations, including the final placement which often takes place in the social work student's future work setting, although the tensions between education and training remain (Harris et al. 2008). It is noteworthy that information on the Frontline programme refers to both a '12-month placement' and 'working full-time' to describe the first year of the programme, perhaps signalling the move to a more distinct apprenticeship model of social work training.

Changes in the name, education and requirements for the role of practice educators equally reflect the debates of the time and tensions between education and training. It has also been argued that the weakening of systems which support teaching and assessment in practice placements compounds the shift towards training further, resulting in the training of practitioners through practice *experience* rather than development of critical practitioners through practice *learning* (Bellinger 2010: 611).

The debate about whether the initial social work qualification should be generic or specialist is a long-standing one and remains current. The CQSW was the foundation of the generic social work qualification which has endured to date, despite numerous reviews and criticisms of the generic model. The arguments for a generic qualification focus mainly on the premise that all social work has a foundation of common values, knowledge and skills which can be applied across service user groups and settings: also reflecting the reality of service users' lives within broader social contexts and communities rather than simply viewing individuals as part of a rigid group classification. However, whereas the unified authorities which developed following Seebohm (1968) were a key factor in the development of a generic qualification, the subsequent separation of services has served to reignite arguments for specialist initial qualifications, as have recruitment and retention problems in certain areas of social work. In addition, funding for employment-based routes has increasingly focused on social work education for those going into children and families in the form of Step-Up and Frontline programmes. The most recent reviews of social work (Croisdale-Appelby 2014; Narey 2014) alongside the development of Frontline have begun to engage with the generic or specialist debate once more.

Presenting the debate as a simple generic or specialist binary is unhelpful; Stevenson articulates its features and complexities well (2005), although she is also critical of the profession for failing to do so externally. Stevenson (1976b) emphasises that there are many ways to 'cut the cake' and that divisions of specialism do not need to be based on administrative rather than professional distinctions. In addition, reference to a generic qualification belies the fact that social work qualifying programmes do offer some specialisation through choice of modules and more particularly through the specialist nature of placement settings. Luckock et al. (2007) suggest that it would be more useful to view generic learning for practice as always being undertaken in the context of specialist settings but at an increasingly sophisticated level of expectation and competence or expertise (Luckock et al. 2007). This approach would also assist in moving the discussion beyond initial qualification to a fuller consideration of the development of specialist knowledge and skills post-qualification, and to the structures and resources required to support such development.

The imbalance in the structures and allocation of resources within social work education, with an emphasis falling on initial education, has been noted from the mid-1970s (Cutmore and Walton 1997), continues to date, and creates further tensions. Changes to the minimum academic level, content and level of specialism at qualifying level naturally impact on post-qualifying education. However, this has resulted in a reactive rather than proactive approach to development of formal post-qualifying education (Stevenson 2005) and contributed to an evolution of post-qualifying structures which has been 'long, difficult and controversial' (Cooper and Rixon 2001: 701). At times, changes in post-qualifying education have been made to enable PQ to 'fit' with qualifying courses and at others to address deficiencies identified in initial training, such as through the Post-Qualifying Child Care Award (PQCCA) (Masson et al. 2008). Given this complex, frequently changing framework, combined with the well-documented challenge in supporting staff to complete assessed post-qualifying studies (Brignall 2001; Brown and Keen 2004; Cooper and Rixon 2001; Lymbery 2009; Taylor et al. 2010; TOPSS 2000), the limited number of social workers completing post-qualifying awards is unsurprising. These factors, combined with a primary focus on initial qualification, have resulted in a failure to properly value and support the development of staff post-qualification (Social Work Task Force 2009), with limited support for professional development unless linked to direct funding or compulsory awards (Cutmore and Walton 1997).

In recent years, there has been more focus on supporting social workers' transition into the workforce through the Newly Qualified Social Worker (NQSW) scheme (CWDC 2008; Skills for Care 2009) and the Assessed and Supported Year in Employment (ASYE) (DfE 2012); both attracting direct funding from central government. Meanwhile, tangible methods to support the development of a strong learning culture (Social Work Task Force 2009) for more experienced workers remain less prevalent. This is perhaps surprising, and certainly short-sighted, given the ongoing difficulties in retaining experienced social workers (Baginsky 2013; Healy et al. 2009; LGA 2009). Although it is a complex area, retention does appear to be supported by opportunities for professional development and clear career pathways (Baginsky 2013; Healy et al. 2009) and yet it fails to be given proportionate or consistent attention or resources.

In contrast to the areas already discussed, the evaluation of social work education is unfortunately an area where there has been too little debate and attention. It is noteworthy how few changes to social work education have been made with the benefit of robust evidence to underpin the changes or the debates which have informed them. The limited evaluation of social work education at both qualifying and post-qualifying levels is widely acknowledged (Carpenter 2005; Doel et al. 2008; Orme et al. 2009; Rixon and Ward 2012). Of the studies which have been undertaken, many are small-scale, focusing on specific groups, programmes or aspects of education. In addition, Carpenter (2005) argues that overall this is an area of research lacking in rigour. The lack of focus on the impact of social work education on outcomes for service users is also noted (Robinson and Webber 2013; Slater 2007).

There are numerous challenges with regard to the evaluation of social work education of which three are briefly outlined. First, this area poses particular methodological and practical challenges (Carpenter 2005; Orme 2012). An illustration of this is the lack of baseline data for studies: a problem exacerbated by frequent changes to education frameworks, content and delivery modes (Orme 2012). Second, the lack of funding is a barrier, particularly to support larger scale studies. There have been some exceptions to this such as the Department of Health funding to evaluate the social work degree (Orme et al. 2009) but there are other examples such as the Department of Health's stated commitment to an evaluation of the Post-Qualifying Child Care Award (Masson et al. 2008) where funding was never forthcoming. Employers have at times been allocated funding to evaluate the impact of centrally funded social work training, for example through the Training Support Programme (TSP) Grant (DH 2001, 2003). Guidance has however provided only limited encouragement to evaluate rather than a requirement to do so, and measurements of effectiveness have tended to remain linked to the achievement of qualifications or number of training days provided (DH 2001, 2003) rather than evaluation of the impact of training activity. Finally, Orme (2012) offers a clear articulation of political influences on the evaluation of social work education. These are manifested through decisions about which aspects of social work education to evaluate and the level of funding to support this, as well as the failure to either wait for the evaluations to be completed before embarking on further changes to social work education or to attend to the conclusion of evaluations when they are available.

The final and arguably most pertinent aspect of social work education to consider is who controls and drives the social work education agenda. All aspects of social work education are made more complex by the number of stakeholders in this area and their varying levels of involvement and influence. The ever-changing landscape of arm's-length bodies, including regulators (CCETSW, GSCC, HCPC [Health and Care Professions Council]) and bodies representing employer interests (TOPSS, Skills for Care, CWDC [Children's Workforce Development Council]) simply compounds this complexity and creates an ongoing state of disequilibrium. Before returning to the question of who drives the agenda, the key stakeholders will be considered briefly in turn.

Although HEIs may be perceived as powerful stakeholders in social work education and training, and at times their position has been reinforced, in reality their position is a precarious one. It has been argued that HEI social work programmes have been under attack since the establishment of CCETSW (Parton 1996; Rogowski 2010). Others emphasise the 'control' of social work programmes through regulatory bodies and processes (Lymbery et al. 2000), arguing that 'Britain is subject to a much greater level of control than in other European countries' (2000: 278). The level and nature of external control of HEI social work programmes is also uncharacteristic when compared to other programmes delivered within British HEIs. Consequently, as well as external pressures on social work programmes, significant internal pressures also exist (Bellinger 2010; Green 2006). Wilson and Campbell (2013) highlight the particular difficulty social work academics experience in balancing the competing demands of teaching, administration and research. This combination of internal and external pressures has recently seen the closure of several social work programmes and an increasing threat to others (Burke 2012).

Two of the most significant stakeholders, the social work profession and service users and carers, have the weakest voices in these debates and therefore remain the least influential players in social work education and training. This is despite the fact that the role of service users and carers in education has been increasing since the 1990s (Molyneux and Irvine 2004) and required since 2002 (DH 2002; GSCC 2005). However, Robinson and Webber (2013) highlight ongoing challenges in this area and also significant gaps in evidence about the effect of involvement in programmes and on direct practice. In addition, although the involvement of service users and carers was identified as an underpinning principle of the Social Work Reform Board (2010), this is subject to a number of threats. The change of regulator to the HCPC initially saw an end to the formal requirement to involve service users and carers, although this was subsequently reversed (HCPC 2014); however, arrangements for funding their involvement remain uncertain (Moriarty and Manthorpe 2014). In addition, Robinson and Webber (2013) warn that changes to funding service user and carer involvement and a move to a continuing professional development (CPD) framework which is likely to involve more employer-based training may result in a diminished role for service users and carers in social work education.

In relation to the social work profession, Hugman (1991) asserts that many of the professions (including social work) are in a triangular, interdependent relationship with the state and the client but that the state has considerably more power than either the professional or the client. The impact of this can be seen in the phases of social work education outlined in this chapter. In addition, Cooper (2012) argues that social work has become steadily identified with child protection, rather than as a whole of which child protection is only part. Challenge to, and revision of, this perspective would enable the profession to be more robust rather than 'still shaped by the dominant public narratives of the recent past – the episodic eruption of child abuse scandals' (Cooper 2012: 146). More recently, both the Social Work Task Force (2009) and Munro (2011) commented on the lack of voice of the social work profession. Although the work of these reviews resulted in the establishment of the College of Social Work which in its strapline proclaimed itself 'The voice of social work in England', the organisation failed to attract a significant proportion of social workers as members and was also criticised for restricted, undemocratic elections to key posts within the College (Jones 2013). Crucially the College remained dependent on government funding and therefore vulnerable to closure. The announcement of withdrawal of government funding and resultant closure of the College (Cleary 2015) means that the immediate future does not appear to signal any likely strengthening of the voice of the profession or of service users and carers in relation to social work education.

Employers, particularly local authority employers, have been identified as exerting an increasing influence on social work education from the 1970s onwards (Bellinger 2010; Jones 1996; Lymbery 2009; Rogowski 2012; Webb 1996). So, although the creation of social services departments bringing together large numbers of social workers was seen by some as a point of optimism, it can also be viewed as the point which signalled the beginning of control of social work and social work education by local government employers. The influence of employers has been facilitated through changes such as an increased representation in bodies such as CCETSW (Webb 1996), the central role identified for employers within social work qualifying programmes (J.M. Consulting 1999) and the expansion of employment-based routes to social work qualification. Most recently, the development of the ASYE could be seen as giving employers the role of final gatekeeper to the profession, given that failing the ASYE is likely to have a significant and detrimental impact on a newly qualified social worker's career.

However, as social work education and training continues to struggle with the impact of complex stakeholder relationships and more formal partnerships (Cutmore and Walton 1997; Lymbery 2009; Lyons 1999), it is central government which retains the balance of power in social work education. This can be seen, for example, from the establishment of social services departments post-Seebohm (1968) which have come under increasing government influence, regulation and control; through the changes of arm's-length bodies directing the course of social work education, at government behest; to the brief endowment of a College of Social Work which was notably *for* the profession rather than established *by* the profession. This does not mean that other stakeholders are unable to influence the agenda and direction of travel for social work education, but that it is likely to be an ongoing labour.

Conclusion

Various terms and phrases are used within the literature to describe some of the key points in social work and social work education and training. These include 'crossroads' (Lymbery 2001), 'watershed' (SWTF 2009), 'high watermark' (Rogowski 2010), 'critical moment in time' (Jones 2014) and 'perfect storm' (Taylor and Bogo 2014). However, Dickens argues that such metaphors are unhelpful given that the 'shape of social work is never fixed, can never be settled for once and for all' (2011: 35).

So, it may be useful instead to consider the challenges facing social work education and training as 'wicked'. Indeed, Lymbery (2011) has already made use of this concept. Among other characteristics 'wicked problems' have innumerable causes, involve many stakeholders, can be considered to be a symptom of another problem and do not have 'a' right answer (Camillus 2008). Whether the term itself appeals or not, many of the messages are helpful, emphasising the need to shift from binaries, to look at the whole and to collaborate and share understanding. Such shared understanding does not necessarily mean that there is agreement about the 'problem' but instead that stakeholders understand each other's perspectives well enough to have intelligent dialogue about different interpretations of position and to exercise collective intelligence about how to solve it. While such an approach is easy to describe, I suspect few stakeholders would deny that in reality the challenges of social work education are experienced as 'ambiguous, fluid, complex, political, and frustrating as hell' (Roberts 2000: 2). The challenge then is to ensure that social workers, and all those who have a stake in the roles they undertake, are well informed about, and engage with, these issues and debates. It will require tenacity, resilience and patience to remain engaged in issues to which there are no obvious solutions and certainly not 'an answer'.

References

Baginsky, M. (2013) *Retaining Experienced Social Workers in Children's Services: The Challenge Facing Local Authorities in England.* Available at: www.kcl.ac.uk/sspp/policy-institute/scwru/pubs/2013/reports/baginsky13retaining.pdf (accessed: 29 July 2015).

Bellinger, A. (2010) 'Studying the landscape: practice learning for social work reconsidered', *Social Work Education: The International Journal,* 29 (6): 599–615.

Blom-Cooper, L. (1985) *A Child in Trust: The Report of the Panel of Inquiry into the Circumstances Surrounding the Death of Jasmine Beckford.* Wembley: London Borough of Brent.

Brewer, C and Lait, I. (1980) 'Can social work survive?', in K. Lyons (1999), *Social Work in Higher Education: Demise or Development?* Aldershot: Ashgate.

Brignall, P. (2001) 'Comparative evaluation of the factors influencing the success of candidates in achieving PQ1 in respect of a variety of routes', *What Works in Post-Qualifying Education for Social Workers?* London: Central Council for Education and Training in Social Work (CCETSW).

Brown, K. and Keen, S. (2004) 'Post-qualifying awards in social work (Part 1): Necessary evil or panacea?', *Social Work Education,* 23 (1): 77–92.

Burke, C (2012) 'Should UK universities take social work education more seriously?', *The Guardian,* 1 October. Available at: www.theguardian.com/social-care-network/2012/oct/01/uk-universities-social-work-education (accessed 31 December 2013).

Camillus, J.C. (2008) 'Strategy as a wicked problem', *Harvard Business Review,* 86 (5): 98–106.

Carey, M. (2007) 'White-collar proletariat? Braverman, the deskilling/upskilling of social work and the paradoxical life of the agency care manager', *Journal of Social Work,* 7: 93.

Carpenter, J. (2005) *Evaluating Outcomes in Social Work Education.* Dundee: Scottish Institute for Excellence in Social Work Education (SIESWE) and the Social Care Institute for Excellence (SCIE).

Central Council for Education and Training in Social Work (CCETSW) (1975) *Second Annual Report.* London: CCETSW.

Central Council for Education and Training in Social Work (CCETSW) (1989) *Requirements and Regulations for the Diploma in Social Work, Paper 30.* London: CCETSW.

Central Council for Education and Training in Social Work (CCETSW) (1991) *Requirements and Regulations for the Diploma in Social Work, Paper 30* (2nd edn). London: CCETSW.

Centre for Workforce Intelligence (CfWI) (2011) *Workforce Risks and Opportunities: Adult Social Care.* London: CfWI.

Children's Workforce Development Council (CWDC) (2008) *Newly Qualified Social Worker Pilot Programme 2008–9.* Leeds: CWDC.

Cleary, J. (2015) *Announcement: Closure of The College of Social Work.* Available at: www.tcsw.org.uk/membership/ (accessed 16 July 2015).

Collins, S., Gutridge, P., James, A., Lynn, E. and Williams, C. (2000) 'Racism and anti-racism in placement reports', *Social Work Education: The International Journal*, 19 (1): 29–43.

Cooper, A. (2012) 'How to (almost) murder a profession', in J. Adlam, A. Aiyegbusi, P. Kleinot, A. Motz. and C. Scanlon (eds), *The Therapeutic Milieu under Fire*. London: Jessica Kingsley Publishers.

Cooper, B. and Rixon, A. (2001) 'Integrating post-qualification study into the workplace: The candidates' experience', *Social Work Education: The International Journal*, 20 (6): 701–716.

Croisdale-Appleby, D. (2014) *Re-visioning Social Work Education*. London: Department of Health. Available at: www.gov.uk/government/publications/social-work-education-review (accessed 6 March 2014).

Cutmore, J. and Walton, R. (1997) 'An evaluation of the postqualifying framework', *Social Work Education*, 16 (3): 74–95.

Davies, M. (1981) 'Social work, the state and the university', *British Journal of Social Work*, 11: 275–288.

Department for Eduction (2012) 'Press release: Funding to support new social workers'. Available at: www.gov.uk/government/news/funding-to-support-new-social-workers (accessed 6 March 2014).

Department for Eduction (2013) 'Press release: First ever chief social worker for children and fast-track training to lead social work reform'. Available at: www.gov.uk/government/news/first-ever-chief-social-worker-for-children-and-fast-track-training-to-lead-social-work-reform (accessed 6 March 2014).

Department for Education and Department of Health (2013) *Office of the Chief Social Worker: New Appointees Start*. Available at: www.gov.uk/government/news/office-of-the-chief-social-worker-new-appointees-start (accessed 30 July 2015).

Department for Education and Schools and Department of Health (DH) (2006) *Options for Excellence: Building the Social Care Workforce of the Future*. London: DH.

Department of Health (DH) (1998) *Modernising Social Services*. London: DH.

Department of Health (DH) (2001) *Information Pack for the 2001/2002 Training Support Programme Circular (LAC(2001)7)*. London: DH.

Department of Health (DH) (2002) *Requirements for Social Work Training*, London: DH.

Department of Health (DH) (2003) *Information Pack for the 2003/2004 Training Support Programme Circular (LAC(2003)5)*. London: DH.

Dickens, J (2011) 'Social work in England at a watershed – as always: From the Seebohm Report to the Social Work Task Force', *British Journal of Social Work*, 41: 22–39.

Doel, M., Nelson, P. and Flynn, E. (2008) 'Experiences of post-qualifying study in social work', *Social Work Education*, 27 (5): 549–571.

Ferguson, I. and Woodward, R. (2009) *Radical Social Work in Practice: Making a Difference*. Bristol: Policy Press.

Frontline (2013) *Frontline: Our Programme*. Available at: www.thefrontline.org.uk/frontline-graduate-programme (accessed 2 November 2013).

General Social Care Council (GSCC) (2005) *Post-Qualifying Framework for Social Work Education and Training*. London: GSCC.

General Social Care Council (GSCC) (2007) *Roles and Tasks of Social Work in England*. London: GSCC.

Green, L.C. (2006) 'Pariah profession, debased discipline? An analysis of social work's low academic status and the possibilities for change', *Social Work Education: The International Journal*, 25 (3): 245–264.

Harris, J., Manthorpe, J. and Hussein, S. (2008) *What Works in 'Grow Your Own' Initiatives for Social Work?* London: General Social Care Council.

Health and Care Professions Council (HCPC) (2014) *Standards of Education and Training*. London: HCPC.

Healy, K., Meagher, G. and Cullin, J. (2009) 'Retaining novices to become expert child protection practitioners: Creating career pathways in direct practice', *British Journal of Social Work*, 39: 299–317.

HM Treasury (2003) *Every Child Matters, Cm 5860*. London: The Stationery Office.

Hugman, R. (1991) *Power in Caring Professions*. London: Macmillan.

J.M. Consulting Ltd (1999) *Review of the Diploma in Social Work*. Bristol: J.M. Consulting.

Jones, C. (1996) 'Anti-intellectualism and the peculiarities of British social work education', in N. Parton (ed.), *Social Theory, Social Change and Social Work*. London: Routledge.

Jones, C. (1999) 'Social work: regulation and managerialism', in M. Exworthy and S. Halford (eds), *Professionals and the New Managerialism in the Public Sector*. Buckingham: Open University Press.

Jones, R. (2013) 'The opportunity to give social work a strong voice is being lost', *The Guardian*, 21 January. Available at: www.theguardian.com/social-care-network/2013/jan/21/social-work-strong-voice-lost (accessed 16 September 2013).

Jones, R. (2014) 'The best of times, the worst of times: social work and its moment', *British Journal of Social Work*, 44 (3): 485–502.

Keating, K. (2000) 'Anti-racist perspectives: what are the gains for social work?', *Social Work Education: The International Journal*, 19 (1): 77–87.

Kelly, J. and Horder, W. (2001) 'The how and the why: competences and holistic practice', *Social Work Education*, 20 (6): 689–699.

Local Government Association (LGA) (2009) *Respect and Protect: Respect, Recruitment and Retention in Children's Social Work*. London: LGA.

Luckock, B., Lefevre, M. and Tanner, K. (2007) 'Teaching and learning communication with children and young people: Developing the qualifying social work curriculum in a changing policy context', *Child and Family Social Work*, 12: 192–201.

Lymbery, M. (2001) 'Social work at the crossroads', *British Journal of Social Work*, 31 (3): 369–384.

Lymbery, M. (2005) *Social Work with Older People*. London: Sage.

Lymbery, M. (2009) 'Troubling times for British social work education?', *Social Work Education: The International Journal*, 28 (8): 902–918.

Lymbery, M. (2011) 'Building a Safe and Confident Future: One year on – reflections from the world of higher education in England', *Social Work Education: The International Journal*, 30 (4): 465–471.

Lymbery, M., Charles, M., Christopherson, J. and Eadie, T. (2000) 'The control of British social work education: European comparisons', *European Journal of Social Work*, 3 (3): 269–282.

Lyons, K. (1999) *Social Work in Higher Education: Demise or Development?* Aldershot: Ashgate.

MacAlister, J. (2012) *Frontline: Improving the Children's Social Work Profession*. London: Institute for Public Policy Research (IPPR).

Malloch, M., Cairns, L., Evans, K. and O'Connor, B.N. (2011) *The SAGE Handbook of Workplace Learning*. London: Sage.

Masson, H., Frost, N. and Parton, N. (2008) 'Reflections from the "frontline": social workers' experiences of post-qualifying child care training and their current work practices in the new children's services', *Journal of Children's Services*, 3 (3): 54–64.

Molyneux, J. and Irvine, J. (2004) 'Service user and carer involvement in social work training: A long and winding road?', *Social Work Education: The International Journal*, 23 (3): 293–308.

Moriarty, J. (2011) 'Whose profession is it anyway? Central government in England and qualifying education in social work', in Proceedings of 9th Annual ESPAnet Conference – Sustainability and Transformation in European Social Policy, 8–10 September, Valencia.

Moriarty, J. and Manthorpe, J. (2014) 'Controversy in the curriculum: What do we know about the content of the social work qualifying curriculum in England?', *Social Work Education: The International Journal*, 33 (1): 77–90.

Munro, E. (2011) *The Munro Review of Child Protection: Final Report: A Child-Centred System*. London, Department for Education.

Narey, M. (2014) *Making the Education of Social Workers Consistently Effective*. London: Department for Education. Available at: www.gov.uk/government/publications/making-the-education-of-social-workers-consistently-effective (accessed 7 February 2014).

Orme, J. (2001) 'Regulation or fragmentation? Directions for social work under New Labour', *British Journal of Social Work*, 31: 611–624.

Orme, J. (2012) 'Evaluation of social work education', in J. Lishman (ed.), *Social Work Education and Training*. London: Jessica Kingsley Publishers, pp. 15–34.

Orme, J., MacIntyre, G., Green Lister, P., Cavanagh, K., Crisp, B.R., Hussein, S., Manthorpe, J., Moriarty, J., Sharpe, E. and Stevens, M. (2009) 'What (a) difference a degree makes: The evaluation of the new social work degree in England', *British Journal of Social Work*, 39: 161–178.

Parsloe, P. (1990) 'The future of social work education', in K. Lyons (1999), *Social Work in Higher Education: Demise or Development?* Aldershot: Ashgate.

Parsloe, P. (2001) 'Looking back on social work education', *Social Work Education: The International Journal*, 20 (1): 9–19.

Parton, N. (ed.) (1996) *Social Theory, Social Change and Social Work*. London: Routledge.

Paton, G. (2013) 'Micheal Gove: Many social workers "not up to the job"', *The Telegraph*, 12 November. Available at: www.telegraph.co.uk/news/uknews/10442309/Michael-Gove-many-social-workers-not-up-to-the-job.html (accessed 17 November 2013).

Phillips, M. (1993) 'Anti-racist zealots drive away recruits', *The Observer*, 1 August. Cited in H. Walker *A Genealogy of Equality: The Curriculum for Social Work Education and Training*. London: Woburn Press, 2002.

Pinker, R. (1993) 'A lethal kind of looniness', *Times Higher Educational Supplement*, 10 September. In H. Walker *A Genealogy of Equality: The Curriculum for Social Work Education and Training*. London: Woburn Press, 2002.

Preston-Shoot, M. (2004) 'Responding by degrees: Surveying the education and practice landscape', *Social Work Education: The International Journal*, 23 (6): 667–692.

Prime Minister's Office (2015) *PM Announces new Taskforce to Transform Child Protection*. Available at: www.gov.uk/government/news/pm-announces-new-taskforce-to-transform-child-protection (accessed 16 July 2015).

Rixon, A. and Ward, R. (2012) 'What difference does it make? Social work practice and post-qualifying awards', *Practice: Social Work in Action*, 24 (3): 147–159.

Roberts, N. (2000) 'Wicked problems and network approaches to resolution', *International Public Management Review*, 1: 1.

Robinson, K. and Webber, M. (2013) 'Models and effectiveness of service user and carer involvement in social work education: A literature review', *British Journal of Social Work*, 43: 925–944.

Rogowski, S. (2010) *Social Work: The Rise and Fall of a Profession?* Bristol: Policy Press.

Sackville, A. (2013) 'Professional Associations in Social Work 1900–1990'. Paper presented to Social Work History Network, May, London.

Seebohm Report (1968) *Report of the Committee on Local Authority and Allied Personal Social Services, Cmnd 3703*. London: HMSO.

Skills for Care (2009) *Employers' Guide to the NQSW Framework*. Leeds: Skills for Care.

Slater, P. (2007) 'The passing of the practice teaching award: History, legacy, prospects', *Social Work Education: The International Journal*, 26 (8): 749–762.

Social Work Reform Board (2010) *Building a Safe and Confident Future: One Year On – Detailed Proposals from the Social Work Reform Board*. London: Department for Education.

Social Work Task Force (2009) *Building a Safe and Confident Future: The Final Report of the Social Work Task Force*. London: Department for Education.

Stevenson, O. (1976a) 'The development of social work education', in A.H. Hasley (ed.), *Traditions of Social Policy*. Oxford: Basil Blackwell.

Stevenson, O. (1976b) 'Some dilemmas in social work education', *Oxford Review of Education*, 2 (2): 149–155.

Stevenson, O. (1979) 'Training, Organisation and Professionalism'. Conference Paper, November, Bournemouth. Available at: www.olivestevenson.com/1970s/unpublished-papers/1979%20-%20Training%20Organisation%20and%20Professionalism.pdf (accessed 16 September 2013).

Stevenson, O. (2005) 'Genericism and specialization: The story since 1970', *British Journal of Social Work*, 35: 569–586.

Taylor, B.J., Mullineux, J.C. and Fleming, G. (2010) 'Partnership, service needs and assessing competence in post-qualifying education and training', *Social Work Education: The International Journal*, 29 (5): 475–489.

Taylor, I. and Bogo, M. (2014) 'Perfect opportunity<perfect storm? Raising the standards of social work education in England', *British Journal of Social Work*, 44: 1402–1418.

Training Organisation for the Personal Social Services (TOPSS) (2000) *Modernising the Social Care Workforce – The First National Training Strategy for England*. Leeds: TOPSS.

Training Organisation for the Personal Social Services (TOPSS) (2002) *The National Occupational Standards for Social Work*. Leeds: TOPSS.

Turner, B. (2000) 'Supervision and mentoring in child and family social work: The role of the first-line manager in the implementation of the post-qualifying framework', *Social Work Education*, 19 (3): 231–240.

Walker, H. (2002) *A Genealogy of Equality: The Curriculum for Social Work Education and Training*. London: Woburn Press.

Webb, D. (1996) 'Regulations for radicals: The state, CCETSW and the academy', in N. Parton (ed.), *Social Theory, Social Change and Social Work*. London: Routledge.

Weinstein, J. (1998) 'The use of National Occupational Standards in professional education', *Journal of Interprofessional Care*, 12 (2): 169–179.

Welbourne, P. (2011) 'Twenty-first century social work: The influence of political context on public service provision in social work education and service delivery', *European Journal of Social Work*, 14 (3): 403–420.

Williams, C. (1997) 'Sharing anti-discriminatory practice through Erasmus', *Social Work Education: The International Journal*, 16 (1): 54–65.

Wilson, G. and Campbell, A. (2013) 'Developing social work education: academic perspectives', *British Journal of Social Work*, 43: 1005–1023.

3

Prevention and Protection: The Development of Safeguarding in Children's Services

Rick Hood

Introduction

Safeguarding can be understood as policies and practices that seek to promote the overall welfare of children as well as protecting them from harm (Davies and Ward 2012; Parton 2006a). Safeguarding is particularly associated with *Every Child Matters*, an influential policy document that set out proposals to reform children's services following the Laming Report into the death of Victoria Climbié (Laming 2003). However, the shift to safeguarding can be seen as part of a broader trend in child welfare policy, both in the UK and other countries. Starting with an examination of the relationship between prevention and protection, this chapter explores the underlying principles of safeguarding as a conceptual framework for policy and practice.

Prevention and protection

Every Child Matters (HM Treasury 2003) was supposed to herald 'a shift to prevention whilst strengthening the protection of children' (Parton 2006a). But what is meant by prevention and protection, and what is the relationship between them? Ostensibly, both terms could describe services which try to avert or minimise harm to children, and to maximise their current and future wellbeing (Munro 2008). In their framework of preventive intervention, Davies and Ward (2012: 56) distinguish between interventions that take place before a child has been maltreated, and those which take place after maltreatment occurs. The former category includes universal services, or *primary prevention*, which all children receive, as well as targeted services, or *secondary prevention*, which help children with additional needs. What Davies and Ward call *tertiary prevention* means services for children who have already experienced maltreatment. These are designed to stop maltreatment from recurring, or in the most severe cases to prevent long-term impairment to children's development.

Within this model, it is the latter category of tertiary prevention that would commonly be understood as child protection. These services might include investigations into cases of suspected abuse, statutory interventions to protect children if abuse is identified, or assessments and care arrangements under the purview of the family court. Child protection is often perceived to be the province of local authority social workers, but is usually carried out in a multi-agency context. A range of non-social work professionals will contribute to formulating and carrying out child protection plans, for instance. Professionals undertaking protective work may experience difficult or adversarial relations with parents and other family members, while families may feel stigmatised or coerced by their involvement with such services (Bell 1999; Turnell and Edwards 1997).

In contrast, prevention is most commonly understood in terms of what Davies and Ward call primary and secondary prevention. It is often linked to the principle of early intervention. 'Early' in this context may be taken to mean in early childhood or at an early stage in the genesis of problems (Allen 2011; Sharp and Filmer-Sankey 2010). While preventive work is often undertaken in the context of protection, and in situations of varying severity, the emphasis is on avoiding the escalation of problems and – more ambitiously – on preventing problems from occurring at all. Prevention is also linked to the idea of social investment, which is discussed later on in this chapter. One rationale for early intervention is to try and reduce the burden on specialist services, such as those undertaking child protection work. For this reason, universal settings such as schools increasingly offer provision for children with additional needs. Preventive services are also provided by non-statutory settings such as Sure Start children's centres. Families are more likely to engage voluntarily with such services and to perceive them as supportive and non-stigmatising. There is an implicit contrast with the statutory context, interventionism and adversarial relations associated with child protection.

The relationship between prevention and protection is emblematic of other dualisms familiar to the children's practitioner. Most obviously, the labels attached to particular services are connected to assumptions about the people who use them. Referrals to preventive services, for example, may emphasise vulnerability and the family's need for support, whereas referrals to tertiary services may emphasise risk or dangerousness (Dale et al. 1986; Spratt 2000; Stevenson 1989). This in turn reflects an ambivalence in public attitudes towards the users of welfare services, which date back to Victorian distinctions between the 'deserving' and 'undeserving' poor. On the one hand, the idealisation of childhood 'innocence' contributes to a view of children as blameless in their family's circumstances, and as potential victims of neglect and abuse. On the other hand, the association of youth with delinquency and deviance cause young people to be seen as a potential threat to the social order (Parton 2006b).

Social constructions of the family and childhood are also tied up with conflicting attitudes towards state intervention, care and control. On a broader scale, family life has been idealised as the quintessential private sphere, into which the state should not intrude unless it is absolutely necessary. Conversely, since the family is the primary site of children's socialisation, it has also been seen as a legitimate target of efforts to tackle social problems. Welfare services are expected to police the behaviour of families, at the same time as providing them with assistance and support. Child protection typically involves elements of coercive intervention in private family life, and in some cases this might lead to the removal of children from their families. The concern to clarify and constrain the state's powers in this regard has been an important part of child welfare policy, as will be seen below.

Points for reflection

What do you understand to be the difference between prevention and protection? To what extent are they distinct concepts or two sides of the same coin?

An overview of child welfare policy

The UK's child welfare system emerged out of the social upheaval of industrialisation and urbanisation from the late 18th century onwards (Denney 1998; Dingwall et al. 1983; Ferguson 2004; Parton 2006b). In the Victorian era, governments passed legislation to reduce the exploitation of child labour in factories, to provide accommodation for pauper children and to expand schooling. The growth of philanthropic societies, often linked to the church and evangelic Christian movements, contributed to the provision of services for homeless children and abandoned babies. As these organisations expanded in scope, volunteers began to visit poor families in order to disseminate ideas about hygiene, education and morality, and to determine their eligibility for material and financial assistance. The National Society for the Prevention of Cruelty to Children (NSPCC) campaigned for legislation to outlaw what was then termed child cruelty, including in the family home, and give public agencies the powers of legal action. Public anxiety about juvenile crime and delinquency also drove 'reformist' work with children and families. These 19th-century developments illustrate the basic principles that underpin the involvement of welfare agencies with children and families to this day.

The Second World War marked a turning point for children's services. The evacuation of children during the Blitz had highlighted the adverse effects of poverty and deprivation, and the importance of parental caregiving. These issues contributed to the drive towards a comprehensive and centrally funded welfare state in line with the Beveridge proposals. Further impetus for reform was provided by the 1946 Curtis Report, following the death of Denis O'Neill in foster care (HMSO 1946). This report highlighted the inadequate and often punitive treatment accorded to children in care. The result was the establishing of local authority children's departments under the 1948 Children Act. For the first time, the state took a principal role in providing services for children, and gradually brought a wide range of voluntary services under the aegis of formal regulation and inspection.

In the aftermath of the 1948 Act, there was a period of optimism about the capacity of new professional human services, such as social work, to contribute to the alleviation of child neglect and other social problems. Partly as a response to burgeoning youth crime, the duties of local authorities and the role of social workers were expanded to include preventive work with 'problem families'. The 1968 Seebohm Report proposed that support for vulnerable groups, including the elderly and infirm, should be amalgamated in order to provide a unitary family-oriented service. As a result, disparate personal services were amalgamated into local authority social service departments in 1970. These departments gave a central role to the emerging profession of social work, and also reinforced the role of the state as service provider. However, the initial optimism was short-lived, succumbing to the economic difficulties of the 1970s and a breakdown in the postwar welfarist consensus. Greater complexity and fluidity of social structures, particularly in the industrialised world, made it increasingly difficult to predicate policy on the traditional, i.e. patriarchal, model of the family, based on the idea of a male breadwinner and maternal caregiver.

For most of the 20th century, perceptions of child maltreatment in the western world were dominated by the issue of neglect. This changed dramatically with the publication in 1962 of a US study into 'battered child syndrome' (Kempe et al. 1962), which drew attention to the physical abuse of babies and young children by their parents. Another seminal event, certainly in the UK, was the public inquiry set up to look into the death of Maria Colwell in 1973 (DHSS 1974). Maria had been in foster care for a number of years before being placed back with her mother and an abusive stepfather. There was extensive media coverage of the circumstances leading up to her death, generating public outrage at the professional failings that were reported. The inquiry's recommendations led ultimately to an overhaul of statutory guidelines and procedures. Sadly, over the next three decades, this was to become a familiar pattern of events. Subsequent inquiries into deaths from child abuse increased public awareness of its prevalence in institutional as well as private family settings (Hallett 1989). The overall result was ever more scrutiny and tighter controls over child protection practice, including a proliferation of guidelines and procedures. Knowledge about forms of abuse began to encompass an ever-broader range of behaviour, including physical, sexual and emotional abuse, as well as neglect (Glaser 2002).

Child abuse inquiries have had enormous influence on the child welfare system in the UK, and particularly on the balance between prevention and protection (Munro 2004). During the 1980s, increasing emphasis was placed on the statutory context of social work, and its overriding responsibility to protect children. Agencies were repeatedly criticised for failing to investigate thoroughly, share information, or collaborate effectively. The pressure to avoid child deaths – and to avoid being blamed for them – led professionals to concentrate on investigating referrals and to lower their thresholds for coercive action. Child protection practice was increasingly shaped by formal protocols to guide decision-making and intervention.

However, the more robust attitude to intervention provoked a backlash against professional intrusion into private family life. The 1988 inquiry into sexual abuse cases in Cleveland (DHSS 1988) reinforced the perception that professionals were acting hastily and excessively to identify abuse and break up families, even as other reports continued to highlight their failure to intervene when abuse had occurred.

As a result of these conflicting pressures, the 1989 Children Act sought to establish a clear remit for statutory intervention, as well as for parental responsibility. The Act emphasised partnership between agencies and families, while also emphasising the paramount importance of the child's welfare.

By the middle of the 1990s, a consensus among researchers and policy-makers had emerged that the system had become skewed towards protection and needed to be rebalanced (DH 1995). Although the 1989 Children Act had imposed a duty on local authorities to provide a broad range of services to children in need, agencies were continuing to focus on identifying and dealing with cases of abuse. As a result, secondary services in particular were being starved of resources, since professionals were implementing a high threshold for support to families. There was talk of a 'crisis' in the child protection system, not just in the UK but also in other English-speaking countries (Cooper et al. 1995). Social workers were seen as working with families in an overly legalistic and adversarial way, reinforced by a culture of institutional anxiety about risk. Comparisons were made to European welfare systems, which appeared to place greater emphasis on social support for families, partnership with parents and therapeutic needs assessment (Stafford et al. 2012).

A perceived contrast between the UK system, geared towards child protection, and European systems with a more preventive 'family service' orientation, was characteristic of the refocusing debate of the mid-1990s (Gilbert 1997). Stafford et al. (2012) point out that the direction of UK policy since then has not been to try and replace one approach with the other, but rather to try and synthesise them. This is line with what has been called an emerging 'child-focused orientation' in modern child protection systems (Gilbert et al. 2011). The child-focused approach implies a focus on overall developmental outcomes, as well as protection from harm, and envisages an active role for the state in promoting children's welfare from an early age. It is influenced by a children's rights perspective, so that the child is seen as an autonomous individual in relation to family, society and the state.

The concept of 'social investment' has been another key principle in the development of child-focused services. Social investment strategies are designed to mitigate and pre-empt the impact of social exclusion by targeting vulnerable groups with extra support from the state (Fawcett et al. 2004; Featherstone 2006). This applies particularly to children, and most particularly young children, for whom 'the benefits of investment are repaid over an extended time in economic productivity and reduction in cost to society through decreased demands on services' (Spratt 2009: 438–9). Needs are equated with short-term and long-term risk factors, which are predicted to have an adverse effect on immediate wellbeing and developmental outcomes in later life. The terminology of social investment reveals a more utilitarian 'cost–benefit' analysis underlying the rights-based perspective referred to above.

To summarise, the policy context to children's services in the early 21st century can be understood in terms of three interrelated strands. First, there is the concern to address systemic failings identified in successive reviews and inquiries into child deaths. Second, there is the need to achieve a balance between protecting children from abuse and fulfilling a broader welfare remit in supporting vulnerable children and families. Third, there is the wish to reorient services around the needs of children, in order to promote a positive developmental path into adulthood and pre-empt the social and financial cost of exclusionary outcomes. This is the context in which a framework for 'safeguarding children' was outlined in *Every Child Matters* and implemented in subsequent legislation and guidance.

It should be noted that *Every Child Matters* was a centrepiece of the New Labour government's strategy for children's services up until the general election of 2010. Since then, social policy under the (Conservative–Liberal Democrat) Coalition has taken a rather different course, shaped by the overarching priority to cut public expenditure and curtail the role of the state in providing services. At the same time, many of the collaborative structures introduced in the wake of *Every Child Matters* have remained in place (Davies and Ward 2012; Department for Education 2013). A similar emphasis on interprofessional care has been evident in the development of services for vulnerable adults (Domac and Haider 2013; Stevens 2013). More will be said at the end of this chapter about the shape of safeguarding in an 'age of austerity' (Sidebotham 2012). For now, our attention turns to the characteristics of the safeguarding system heralded by *Every Child Matters* and the 2004 Children Act.

Every Child Matters and the 2004 Children Act

Every Child Matters (ECM) set out the New Labour government's strategy to reform children's services, partly in response to the Laming Report but also in line with long-standing policy concerns. As we have seen, these included the refocusing debate around prevention and protection, and the application of social investment ideas to welfare policy. A key criticism made by Laming was the inability of services to share information and collaborate effectively across organisational boundaries. Similar failings had been echoed in other inquiries and case reviews, stretching back to the 1946 Curtis Report (HMSO 1946). In *Every Child Matters*, the need to improve inter-agency working in child abuse cases was linked to a more general ambition to enhance the coordination of services for vulnerable children. This was to be achieved through a process of integration, making services more child-centred instead of being organised around single agency remits or professional areas of expertise (DCSF 2007, 2008). Integrated processes were to be focused on outcomes for children, which were articulated in ECM as six broad categories of wellbeing: being healthy, staying safe, enjoying and achieving, making a positive contribution and achieving economic wellbeing (DfES 2004: 8).

The 2004 Children Act introduced a range of measures to promote integration. The overall aim was to promote joint leadership, planning and accountability among agencies providing services to children. New arrangements included children's trusts, local child safeguarding boards (LCSBs), and directors of children's services in local authorities. Children's trusts brought together bodies such as district councils, schools, health authorities, youth offending teams and probation services, with partnership arrangements to be maintained through a statutory body called the children's trust board (DCSF 2010).

Figure 3.1 illustrates the cooperative arrangements of a children's trust. The onion-shaped model can be envisaged as a type of ecological system of care (Bronfenbrenner 1979). At its centre are the various microsystems that produce outcomes for the child and family, which are embedded within frontline professional

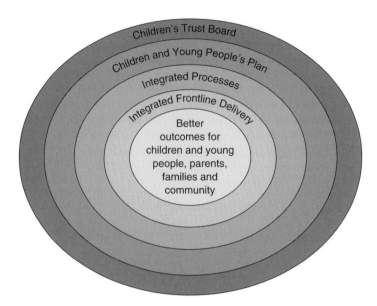

Figure 3.1 The 'onion' model: cooperative arrangements under children's trusts
(DCSF 2010: 8)

services and strategic partnerships within the community. The concept of nested
systems conveys the dual emphasis on containment and control, since these
arrangements are designed to protect children as well as to shape their future.
The government's plan was to build a 'preventive system' (DCSF 2007: 92) that
would deal with problems at an early stage in children's development, through
a combination of universal and specialist services. Professionals involved in
delivering these services, collectively known as the 'children's workforce', would
be educated to have a 'common core' of knowledge, values and aspirations. New
'integrated' procedures and tools were introduced to facilitate collaboration and
information sharing. These included the common assessment framework (CAF),
and IT-based case management systems such as the integrated children's system
(ICS). The significance of these developments, and other principles of safeguarding,
are discussed in the next section.

The principles of safeguarding

The safeguarding system advocated by *Every Child Matters* serves as a conceptual framework for child welfare services. Its overarching aim is to bring
specialist services for vulnerable children, and children at risk of maltreatment,
within the broader spectrum of universal services. Theoretically this should allow
the system as a whole to move away from a narrow focus on abuse and protection,
and enable a shift to preventive strategies based on the principle of early intervention. As such, it represents an effort to address some of the long-standing social
policy issues that were explored earlier. The system's organising principles can be
summarised as follows.

Tiered spectrum of need

It was seen earlier that ambivalent public attitudes towards the providers and recipients of welfare services have tended to manifest themselves in dualistic premises, such as vulnerability and dangerousness, care and control, protection and prevention. In children's services, these divisions have been reproduced in the distinction between statutory agencies dealing with child protection or youth offending, and other services, often non-statutory, oriented towards family support or therapeutic care. The preventive system envisaged by ECM marked an attempt at depolarisation, defining the remit for services in terms of a spectrum of need rather than by the threshold between protection and non-protection.

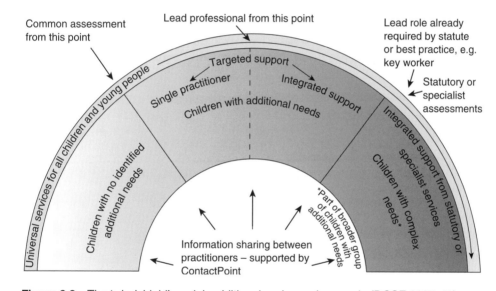

Figure 3.2 The 'windshield' model: additional and complex needs (DCSF 2007: 11)

This idea is illustrated in the 'windshield model' shown in Figure 3.2. The spectrum of need ranges from 'children with no identified additional needs', on the left, to 'children with complex needs', on the right. The type of service is linked to the level of need. Children with no additional needs are catered for by universal services such as schools and primary health care. Children with additional needs are provided with more specialist support, often in universal settings. A minority of children have multiple difficulties requiring input from several different agencies. As the level of need increases, assessment and provision are (or should be) coordinated by a 'lead professional' (Easton 2012). At the far end of the scale, children with the most complex needs may be at significant risk of impaired development, and possibly of maltreatment. At this point the statutory agency is expected to take over as lead professional in order to coordinate multi-agency assessment and intervention. However, this model shows a 'tiered spectrum' of need, rather than a smooth continuum. There are three main categories – universal, additional and complex needs – and the boundaries between them are marked by a shift to different forms of service provision.

Targeted intervention

The tiered model of need has obvious links to the primary–secondary–tertiary model of preventive intervention that was introduced at the start of the chapter. In fact, this model draws on a familiar concept in modern health care systems. The idea is to separate services into different categories of knowledge and expertise, which roughly correspond to people at different stages of health and illness (Hardiker et al. 1991). In the UK, for example, people who get symptoms of illness first go to see their general practitioner (primary care), who, if necessary, will refer patients with additional or complex health needs onto an appropriate specialist (secondary and tertiary care). *Every Child Matters* suggests a similar system of targeted intervention, which is reproduced in Figure 3.3. It shows a pyramid of services, in which the preventive levels – universal, targeted and specialist – match the categories of need described above. The binary distinction between protection and prevention has become a series of referral thresholds between services and across different tiers of provision. Need is explicitly equated with risk, since an

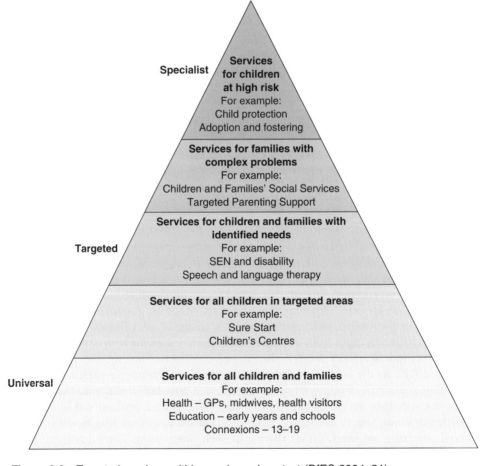

Figure 3.3 Targeted services within a universal context (DfES 2004: 21)

increase in the level or complexity of need is associated with an increased risk of adverse outcomes in the future. This is recognised in the ECM model, in which 'children at high risk' constitute the 'top' of the pyramid.

Targeted intervention also enables policy-makers and practitioners to obtain information about whether specific models of provision are effective or not. Keeping track of outcomes can therefore help to guide future decision-making, as advocated by the 'evidence-based' movement in medicine and other health and social care professions (Sackett et al. 1996). As we shall see, governments have been concerned to pilot and evaluate new forms of provision, generating a plethora of research into 'what works for children' (Liabo et al. 2006). Using scientific methods to establish a body of evidence means that successful models of intervention can be validated and promulgated. It also means that professionals can base their activity on knowledge about 'best practice' in their fields. In this way, needs are targeted with interventions that have been independently proven to be effective, improving consistency and reducing the risk of individual variations in the quality of service (Sheldon 2001). IT-based assessment templates and workflow systems can also be designed to generate statistical data on outcomes and processes, with the aim of improving performance management and the inspection of services (Shaw et al. 2009). These developments have therefore been seen as increasing the extent of managerial control over the work of children's professionals (Chard and Ayre 2010).

Integrated working

Proposals to integrate services for children and young people were fundamental to the *Every Child Matters* reforms. In part this was a response to the perceived lack of inter-agency collaboration in child abuse cases. More generally, the growth of specialised professions and the separation of purchaser–provider functions had led to a fragmentation of welfare services, making them more difficult for users to navigate. Case management had become increasingly important as services tried to coordinate their activities and provide continuity of care for their users (DH 2005). In children's services, a key concept was the 'team around the child', which had originally developed in early years settings as a key worker model of family support around babies and young children with disabilities (Limbrick 2001). In the statutory guidance that followed the 2004 Children Act the team around the child became the preferred designation for groups of professionals providing support to children with additional or complex needs (e.g. DCSF 2008, 2010). The responsibility of the 'lead professional' in such teams was to coordinate the 'package of support' and serve as a single point of contact for the family.

Like the earlier emphasis on partnership (Percy-Smith 2005), integration was seen as intrinsic to the preventive system as a whole. The government launched a range of initiatives aimed at breaking down professional and institutional 'silos' and barriers to collaboration. One example was the common assessment framework (CAF), which set out a standardised approach to identifying children's additional needs and arranging support (Pithouse et al. 2009). On the non-statutory side, preventive programmes such as Sure Start and the Children's Fund were based on multi-agency models of working. Statutory social workers began to manage cases using the Integrated Children's System (ICS), an IT-based workflow process designed to systematise assessment and planning for children in need. It was largely through these and other integrated 'tools' that safeguarding practice changed in the years following the 2004 Children Act.

Points for reflection

Think of your current role or placement. Where does it fit within the model of safeguarding described here? For example, do you work within a universal or specialist service, and how do you know this to be the case?

Evaluation and critique

Safeguarding itself is perhaps too amorphous a concept to be evaluated directly. Nevertheless, there is a considerable body of literature examining the impact of integrated services and other initiatives associated with the ECM agenda (Brown and White 2006; NESS 2008; O'Brien et al. 2009; Tunstill et al. 2007). However, caution must be exercised when examining the 'evidence base' for any particular type of provision. There are methodological challenges in evaluating outcomes in complex real-life situations, in which there are a huge number of interacting variables (Sanderson 2006). National programmes such as Sure Start actually consist of a large number of individual projects, each influenced by local contexts and contingencies. Pilot projects may prove effective while they are well resourced and delivered by motivated staff, but may become less so when rolled out on a wider basis (Anning et al. 2006). The use of case studies raises questions of generalisability, since findings in one area may not be applicable to another. For this reason, large-scale evaluations usually have a quantitative component, using measurable indicators to represent outcomes. However, this in turn raises questions about what is being measured and whether these indicators actually reflect the experiences or wellbeing of service users.

With these reservations in mind, there is some evidence that families can and do benefit from integrated services. Lord et al. (2008: 5) summarise these benefits as follows: 'early identification and intervention; easy access to services and to information about available provision; respectful and reliable support; and the greater understanding of their child's needs'. Evaluations of government programmes have reported qualified progress in achieving specified objectives, such as reducing school exclusions and improving pupil attainment (Halsey et al. 2005; Webb and Vuillamy 2004), reducing criminal activity and improving behaviour and parenting (Ghate et al. 2008), or more broadly tackling social exclusion (Edwards et al. 2006). Robinson et al. (2008) point out that professionals also derive benefits from integrated working, such as a better understanding of clients' issues, greater awareness of other agencies' work and the role of networks, and more leeway for developing local solutions.

In general, however, there is only 'sparse' empirical evidence that multi-agency working on its own improves outcomes for service users (Atkinson et al. 2007). Particularly when it comes to very disadvantaged families, those with a long history of involvement with services, or with significant and multiple problems, agencies have found it difficult to produce sustainable outcomes (Brodie 2010; Daniel et al. 2011; Davies and Ward 2012; Farmer and Lutman 2012). Another limitation of the changes brought about by *Every Child Matters* was that while time-limited funding streamed into new preventative models of service delivery, such as Sure Start, the 'core' duties and practices of statutory services have remained largely unchanged (Morris 2010). The child protection system has continued to labour under the impact of high profile child abuse cases, with a surge in referrals and care proceedings in the aftermath of the Peter Connelly case (Association of Directors of Children's Services 2010).

A further criticism of the safeguarding agenda has been its failure to address the proliferation of procedures and the administrative burden on practitioners, especially in child protection work. This has been attributed to various causes: reliance on technocratic and managerial solutions, a pervasive culture of blame and defensive practice driven by institutional attitudes to risk, and the continued tendency of public inquiries and serious case reviews to produce bureaucratic recommendations (Ayre and Preston-Shoot 2010). It could also be argued that some of the ECM reforms have themselves made matters worse, for example in relying on IT-enabled initiatives such as ICS to resolve practice-related issues (Wastell and White 2010). The Munro Review of Child Protection (Munro 2011), which will be discussed below, drew attention to some of these systemic failings.

The Munro Review and developments under the Coalition

As noted already, the Coalition government elected in 2010 made cuts in public expenditure an overarching policy objective. The New Labour vision of fostering social inclusion through a preventative state has accordingly been trimmed into something rather more austere. Resources have increasingly been targeted at individuals and families who are considered incur the most costs to the community (Casey 2012; Churchill 2013). Pressure on services has also been mounting since a child death scandal in 2008, which set in motion a steady rise in child protection referrals and accommodation of children into statutory care (Association of Directors of Children's Services 2010; Pemberton 2013). A combination of these factors has arguably prompted a shift back towards some of the old emphasis on child protection under the Coalition (Parton 2011).

In the light of continuing public concern about deaths from child abuse, one of first acts of the Coalition was to commission a high profile review of child protection (Munro 2011). The review began by examining the highly procedural and risk-averse culture that has developed in the years since the death of Maria Colwell (Munro 2010). The unintended consequences of this culture have been a general erosion of skills and confidence, exacerbated by an exodus of senior practitioners from the more exposed areas of frontline practice (Ayre and Preston-Shoot 2010). Munro called for a cultural shift away from compliance and a renewed focus on professional standards, highlighting the value of reflective practice, relationship-based casework and the capacity to make judgements in complex and uncertain situations.

In the wake of the Munro Review, there have been efforts to move away from overly rigid and prescriptive working practices in child protection (Munro 2012). The government has produced a 'slimmed down' version of statutory guidance for agencies and practitioners (Department for Education 2013), while some local authorities have experimented with timescales for assessments (Stanley et al. 2012). Others have endeavoured to develop alternative approaches to delivering early intervention, for example through integrated multi-professional teams (Local Government Leadership and City of Westminster 2010) or 'social work units' (Goodman and Trowler 2012). Despite such innovations, it remains to be seen whether a preventive system of safeguarding will develop as envisaged in *Every Child Matters*, or whether the old fault-lines between prevention and protection will re-emerge in a harsher financial climate.

Conclusion

Safeguarding can be considered as a conceptual framework for the provision of welfare services to children. It is closely associated with the *Every Child Matters* agenda and the subsequent development of integrated children's services in the UK. In policy terms, safeguarding is characterised by the effort to locate child protection within a broader system of preventive intervention. Universal and specialist services are expected to work in a child-centred way, which means coordinating a multi-agency response to additional and complex needs. In practice terms, these requirements have largely been translated into a set of inter-agency protocols and case management tools designed to encourage collaboration and information sharing. Although certain types of integrated provision have been shown to be effective in particular contexts, there is insufficient evidence to say whether or how the safeguarding system has improved outcomes for service users. In recent years, there has arguably been a shift back towards protection, due to policy changes under the Coalition government, as well as a steady rise in the number of cases requiring statutory intervention. While safeguarding continues to provide an overall framework for children's services, the emphasis has shifted towards targeting particularly 'high risk' individuals and families. The Munro Review of Child Protection has provided an influential critique of safeguarding practice, and has proposed systemic changes to the way that social workers and other practitioners carry out their work.

References

Allen, G. (2011) *Early Intervention: The Next Steps*. London: Cabinet Office.

Anning, A., Cottrell, D., Frost, N., Green, J. and Robinson, M. (2006) *Developing Multiprofessional Teamwork for Integrated Children's Services*. Maidenhead: Oxford University Press.

Association of Directors of Children's Services (ADCS) (2010) *Safeguarding Pressures Report Phase 2: Exploring Reasons and Effect*. Manchester: ADCS Ltd.

Atkinson, M., Jones, M. and Lamont, E. (2007) *Multi-Agency Working and its Implications for Practice: A Review of the Literature*. Reading: Centre for British Teachers (CfBT).

Ayre, P. and Preston-Shoot, M. (eds) (2010) *Children's Services at the Crossroads: A Critical Evaluation of Contemporary Policy for Practice*. Lyme Regis: Russell House Publishing.

Bell, M. (1999) 'Working in partnership in child protection: The conflicts', *British Journal of Social Work*, 29 (3): 437–455.

Brodie, I. (2010) 'Inadmissible evidence? New Labour and the education of children in care', in P. Ayre and M. Preston-Shoot (eds), *Children's Services at the Crossroads: A Critical Evaluation of Contemporary Policy for Practice*. Lyme Regis: Russell House Publishing.

Bronfenbrenner, U. (1979) *The Ecology of Human Development*. Cambridge, MA: Harvard University Press.

Brown, K. and White, K. (2006). *Exploring the Evidence Base for Integrated Children's Services* [Online]. Available at: www.gov.scot/resource/doc/90282/0021746.pdf (accessed 22 July 2015).

Casey, L. (2012) *Listening to Troubled Families*. London: Department for Communities and Local Government Leadership and City of Westminster.

Chard, A. and Ayre, P. (2010) 'Managerialism – at the tipping point?', in P. Ayre and M. Preston-Shoot (eds), *Children's Services at the Crossroads: A Critical Evaluation of Contemporary Policy for Practice*. Lyme Regis: Russell House Publishing.

Churchill, H. (2013) 'Retrenchment and restructuring: Family support and children's services reform under the Coalition', *Journal of Children's Services*, 8 (3): 209–222.

Cooper, A., Hetherington, R., Bairstow, S., Pitts, J. and Spriggs, A. (1995) *Positive Child Protection: A View from Abroad*. Lyme Regis: Russell House Publishing.

Dale, P., Davies, M., Morrison, T. and Waters, J. (1986) *Dangerous Families: Assessment and Treatment of Child Abuse*. London: Tavistock Publications Ltd.

Daniel, B., Taylor, J. and Scott, J. (2011) *Recognizing and Helping the Neglected Child*. London: Jessica Kingsley

Davies, C. and Ward, H. (2012) *Safeguarding Child across Services: Messages from Research*. London: Jessica Kingsley.

Denney, D. (1998) *Social Policy and Social Work*. Oxford: Oxford University Press.

Department for Children Schools and Families (DCSF) (2007) *The Children's Plan*. London: The Stationery Office.

Department for Children Schools and Families (DCSF) (2008) *Building Brighter Futures: Next Steps for the Children's Workforce*. Nottingham: DCSF.

Department for Children Schools and Families (DCSF) (2010) *Children's Trusts: Statutory Guidance on Cooperation Arrangements, Including the Children's Trust Board and the Children and Young People's Plan*. London: The Stationery Office.

Department for Education (DfE) (2013) *Working Together to Safeguard Children: A Guide to Inter-agency Working to Safeguard and Promote the Welfare of* Children. London: The Stationery Office.

Department for Education and Skills (DfES) (2004) *Every Child Matters: Change for Children*. London: HMSO.

Department of Health (DH) (1995) *Messages from Research*. London: HMSO.

Department of Health (DH) (2005) *Supporting People with Long Term Conditions: An NHS and Social Care Model to Support Local Innovation and Integration*. London: HMSO.

Department of Health and Social Security (DHSS) (1974) *Report of the Committee of Inquiry into the Care and Supervision Provided in Relation to Maria Colwell*. London: HMSO.

Department of Health and Social Security (DHSS) (1988) *Report of the Inquiry into Child Abuse in Cleveland*. London: HMSO.

Dingwall, R., Eekelaar, J. and Murray, T. (1983) *The Protection of Children*. Oxford: Basil Blackwell.

Domac, S. and Haider, S. (2013) 'Interagency safeguarding adults training for protection and prevention', *Journal of Interprofessional Care*, 27 (6): 520–522.

Easton, C., Featherstone G,. Poet, H., Aston, H., Gee, G. and Durbin, B. (2012) *Supporting Families with Complex Needs: Findings from LARC 4*. Slough: National Foundation for Educational Research (NFER).

Edwards, A., Barnes, M., Plewis, I. and Morris, K. (2006) *Working to Prevent the Social Exclusion of Children and Young People: Final Lessons from the National Evaluation of the Children's Fund*. Nottingham: Department for Education and Schools.

Farmer, E. and Lutman, E. (2012) *Working Effectively with Neglected Children and their Families: Understanding their Experiences and Long-Term Outcomes*. London: Jessica Kingsley.

Fawcett, B., Featherstone, B. and Goddard, J. (2004) *Contemporary Child Care Policy and Practice*. Basingstoke: Palgrave Macmillan.

Featherstone, B. (2006) 'Rethinking family support in the current policy context', *British Journal of Social Work*, 36: 5–19.

Ferguson, H. (2004) *Protecting Children in Time*. Basingstoke: Palgrave Macmillan.

Ghate, D., Asmussen, K., Tian, Y. and Hauari, H. (2008) *'On Track' Phase Two National Evaluation: Reducing Risk and Increasing Resilience – How Did 'On Track' Work? Research Report DCSF-RR035*. London: Policy Research Bureau.

Gilbert, N. (ed.) (1997) *Combating Child Abuse: International Perspectives and Trends*. New York: Oxford University Press.

Gilbert, N., Parton, N. and Skivenes, M. (2011) 'Changing patterns of response and emerging orientations', in N. Gilbert, N. Parton and M. Skivenes (eds), *Child Protection Systems: International Trends and Orientations*. New York: Oxford University Press.

Glaser, D. (2002) 'Emotional abuse and neglect (psychological maltreatment): A conceptual framework', *Child Abuse & Neglect*, 26 (6–7): 697–714.

Goodman, S. and Trowler, I. (eds) (2012) *Social Work Reclaimed*. London: Jessica Kingsley.

Hallett, C. (1989) 'Child-abuse inquiries and public policy', in O. Stevenson (ed.), *Child Abuse: Public Policy and Professional Practice*. London: Harvester Wheatsheaf.

Halsey, K., Gulliver, C., Johnson, A., Martin, K. and Kinder, K. (2005) *Evaluation of Behaviour and Education Support Teams. Research Brief RB706*. Nottingham: Department for Education and Schools Publications.

Hardiker, P., Exton, K. and Barker, M. (1991) *Policies and Practices in Preventive Child Care*. Ashgate: Aldershot.

HM Treasury (2003) *Every Child Matters, Cm 5860*. London: The Stationery Office.

HMSO (1946) *Report of the Care of Children Committee (Curtis Report), Cmnd. 6922*. London: HMSO.

Kempe, C.H., Silverman, F.N., Steele, B.F., Droegemueller, W. and Silver, H.K. (1962) 'The battered-child syndrome', *Journal of the American Medical Association*, 181 (1): 17–24.

Laming, L. (2003) *The Victoria Climbié Inquiry* [Online]. Available at: www.victoria-climbie-inquiry.org.uk (accessed 10 November 2009).

Liabo, K., Frost, S., McNeish, D., Sheldon, T. and Roberts, H. (2006) 'What works for children?', in A. Killoran (ed.), *Public Health Evidence: Tackling Health Inequalities*. Oxford: Oxford University Press.

Limbrick, P. (2001) *The Team Around the Child: Multi-agency Service Co-ordination for Children with Complex Needs and Their Families*. Worcester: Interconnections.

Local Government Leadership and City of Westminster (2010) *Repairing Broken Families and Rescuing Fractured Communities: Lessons from the Front Line*. London: Local Government Leadership and City of Westminster.

Lord, P., Kinder, K., Wilkin, A., Atkinson, M. and Harland, J. (2008) *Evaluating the Early Impact of Integrated Children's Services: Round 1 Final Report*. Slough: National Foundation for Educational Research (NFER).

Morris, K. (2010) 'Children in need: The challenge of prevention for social work', in P. Ayre and M. Preston-Shoot (eds), *Children's Services at the Crossroads: A Critical Evaluation of Contemporary Policy for Practice*. Lyme Regis: Russell House Publishing.

Munro, E. (2004) 'The impact of child abuse inquiries since 1990', in N. Stanley and J. Manthorpe (eds), *The Age of the Inquiry: Learning and Blaming in Health and Social Care*. London: Routledge.

Munro, E. (2008) *Effective Child Protection*. London: Sage.

Munro, E. (2010) *The Munro Review of Child Protection, Part One: A Systems Analysis*. London: Department for Education.

Munro, E. (2011) *The Munro Review of Child Protection: Final Report: A Child-Centred System*. London: The Stationery Office.

Munro, E. (2012) *The Munro Review of Child Protection: Progress Report: Moving towards a Child-Centred System*. London: DfE.

National Evaluation of Sure Start (NESS) (2008) *The Impact of Sure Start Local Programmes on Three-Year-Olds and Their Families*. Nottingham: Department for Education and Schools Publications.

O'Brien, M., Bachmann, M.O., Jones, N.R., Reading, R., Thoburn, J., Husbands, C., Shreeve, A. and Watson, J. (2009) 'Do integrated childrens services improve childrens outcomes?: Evidence from Englands childrens trust pathfinders', *Children & Society*, 23: 320–335.

Parton, N. (2006a) '"Every Child Matters": The shift to prevention whilst strengthening protection in children's services in England', *Children and Youth Services Review*, 28 (8): 976–992.

Parton, N. (2006b) *Safeguarding Childhood: Early Intervention and Surveillance in a Late Modern Society*. Basingstoke: Palgrave Macmillan.

Parton, N. (2011) 'Child protection and safeguarding in England: Changing and competing conceptions of risk and their implications for social work', *British Journal of Social Work*, 41 (5): 854–875.

Pemberton, C. (2013) *Care Applications Rise 70% in Years since Baby P Case*. Available at: www.communitycare.co.uk/articles/09/05/2013/119162/care-applications-rise-70-in-years-since-baby-p-case.htm (accessed 22 July 2015).

Percy-Smith, J. (2005) *What Works in Strategic Partnerships for Children?* Ilford: Barnardos.

Pithouse, A., Hall, C., Peckover, S. and White, S. (2009) 'A tale of two CAFs: The impact of the electronic Common Assessment Framework', *British Journal of Social Work*, 39 (4): 599–612.

Robinson, M., Atkinson, M. and Downing, D. (2008) *Supporting Theory Building in Integrated Services Research*. Slough: National Foundation for Educational Research (NFER).

Sackett, D.L., Rosenberg, W.M.C., Gray, J.A.M., Haynes, R.B. and Richardson, W.S. (1996) 'Evidence-based medicine: What it is and what it isn't', *BMJ*, 312 (7023): 71–72.

Sanderson, I. (2006) 'Complexity, "practical rationality" and evidence-based policy-making', *Policy and Politics*, 34 (1): 115–132.

Sharp, C. and Filmer-Sankey, C. (2010) *Early Intervention and Prevention in the Context of Integrated Services: Evidence from C4EO and Narrowing the Gap Reviews (Early Intervention Desk Study)*. London: Centre for Excellence and Outcomes (C4EO).

Shaw, I., Bell, M., Sinclair, I., Sloper, P., Mitchell, W., Dyson, P., Clayden, J. and Rafferty, J. (2009) 'An exemplary scheme? An evaluation of the integrated children's system', *British Journal of Social Work*, 39: 613–626.

Sheldon, B. (2001) 'The validity of evidence-based practice in social work: A reply to Stephen Webb', *British Journal of Social Work*, 31 (5): 801–809.

Sidebotham, P. (2012) 'Safeguarding in an age of austerity', *Child Abuse Review*, 21 (5): 313–317.

Spratt, T. (2000) 'Decision-making by senior social workers at point of first referral', *British Journal of Social Work*, 30 (5): 597–618.

Spratt, T. (2009) 'Identifying families with multiple problems: Possible responses from child and family social work to current policy developments', *British Journal of Social Work*, 39: 435–450.

Stafford, A., Parton, N., Vincent, S. and Smith, C. (2012) *Child Protection Systems in the United Kingdom*. London: Jessica Kingsley.

Stanley, T., McGee, P. and Lincoln, H. (2012) 'A practice framework for assessments at Tower Hamlets children's social care: Building on the Munro Review', *Practice*, 24 (4): 239–250.

Stevens, E. (2013) 'Safeguarding vulnerable adults: Exploring the challenges to best practice across multi-agency settings', *Journal of Adult Protection*, 15 (2): 85–95.

Stevenson, O. (ed.) (1989) *Child Abuse: Public Policy and Professional Practice*. London: Harvester Wheatsheaf.

Tunstill, J., Aldgate, J. and Hughes, M. (2007) *Improving Children's Services Networks: Lessons from Family Centres*. London: Jessica Kingsley.

Turnell, A. and Edwards, S. (1997) 'Aspiring to partnership: The signs of safety approach to child protection', *Child Abuse Review*, 6 (3): 179–190.

Wastell, D. and White, S. (2010) 'Technology as magic: Fetish and folly in the IT-enabled reform of children's services', in P. Ayre and M. Preston-Shoot (eds), *Children's Services at the Crossroads: A Critical Evaluation of Contemporary Policy for Practice*. Lyme Regis: Russell House Publishing.

Webb, R. and Vuillamy, G. (2004) *A Multi-Agency Approach to Reducing Disaffection and Exclusions from School. DfES Research Report No. 568*. York: University of York.

4

Children Like Ours? Policy and Practice Responses to Children Looked After

Anna Gupta

Introduction

How a society responds to its most vulnerable children is central to the debate about the relationship between children, families and the state. When and how the state should intervene in private family life are dilemmas that continue to challenge policy-makers and practitioners. The previous chapter examines policy in relation to safeguarding and family support. The focus of this chapter is on children who are unable to live with their birth parents and become looked after by the state. The terms 'children in care' and 'children looked after' are used interchangeably to refer to children living away from their birth parents in placements organised by statutory authorities.

The United Nations Convention on the Rights of the Child (UNCRC) (1989) provides a set of standards and obligations in relation to vulnerable children. However, the ways in which governments interpret these requirements reflect the particular historical, social and political contexts of the country (Frost and Parton 2009). This chapter explores contextual issues and forces of wider society that shape policies and practices developed to respond to the needs of children at risk of significant harm and unable to live with their birth parents. The focus is thresholds for care and substitute care placements; crucial issues when considering compulsory state intervention to safeguard and promote the welfare of children. While this chapter primarily concerns policy responses in England, reference is made to other countries in the UK, Europe and beyond.

Value perspectives in child welfare

While there are many similar components to contemporary child welfare systems in modern industrialised countries, there are also great differences. Fox-Harding (1997) explored the historical development of contemporary child protection systems and developed a useful framework for considering value perspectives and how these influence policy. The four broad perspectives Fox-Harding (1997) identified are:

1. *Laissez-faire and patriarchy* – This perspective prioritises the moral authority of the family and sees state intervention as inherently problematic. Disruption of the privacy of family life should only occur in the most extreme cases of child maltreatment. In such cases state intervention is not only acceptable but of a strong and authoritative kind, transferring the child to a secure placement with a new set of parent figures.
2. *State intervention and child protection* – This perspective favours extensive state intervention to protect children from poor parental care. The rights and liberties of parents are given a low priority; the child is paramount. There is a tendency to be more punitive towards parents who fall short of particular norms and standards. This perspective tends to favour the idea of the 'rescue' of suffering children to other, better homes.
3. *Modern defence of the birth family* – This perspective emphasises the importance of birth families not only from the perspective of their rights but also identifies some of the negative results of state intervention. The role of the state should play is neither paternalistic nor *laissez-faire*, but supportive of families, providing various services to enable families to remain together. Where children do, as a last resort, come into state care, considerable effort should be devoted to helping families deal with problems and maintaining links so that children can return home again.
4. *Children's rights and participation* – In its purest form this perspective would promote children's rights as indistinguishable from those of adults but more generally promotes the rights and participation of children in decisions made about their lives. The distinguishing characteristic of this perspective, is the emphasis on the child's own viewpoint, feelings, wishes, definitions, freedoms and choices; rather than on the attribution by adults of what is best for the child.

Frost et al. (1999) provide another useful analysis that specifically considers children in care. They argue that three main themes emerge from a historical analysis. First the enduring effect of the Poor Law, which made the provision that state welfare should be of a lower standard than life in the community, is reflected in the continuing stigma associated with being 'in care'. Second, there has been an emphasis on education and training as methods of rescuing children from poverty, which in more recent times is often framed as addressing 'poor outcomes'. Finally, there is the continuing tension between family-based care and residential provisions.

　　Both of these frameworks are relevant to current policy and practice considerations for children looked after, and assist our understanding of the contextual influences that are analysed further in this chapter.

Points for reflection

Before reading about policy and practice contexts over the years, think about your own values regarding families and the state. Which of Fox-Harding's (1997) value perspectives best reflects your values? What has influenced the development of your values, for example your family history, politics, religion, or professional experience? How might your values influence your work with children and families?

Historical context

Prior to considering more recent policy contexts and debates in relation to children in care, a brief historical overview is provided. Hendrick (2005) identifies a shift, beginning around the 1870s, from a simple concern with the rescue of destitute children into Poor Law institutional care, to a more complex notion and practice of welfare, education and instruction into 'citizenship'. Increasing attention was being paid at the time to child cruelty and the late 19th century saw the development of the first child protection legislation. Children placed in institutions were there to protect them from life on the streets, as well as from maltreatment at home (Ferguson 2004). These children were inevitably from poor backgrounds, and residential care provisions emphasised children's physical and moral welfare rather than their emotional wellbeing. Many were prepared for work, such as domestic service or labouring, reflecting what Frost et al. (1999) identify as the emphasis on education and training.

From the middle of the 20th century there was a change in policy from residential care to greater use of family-based care. The Children Act 1948 was influenced by the work of child development theorists such as Bowlby, and the experiences of evacuated children separated from their families during the Second World War. The Curtis Committee, from whose recommendations the 1948 Children Act emerged, was critical of residential care, stating that 'the child in these homes was not regarded as an individual with his rights and possessions, his own life to live, and his contribution to offer' (Secretary of State for the Home Department et al. 1946: 450). The main principles of the Children Act 1948 included the emphasis on family-based care or 'boarding out'; reunification of children with their birth families; and greater promotion of adoption (Hendrick 2005).

While children continued to be placed in residential care, this was increasingly seen as a residual service, which Frost and Parton (2009) argue led in part to many homes being poorly managed and, on occasion, becoming abusive environments. Two reports in the 1990s by Sir William Utting, *Children in the Public Care* (1991) and *People Like Us* (1997), provide powerful and damning testimony to the extent of the abuse of children in residential care. The extent of physical and sexual abuse of children, documented by Utting as well as Waterhouse (2000), reflected a historical theme of residential care being neglected, and children in the homes being 'less eligible' and less deserving (Frost and Parton 2009: 99).

Tensions between different family-based care options are also reflected in differing policy contexts. Whether adoption, with all legal rights over the child awarded to adopters, or long-term fostering, where parental responsibility is usually shared between the local authority and parents, should be the preferred option for children requiring permanent substitute care has been much debated over the past five decades. There was a shift in focus from foster care to permanence and adoption in the 1970s. The Children Act 1975 reflected a move away from 'holding open the door to eventual return to the birth family for most children in foster care' (Fox-Harding 1997: 106), towards easier adoption and the assumption of parental rights. This marked a shift from the pro-birth family approaches of the 1950s and 1960s to one of state paternalism and child protection (Fox-Harding 1997).

From the 1960s onward, the profile of children available for domestic adoptions changed in the context of changing attitudes to single parenthood and children born out of wedlock. There were fewer babies relinquished at birth and more children who were older and in care because of abuse. Before the mid-1960s it was commonly accepted that Black children were not 'suitable' for adoption (Thoburn et al. 2000). During the 1960s, as the numbers of White babies decreased; Black children slowly became viewed as acceptable for White childless couples to adopt, usually as a last resort (Gill and Jackson 1983). Transracial adoption was also advocated as a way of reducing the disproportionately high number of Black children in residential care (Dale 1987). Gradually the critics of transracial adoption were getting their views heard. With increasing numbers of Black young people brought up in transracial placements talking of their struggles with identity confusion and alienation (Black and In Care 1984), supporters of same-race placements contended that psychological and political concerns could not be separated when considering children's development of positive Black identities (Maxime 1986; Small 1986). A highly polarised debate followed, that has been recently reignited by the Coalition government's lessening of the requirement in the Children and Families Act 2014 that due consideration be given to the racial, cultural, religious and linguistic needs of children when placing for adoption (Barn and Kirton 2012).

Fox-Harding (1997: 185) argues that in the 1980s, both the 'paternalist and birth parent perspectives were in evidence, while laissez-faire and child liberation had a more minor influence'. The Children Act (CA) 1989 is an uneasy synthesis of the different perspectives. In the 1990s, following the implementation of the CA 1989, extended families and kinship networks became more central to the decision-making processes for children looked after. The Act also strengthened the duty of local authorities to safeguard and promote the welfare of all children in their care, with an increase in focus on the collective responsibility of local councils, often referred to as 'corporate parenting'. The past two decades have seen complex shifts in perspectives within and across different governments.

Children looked after and New Labour

In their first year, the Labour government was forced to respond to Utting's (1997) damning report on residential care. The *Quality Protects* programme between 1998 and 2003 aimed at improving standards of local authority 'corporate parenting'. The focus on adoption was once again affirmed by an initiative to promote adoption led by Tony Blair. Specified outcomes were linked to performance indicators that reflected New Labour's emphasis on managerialism and the 'modernisation' programme (Frost and Parton 2009). However the *Quality Protects* targets, including the proportion of children adopted from care, implemented in the context of an audit system linked to financial and status gains, have been criticised for creating simplistic descriptions of practice focusing on achieving service outputs with little attention to user outcomes (Munro 2004).

During the course of the New Labour government a range of new laws were implemented. Three key pieces of legislation in relation to children in care were the Children (Leaving Care) Act 2000, the Adoption and Children Act 2002 and the Children and Young Persons Act 2008. The issue of leaving care had received attention in the 1980s following the publication of a study by Stein and Carey (1986) and the duties of local authorities were extended under the CA 1989. However, when the Labour government came to power in 1997 outcomes and services for young people leaving care remained problematic. Leaving care was reframed as a social exclusion issue, and young people leaving care seen as vulnerable to a number of indicators of social exclusion (Frost and Parton 2009). However leaving care services continued to be a challenging area of work, and was returned to by New Labour as a theme in the *Care Matters: Time for Change* (DfES 2007) initiative.

The focus on adoption, with the severance of legal ties to the child's birth family, could be viewed as a move away from the pro-birth family perspective, however it was implemented by New Labour alongside initiatives such as Sure Start and *Every Child Matters* (DfES 2004) that aimed at increasing support to vulnerable families. These policies were arguably an attempt to reconcile the pro-birth family and child protection perspectives. The Adoption and Children Act 2002 brought in changes that included a duty on local authorities to provide post-adoption support, and allowing unmarried, including same-sex, couples to adopt. These changes reflected the complex needs of children adopted from care and importance of support, as well as a greater societal acceptance of co-habitation and same-sex parenting. Post-adoption support raises complex questions about the role of the state in private family life where adoption involves a transfer of parental responsibility to adoptive parents, who in law are treated as if they were the child's birth family. Luckock and Hart (2005) argue that the development of post-adoption support can be seen as part of a movement from a 'privacy/autonomy' model to a 'contract/services' model thereby placing the post-adoption family in a different position from other families.

The Children and Young Persons Act 2008 came on to the statute book in the final years of the Labour government. It followed the White Paper *Care Matters: Time for Change* (DfES 2007). Frost and Parton (2009) consider how the White Paper addresses three themes arising from Frost et al.'s (1999) historical analysis of the care system. They conclude that the White Paper indicates a 'rhetorical break with the Poor Law – no hint here of "less eligibility", indeed the highest level of state parenting is called for' (Frost and Parton 2009: 106). Considerable attention in the White Paper is given to educational attainment for children looked after, strongly resonant of the historical focus on education and training. Finally, Frost and Parton (2009: 108) observe that the White Paper continues the focus on foster care at the expense of residential care, 'despite Utting's (1997) plea that choice and diversity in this sector is key to maintaining quality'.

Children looked after and the Coalition government

Most elements of the Children and Young Persons Act 2008 (CYPA 2008) were implemented following the election of the Coalition government in 2010. The ideological and economic agendas of the Coalition government have inevitably impacted on how the reforms are implemented in practice. For example, a survey by the National Care Advisory Service (2012) raised concerns about local authorities' ability to deliver their statutory duties in times of significant cuts to their funding.

The Coalition government's focus of attention for children looked after has been on increasing adoption. This marks a dramatic shift towards the child protection and even *laissez-faire* perspectives, as it is accompanied by severe cuts to family support services and welfare benefits for vulnerable families. Following the election of the Coalition government, Parton (2014: 22) asserts that what has emerged is an *'authoritarian neoliberal state'* that is changing the nature of relationships between the state and families, particularly families from lower socio-economic backgrounds. The new *Working Together* guidance identifies the need to 'rescue children from chaotic, neglectful and abusive homes' (HM Government 2013: 22). The government has also sought to 'speed up' the family court system, giving less opportunity for parents to be supported to care for their children. The changes brought in by the Children and Families Act 2014 includes limiting the time frame for proceedings in all but exceptional cases to 26 weeks and lessening the requirement to consider a child's racial, religious, linguistic and cultural background. The Act does, however, also include provision for children to remain in foster care until they turn 21.

Who are 'children looked after'?

The Department for Education produces annual statistics on children looked after in England. The data for the period ending 31 March 2014 highlight the diversity of the backgrounds, needs and circumstances of the 68,840 children looked after. Most are in care due to abuse or neglect (62%); however, others are looked after because of family breakdown, being disabled or are unaccompanied children seeking asylum. The majority of children are from White British backgrounds, although some minority ethnic groups, such as children of mixed parentage and from Black African or Caribbean communities are over-represented among the care population. Some children will only remain in care for short periods of time, while others will grow up in care. Three-quarters are living in a foster placement, mainly with unrelated foster carers. Residential care continues to be a placement option for around 6360 children. Residential provision includes secure units, children's homes and hostels (www.gov.uk/government/uploads/system/uploads/attachment_data/file/35 9277/SFR36_2014_Text.pdf).

Meeting the diverse needs of these children presents challenges for social workers and other professionals. While the wider social policy environment has a profound impact on practice, so too do other factors, such as legal frameworks, organisational cultures, theoretical ideas, values and the exercise of professional discretion for individual children and their families. In the following sections the complexities and dilemmas inherent in decisions about thresholds for compulsory care and placement options for children requiring permanent substitute care are explored.

Thresholds for care

Children in England become looked after primarily through one of three routes: an order of a court; via a voluntary agreement with parents; or through the criminal justice process. The majority of children (72%) are in care on an order of the court, with 28% in care with their parents' consent or because there is no one with parental responsibility (DfE 2014). The distinction between compulsion and consent has, though, been called into question, with the use of the Section 20 'voluntary' care provision of the CA 1989 on occasions being 'compulsion in disguise', especially where the parents have mental health or learning difficulties (Re [2012] EWHC 2190 (Fam)).

The proportion of children coming into care with parental agreement varies greatly across different countries. In Japan over 90% and Sweden around 85% of those who enter care do so under arrangements agreed with parents and/or the young people themselves (Thoburn 2000). In these and other countries, including Denmark, France and Germany, placement away from home is seen as a necessary part of their family support systems, not as a last resort. Adoption from care without parental consent is far less common, and there is a greater reluctance to break family ties (Boddy et al. 2009).

The permanent removal of a child from his or her birth family has life-long consequences and is one of the most draconian actions of the state. The legal threshold for compulsory state intervention in private family life in England and Wales is the concept of 'significant harm' that was introduced in the CA 1989. The 'significant harm' threshold has to be established on the basis of the balance of probability before a court can consider whether making a care order is in the best interests of the child. The harm or likelihood of harm needs to be attributable to parental care, 'not being what it would be reasonable to expect a parent to give to him' (s. 31, CA 1989). Any breach of a person's right to respect for private and family life (Article 8 of the European Convention on Human Rights [ECHR]) must be proportionate, and uphold parents' and children's rights to a fair trial (Article 6 of the ECHR). The ECHR, since its incorporation into domestic law in the Human Rights Act 1998, has been an important influence on decision-making about children coming into care and the balance between parents' rights, children's welfare and the role of the state (Masson 2012).

There are no absolute criteria for making an assessment of significant harm. Harwin and Madge (2010) argue that the absence of a clear operational definition of significant harm is both a strength and a weakness. It allows for professional discretion given the complex and varied circumstances of children, but discretion is also vulnerable to external contextual factors in its application. The majority of families involved in care proceedings share common experiences of low income, housing difficulties and social exclusion. Many parents also struggle with problems such as mental health, substance misuse, learning difficulties and domestic violence

(Brophy 2006; Masson et al. 2008). However, families from different communities can have varied experiences of the family court system. Brophy et al.'s (2003) study of minority ethnic families' experiences found that communication difficulties and poor interpretation services raise serious questions about access to justice for parents whose first language is not English. Parents with learning difficulties are most likely to lose their children to the state, and there is evidence that these parents meet with a presumption of incompetence that too easily leads to their child being deemed at risk without the provision of compensatory support services (Booth et al. 2005).

Neglect is the most common form of harm experienced by children involved in care proceedings (Masson et al. 2008), however the chronic and cumulative nature of neglect means that decision-making about timing and attribution is complex (Harwin and Madge 2010). Analysis of serious case reviews into child deaths or serious harm has found that neglect is disproportionally represented in these cases, and suggests that the concept of significant harm contributes to the identification of many, but not all neglected children (Brandon et al. 2009). Neglect is frequently linked to poverty and social deprivation, and decisions about parental culpability are likely to become increasingly problematic in the context of the severe cuts to welfare benefits and family support services being brought in by Coalition government policies.

The variable pattern of care applications suggests that the interpretation of the threshold criteria and need for compulsory state intervention are also influenced by wider social and policy contexts. In the period from April to July 2008 applications for care orders fell by 25% compared with the same period in the previous year (Lloyd-Jones 2008). This coincided with the implementation of the Public Law Outline by the Ministry of Justice, which required more emphasis to be given to the prevention of cases coming to court. At the end of that year there was a dramatic increase in the numbers of care proceedings. This followed publicity surrounding the death of Peter Connelly, which was highly critical of social workers and other professionals (Gupta and Lloyd-Jones 2010).

In 2014 there were many changes to the family court system, primarily as a result of the Family Justice Review (Ministry of Justice 2011). The principal proposals of the Family Justice Review are contained in the Children and Families Bill and include the limitation of all but exceptional care cases to 26 weeks. District Judge Crichton, a family court judge, has described as 'tyranny' the government's demand for rigid adherence to a 26-week time limit for care cases. He warns that process is taking over outcomes and suggests that children who could return to their birth families may be placed for adoption due to rigid adherence to the timescales (Baksi 2013). The implementation of these policies and the basis on which decisions are being made have caused much disquiet and some challenge (Featherstone et al. 2013). Evidence from neuroscience research, for instance, which is being used to argue for early and decisive intervention (Brown and Ward 2012) has been criticised for being partial and simplified, and designed to promote a moral mission (Lloyd-Jones 2013; Wastell and White 2012). In September 2013, the Court of Appeal issued a landmark judgement, *Re B-S (Children)* [2013] EWCA Civ. 813. This judgement reaffirms that fundamental principle that adoption is the 'last resort' and urges judges to be alert to resource issues affecting local authorities' plans for adoption, and to go beyond the 26 weeks if necessary. This judgement directly challenges key aspects of the government's stance.

There are many contradictory demands facing social workers making recommendations about thresholds for compulsory care for individual children. Legal and policy frameworks can raise conflicts, and the lack of objective criteria has benefits as well as disadvantages. Ultimately, the overriding principle of the law is that the welfare of the child is paramount, and social workers have a professional responsibility to draw on multiple sources of evidence, critically reflect on their values and assumptions and analyse the options before making recommendations about children coming into care.

Points for reflection

Imagine you are working with Charmaine, a 17-year-old young woman of mixed parentage, who is in care. She has recently moved into a hostel for young people. She has had a troubled past few years after being placed in foster care following sexual abuse by her stepfather. She has had a number of placement breakdowns and has been convicted for possession of cocaine. She has been in a relationship with her boyfriend that has been characterised by frequent arguments and on occasions violence. She is now seven months pregnant and wants to care for the baby on her own. She said that she has separated from her boyfriend and no longer takes drugs. What are the issues that you would need to think about when making decisions about Charmaine and her baby's future?

Placements for children looked after

Placements for children in care are varied, as the children who use them have very diverse needs. For some children their time in care is short due to an acute family crisis, others are not able to return home to their parents, at least in the short term. The placement options for these children vary. With Special Guardianship Orders, children are placed with carers who hold parental responsibility, but the parents still retain some rights. In adoption the adopters hold sole parental responsibility, and birth parents' rights are extinguished. For children on care orders, the local authority shares parental responsibility with parents, and parents retain sole parental responsibility for children in s. 20 accommodation. The discussion in this section examines children for whom a decision has been made that they are unable to return to their parents' care and are in the looked after system or alternative substitute care placements.

The importance of children requiring security, stability and love throughout their childhood and beyond is recognised in child development literature and should provide a framework for all social work with children and families (Boddy 2013). Children coming into care generally come from socially disadvantaged backgrounds and many will have experienced abuse and neglect. All will have experienced loss and separation from caregivers. It is therefore not surprising that on a number of measures, such as educational attainment, employment and health, these children fare worse when compared to the general population. However, Forrester et al. (2009) reviewed the research and found that there was little evidence of the care system having a negative impact on children's welfare. In most of the studies improvement was noted and there was no evidence that children's welfare deteriorated. Key themes that emerge from the literature are the importance of stability and a secure base (Boddy 2013; Munro and Hardy 2006). Stability is important but it is not an end in itself, and the quality of the care is also crucial. Children need to be able to develop a positive sense of identity and belonging (Schofield et al. 2012), and the promotion of resilience through relationships in their wider network is also important (Gilligan 2009).

Kinship care

The involvement of family members in a child's life is something that most people and communities take for granted. Where a child requires care away from their parents, a placement within their wider family network can be used to assist in safeguarding and promoting their welfare. The CA 1989 requires that children who cannot live with their parents should be placed with wider family or friends, so long as this is consistent with their welfare. Family or friends can be approved as foster carers, or hold Special Guardianship, residence orders or adoption orders.

Societies and cultures vary greatly in the value that is placed on individual versus collective care responsibilities. Kinship care can be particularly important when working with families from minority ethnic backgrounds, such as families from the Indian sub-continent or Africa, whose cultural values put particular emphasis on wider family and kinship responsibility (Dwivedi 2002). In Australia and New Zealand in recent years, policy and practice have focused on maintaining indigenous Maori and Aboriginal children within their kinship networks (Thoburn 2000).

Research studies on kinship care in the UK suggest that placements with family or friends can be more stable than care with adults previously unknown to the child; the child can more easily maintain a sense of family and cultural identity and is more likely to retain contact with parents and siblings. Generally, the outcomes in kinship care are favourable for young people (Hunt and Waterhouse 2013; Hunt et al. 2008). However, while studies indicated that kinship care could be a positive option for many children it is not straightforward and requires careful assessment and support. Kinship carers tend to be older, in poorer health and in more disadvantaged circumstances than unrelated foster carers. However, in Britain there is evidence to suggest they are also less likely to receive adequate support (Hunt and Waterhouse 2013; Richards and Tapsfield 2003).

Adoption/long-term fostering

The concept of 'permanence' has for many years been part of the discourse for children in care in England. However 'permanence' has primarily been associated with 'legal' permanence (i.e. the carers hold parental responsibility and the child is no longer looked after), particularly adoption. Over the years this 'gold standard' of permanently transferring legal responsibility for the child to the new carers via adoption has been come under some criticism, with the 'care bad/adoption good' dichotomy seen as reinforcing stigma for children in care (Boddy 2013).

In relation to whether a child should be placed for adoption or placed in long-term foster care there is great variation in policies and practices across different countries. For example, in Austria, Denmark, Finland, the Netherlands and Sweden, long-term foster care is the preferred placement and maintaining links with the birth family is given the highest priority. Adoption from care is also rare in Australia and New Zealand, and if it occurs there is an expectation of ongoing family contact (Thoburn 2000). Australia has a painful history of the forced removal of indigenous children from their birth families, which has had an influence on policy considerations. On the other hand, in the US, children unable to return to their birth families are placed whenever possible for adoption (Selwyn and Sturgess 2000). As indicated, above this is also the policy of the Coalition government in the UK; however, in reality only a small proportion (around 5%) of children in care are placed for adoption each year.

Any plans for permanent substitute care away from parents must consider the child's developmental needs, his or her wishes and feelings and family relationships. These decisions are complex, involving competing needs and priorities and involve value judgements regarding the importance of birth family ties. Pro-adoption policies can be seen as being more aligned with the *laissez-faire* and child protection perspectives, whereas long-term fostering, where birth family contact is more likely to be retained, is more reflective of a pro-birth family perspective. Interestingly, the involvement and responsibility of the state, both in financial and professional terms, are much greater with long-term fostering than with adoption; in short, fostering is far costlier for the state.

Comparison of these two options on the basis of available empirical data is very difficult as the characteristics and experiences of children, as well as outcome measures, vary greatly. In the UK, there is much disagreement in the academic literature about the benefits of one of these options over another, particularly for children who are no longer babies (Biehal et al. 2010; Sellick et al. 2004; Tresiliotis 2002). One of the few areas of agreement is that ideology and dogma should not lead to 'blanket policies'. Researchers have consistently emphasised the need to recognise the complexity of adoption, and to acknowledge that adoption is not an appropriate pathway to permanence for all children in the system (Boddy 2013). A number of authors have argued for the need for clear policy and practice guidance on permanence planning within foster care; they express concern that insufficient attention has been given to ensuring that children in long-term foster placements *do* have a sense of permanence (Schofield et al. 2012; Sinclair et al. 2007).

Points for reflection

Imagine you are working with a sibling group of three children of Nigerian origin. Samuel (aged 9), Josephine (aged 6) and Daniel (aged 3). They are the subject of care proceedings and are unable to return to either parent's care. There are also no kinship carers available to look after them. Their current foster carer, Claudette, is a 60-year-old Jamaican woman. The children are very settled and making good developmental progress in her

(Continued)

(Continued)

care. Claudette's three daughters, who all live close by, support her with the children's care. The local authority would like all three children to be placed for adoption, but if that is not possible, at least the youngest two. Claudette is willing to care for all three children on a permanent basis, but only as a foster carer as she requires continuing financial and practical support. What do you think are the advantages and disadvantages of the options available? What do you think should be the plan for the children?

Residential care

Fewer than 10% of children looked after in England are in residential care, as indicated above. The numbers have decreased dramatically over the past few decades, and residential care is now seen as a placement of last resort. It is often used for adolescents with more challenging needs and when foster placements have broken down. Berridge et al.'s (2012) study found that children in residential care had high levels of need, and presented with significant emotional and behavioural difficulties, but many were not receiving a specialist service that met their needs. Most homes in the study had both short- and long-term placements and were described as 'turbulent environments with rapid turnover' (Berridge et al. 2012: 93).

The Utting Report (1997) and numerous research studies in the UK have highlighted the importance in residential care provision of a planned approach, proper management, inspection and monitoring of the service, more professionally qualified staff, and the provision of therapeutic and treatment programmes for children with high levels of emotional disturbance (DH 1998; Kendrick 2006). However, as long as these requirements are missing, residential care is likely to remain a marginal service of last resort. There is wide variation in the use of residential care across different countries. In the UK, US and Norway, most children are placed in foster care; however, in Denmark, France and Holland, there is a more equal balance between residential and foster care (Browne et al. 2005; Selwyn and Sturgess 2000). In Boddy et al.'s (2009) study of France, Germany and Denmark, residential care was seen as a placement of choice for young people with complex and challenging needs, and this was reflected in the specialised nature of the service with a more highly trained workforce. The Care Inquiry (2013: 8) recommends urgent attention be given to how residential care in England can create a sense of 'permanence' for children by providing stability and security and high quality care for the time they are in the placement.

Children's voices

There has been increasing recognition of the importance of involving children in decision-making that affects them. A child's right to participate is encapsulated in Article 12 of the UNCRC and in many countries, including the UK, this has been incorporated into domestic legislation and guidance. In addition to being a legal requirement, there is also increasing evidence that the participation of children can improve decision-making, engagement with plans and help promote positive developmental outcomes (Luckock and Lefevre 2008). Gilligan (1998) explains that one of the three 'building blocks of resilience' is a sense of self-efficacy and child welfare professionals can promote this by involving them in the planning process.

The CA 1989 resulted in many positive changes to the way children's views are represented in public law proceedings. Many of these changes continue to influence practice today, however Gupta and Lloyd-Jones (2010) argue that the context and culture of public service provision over the past decade have reduced the scope for independent representation for children in care proceedings. The reduction in the scrutiny of care plans by the court being proposed in the Children and Families Bill further undermines children's rights to representation in the legal arena. A study on the work of independent reviewing officers found that heavy caseloads and a working culture that did not value their work led to them often struggling to maintain scrutiny of the implementation of the child's care plan following proceedings (Jelicic et al. 2013). The Care Inquiry (2013) found that children said that they were too often not listened to or involved in decisions about their lives. The children spoke positively about social workers when they were able to build up a relationship based on trust. As one young man explains: 'A good social worker is calm … someone who can sit and talk to you all day, not trying to throw you out and don't give you time slots. They let you know you're not just a case. … It's about them accepting your situation and you for who you are' (Care Inquiry 2013: 5).

Conclusion

This chapter has examined the historical and current policy context in relation to some key issues for children looked after. The chapter has highlighted the diversity in characteristics and needs of children in care, as well as the various ways in which different societies interpret and implement policies to meet the requirements of the UNCRC that a child's best interests must be the primary concern. For social workers, the policy context is highly relevant to their work, but individual children need individualised solutions. In order to achieve this, practitioners must draw upon other sources of knowledge, such as legal frameworks, theory and research; critically reflect upon their own and others' values and assumptions; and make recommendations based on a detailed analysis of the options.

References

Baksi, C. (2013) 'Pioneering family court on the edge', *The Law Gazette,* 4 November.

Barn, R. and Kirton, D. (2012) 'Transracial adoption in Britain: Politics, ideology and reality', *Adoption and Fostering,* 36 (3–4): 25–37.

Berridge D., Biehal N. and Henry L. (2012) *Living in Children's Residential Homes,* Department for Education (DfE) Research Report 201. London: DfE.

Biehal, N., Ellison, S., Baker, C. and Sinclair, I. (2010) *Belonging and Permanence: Outcomes in Long-Term Foster Care and Adoption.* London: British Association for Adoption and Fostering (BAAF).

Black and In Care (1984) *Black and In Care.* London: Blackrose Press.

Boddy, J. (2013) *Understanding Permanence for Looked After Children: A Review of Research for the Care Inquiry.* Available at: www.frg.org.uk/images/Policy_Papers/understanding-permanenc-review-of-evidence.pdf (accessed 19 September 2013).

Boddy, J., Statham, J., McQuail, S., Petrie, P. and Owen, C. (2009) *Working at the 'Edges' of Care? European Models of Support for Young People and Families.* London: Institute of Education, University of London.

Booth, T., Booth, W. and McConnell, D. (2005) 'The prevalence and outcomes of care proceedings involving parents with learning difficulties in the family courts', *Journal of Applied Research in Intellectual Disabilities*, 18 (1): 7–17.

Brandon, M., Bailey, S., Belderson, P., Gardner, R., Sidebottom, P. Dodsworth, J., Warren, C. and Black, J. (2009) *Understanding Serious Case Reviews and Their Impact: A Biennial Analysis of Serious Case Review 2005–07.* London: Department for Children, Schools and Families.

Brophy, J. (2006) *Research Review: Child Care Proceedings under the Children Act 1989.* London: Department for Constitutional Affairs.

Brophy, J., Jhutti-Johal, J. and Owen, C. (2003) *Significant Harm: Child Protection Litigation in a Multi-Cultural Setting.* London: Department for Constitutional Affairs.

Brown, R. and Ward, H. (2012) *Decision-Making within a Child's Timeframe.* London: Childhood Wellbeing Research Centre.

Browne, K., Hamilton-Giachritis, C., Johnson, R., Agathonos-Georgopoulou, H., Anaut, M., Herczog, M., Keller-Hamela, M., Klimackova, A., Leth, I., Ostergren, M., Stan, V. and Zeytinoglu, S. (2005) *Mapping the Number and Characteristics of Children under Three in Institutions across Europe at Risk of Harm.* European Commission Daphne Programme, World Health Organization (WHO) Regional Office for Europe and University of Birmingham.

Care Inquiry (2013) *Making not Breaking: Building Relationships for Our Most Vulnerable Children.* Available at: www.frg.org.uk/images/Policy_Papers/care-inquiry-full-report-april-2013.pdf (accessed 19 September 2013).

Dale, D. (1987) *Denying Homes to Black Children: Britain's New Race Adoption Policies.* London: Social Affairs Unit.

Department for Education (DfE) (2014) *Children Looked After in England (Including Adoption and Care Leavers) Year Ending 31 March 2014*, SFR 36/2014. Available at: www.gov.uk/government/statistics/children-looked-after-in-england-including-adoption (accessed 2 June 2015).

Department for Education and Skills (DfES) (2004) *Every Child Matters: Change for Children.* London: The Stationery Office.

Department for Education and Skills (DfES) (2007) *Care Matters: Time for Change.* London: The Stationery Office.

Department of Health (DH) (1998) *Caring for Children Away from Home: Messages from Research.* Chichester: John Wiley.

Dwivedi, K.N. (ed.) (2002) *Meeting the Needs of Ethnic Minority Children* (2nd edn). London: Jessica Kingsley.

Featherstone, B., Morris, K. and White, S. (2013) 'A marriage made in hell: Early intervention meets child protection', *British Journal of Social Work*. doi: 10.1093/bjsw/bct052. First published online: 19 March.

Ferguson, H. (2004) *Protecting Children in Time.* Basingstoke: Palgrave Macmillan.

Forrester, D., Goodman, K., Cocker, C., Binnie, C. and Jensch, G. (2009) 'What is the impact of public care on children's welfare? A review of research findings from England and Wales and their policy implications', *Journal of Social Policy*, 38 (3): 439–456.

Fox-Harding, L. (1997) *Perspectives in Child Care Policy* (2nd edn). Harlow: Longman.

Frost, N. and Parton, N. (2009) *Understanding Children's Social Care: Politics, Policy and Practice*. London: Sage.

Frost, N., Mills, S. and Stein, M. (1999) *Understanding Residential Child Care*. Aldershot: Ashgate.

Gill, O. and Jackson, B. (1983) *Adoption and Race*. London: Batsford/BAAF.

Gilligan, R. (1998) 'Beyond permanence? The importance of resilience in child placement practice and planning', in M. Hill and M. Shaw (eds), *Signposts in Adoption: Policy, Practice and Research Issues*. London: British Association for Adoption and Fostering.

Gilligan, R. (2009) *Promoting Resilience: A Resource Guide on Working with Children in the Care System*. London: British Association for Adoption and Fostering.

Gupta, A. and Lloyd-Jones, E. (2010) 'The representation of children and their parents in public law proceedings since the Children Act 1989: High hopes and lost opportunities?', *Journal of Children's Services*, 5 (2): 64–72.

Harwin, J. and Madge, N. (2010) 'The concept of significant harm in law and practice', *Journal of Children's Services*, 5 (2): 73–83.

Hendrick, H. (ed.) (2005) *Child Welfare and Social Policy: An Essential Reader*. Bristol: Policy Press.

HM Government (2013) *Working Together to Safeguard Children*. London: Department for Education.

Hunt, J. and Waterhouse, S. (2013) *It's Just Not Fair! Support, Need and Legal Status in Family and Friends Care*. London: Family Rights Group.

Hunt, J., Waterhouse, S. and Lutman, E. (2008) *Keeping Them in the Family: Outcomes for Children Placed in Kinship Care through Care Proceedings*. London: British Association for Adoption and Fostering.

Jelcic, H., Hart, D., La Valle, I. with Fauth, R., Gill, C. and Shaw, C. (2013) *The Role of Independent Reviewing Officer (IROs) in England: Findings from a National Survey*. London: National Children's Bureau.

Kendrick, A. (2006) 'Working with children and young people', in A. Mainey and D. Crimmens (eds), *Fit for the Future? Residential Care in the United Kingdom*. London: National Children's Bureau.

Lloyd-Jones, E. (2008) *The Forward March of Children's Justice Halted*. Axminster: Triarchy Press.

Lloyd-Jones, E. (2013) 'Decision-making within a child's timescale: Who decides?', *Family Law*, 1 August.

Luckock, B. and Hart, A. (2005) 'Adoptive family life and adoption support: Policy ambivalence and the development of effective services', *Child and Family Social Work*, 10 (2): 125–134.

Luckock, B. and Lefevre, M. (eds) (2008) *Direct Work: Social Work with Children and Young People in Care*. London: British Association for Adoption and Fostering.

Masson, J. (2012) 'What are care proceedings really like?', *Adoption and Fostering*, 36 (1): 5–12.

Masson, J.M., Pearce, J. and Bader, K. (2008) *Care Profiling Study*. London: Ministry of Justice.

Maxime, J. (1986) 'Some psychological models of Black self-concept', in S.Ahmed, J. Cheetham and J.Small (eds), *Social Work with Black Children and their Families*. London: Batsford/British Association for Adoption and Fostering.

Ministry of Justice (2011) *The Family Justice Review: Final Report*. London: Ministry of Justice, the Department for Education and the Welsh Assembly Government.

Munro, E. (2004) 'The impact of audit on social work practice', *British Journal of Social Work,* 34: 1077–1097.

Munro, E.R. and Hardy, A. (2006) *Placement Stability: A Review of the Literature.* Loughborough: The Centre for Child and Family Research (CCFR).

National Care Advisory Service (NCAS) (2012) *Funding Leaving Care – Making the Cut: One Year On.* London: NCAS.

Parton, N. (2014) *The Politics of Child Protection: Contemporary Developments and Future Directions.* Basingstoke: Palgrave Macmillan.

Richards, A. and Tapsfield, R. (2003) *Family and Friends Care: The Way Forward.* London: Family Rights Group.

Schofield, G., Beek, M. and Ward, E. (2012) 'Part of the family: Planning for permanence in long-term family foster care', *Children and Youth Services Review,* 34: 244–253.

Secretary of State for the Home Department, Minister of Health and Minister of Education (1946) *Report of the Care of Children Committee (Curtis Report), Cmd. 6922.* London: HMSO.

Sellick, C., Thoburn, J. and Philpot, T. (2004) *What Works in Adoption and Foster Care?* London: Barnados.

Selwyn, J. and Sturgess, W. (2000) *International Overview of Adoption: Policy and Practice.* Bristol: School for Policy Studies.

Sinclair, I., Baker, C., Lee, J. and Gibbs, I. (2007) *The Pursuit of Permanence: A Study of the English Child Care System.* London: Jessica Kingsley.

Small, J. (1986) 'Transracial placements: Conflicts and contradictions', in S. Ahmed, J. Cheetham and J. Small (eds), *Social Work with Black Children and Their Families.* London: Batsford/British Association for Adoption and Fostering.

Stein, M. and Carey, K. (1986) *Leaving Care.* Oxford: Blackwell.

Thoburn, J. (2000) *A Comparative Study of Adoption.* Norwich: University of East Anglia.

Thoburn, J., Norford, L. and Rashid, S. (2000) *Permanent Family Placement for Children of Minority Ethnic Origin.* London: Jessica Kingsley.

Tresiliotis, J. (2002) 'Long-term foster care or adoption? The evidence examined', *Child and Family Social Work,* 7: 23–33.

Utting, W.B. (1991) *Children in the Public Care.* London: HMSO.

Utting, W. (1997) *People Like Us: The Report of the Review of the Safeguards for Children Living Away from Home.* London: HMSO.

Wastell, D. and White, S. (2012) 'Blinded by neuroscience: Social policy, the family and the infant brain', *Families, Relationships and Societies,* 1 (3): 397–414.

Waterhouse, R. (2000) *Lost in Care, Report of the Tribunal of Inquiry into the Abuse of Children in Care in the Former County Council Areas of Gwynedd and Clwyd since 1974.* London: The Stationery Office.

Some useful links and websites

The following Department for Education guidance documents are available from: www.gov.uk/government/publications/children-act-1989-court-orders--2

- Volume 1 – Children Act 1989: Court Orders
- Volume 2 – Children Act 1989: Care Planning, Placement and Case Review
- Volume 3 – Children Act 1989: Transition to Adulthood for Care Leavers
- Volume 4 – Children Act 1989: Fostering Services
- Volume 5 – Children Act 1989: Children's Homes

Further guidance is available from: www.gov.uk/government/uploads/system/uploads/attachment_data/file/306282/Statutory_guidance_on_court_orders_and_pre-proceedings.pdf

The C4EO website (www.c4eo.org.uk) contains useful publications on children in care, including guidance on promoting the quality of life for looked after children and young people: archive.c4eo.org.uk/themes/vulnerablechildren/files/promoting_the_quality_of_life_of_looked_after_children_and_young_people.pdf

The Social Care Institute for Excellence (SCIE) website also contains useful research reviews and guidance on work with children looked after: www.scie.org.uk/topic/careneeds/lookedafterchildrenyoungpeople

Key organisations include:

British Association for Adoption and Fostering (BAAF): www.baaf.org.uk

Family Rights Group (FRG): www.frg.org.uk

The Fostering Network: www.fostering.net

The Office of the Children's Commissioner in England: www.childrenscommissioner.gov.uk

5

Personalisation

Maria Brent

Adult social care is the overarching term to describe the provision of community care services in the United Kingdom and is in the process of a fast paced transformational change which has arguably not been seen since the introduction of the NHS and Community Care Act 1990. The nature of these changes comes under the banner of the Personalisation agenda. Personalisation heralds a radical shift in the provision of community care services from a collective paternalistic model of social care towards a more individualised, person-centred approach to support. The overarching statement of this new agenda is to provide service users with more choice and control through the allocation of an individual budget that will enable them, with support, to purchase their own care (Carr 2010a). This shift towards individualised services is altering the relationship between the state, the service user and social work and is fundamentally changing the role of traditional welfare services (Ferguson 2007; Lymbery 2012; Scourfield 2007). This chapter provides an introduction to some of these developments by exploring how these changes are affecting those who are eligible for community care services, who for the purpose of this chapter will be described as 'service users'. It is not exhaustive or conclusive but aims to provide a broad overview of these developments by exploring:

- the origins of personalisation and its development through legislation and government policy;
- the changing relationship between the welfare state and the service user; and
- the impact of personalisation for social work.

What is personalisation and where has it come from?

The term 'personalisation' has become popularised as a 'catch-all' label to describe a range of policy reforms and practices and is often used interchangeably in a range of different settings (Glasby and Littlechild 2009). There are a plethora of descriptors associated with personalisation and as it has grown it has developed its own language with new terms and processes. In its simplest form, it is about working with service users in a person-centred way, supporting them to achieve their full potential while valuing their strengths, listening to their preferences and giving them choice and control to determine how they want to live their lives (Duffy 2010; Glasby and Littlechild 2009). Personalisation is not only about social care but also aims to ensure that people and communities have advice, advocacy and support to access wider universal services including housing, transport, health, employment and education regardless of their age or disability. The aim of personalisation is to develop new ways of partnership working. It plans to deliver a total transformation of social care that will provide service users and carers with an upfront allocation of funds called an individual budget, which will enable them to have more choice and control over the co-production, design, delivery and evaluation of their community services (Carr 2010a).

Although personalisation is presented as a new agenda for transforming social care, the underpinning philosophy is informed by the work of Carl Rogers and a humanistic, person-centred approach. This is also supported by the work of O'Brien (1987) and Wolfensberger (1972), who championed a social model of disability, promoting choice, independence and a valued role in society for people with learning disabilities. Personalisation's foundations can be traced back to the early 1970s in the US and the effective campaigning of disabled people for more choice and control to live independently. One of the key catalysts for change was brought about by disabled students in the US who demonstrated that with the support of personal assistants (PAs) they were able to study successfully at Berkeley University, California. As this proved so successful the students created the first Center for Independent Living (CIL) which was an organisation run by disabled people for disabled people to support and empower each other to take more control of their lives. The concept spread across Europe and by the early 1980s CILs were being founded in the UK (Glasby and Littlechild 2009). The independent living and disability movements championed a social model of disability and developed a growing market for 'cash-for-care' schemes, equivalent to services in kind, where service users were provided with cash payments to purchase their care from a broader range of commercial options. Cash-for-care schemes were introduced across Europe and were also adopted in Canada and America where governments were more aligned to a market approach to social care. A range of cash-for-care schemes are associated with personalisation, including direct payments, individual budgets and personal budgets (Arksey and Baxter 2012); these are explored later in the chapter.

A significant turning point for the Independent Living Movement and a mark of its success in campaigning for the rights of disabled people was the introduction of the Community Care (Direct Payments) Act 1996, which set out to provide a budget for all eligible adult service users to purchase their own care, either independently or with support. The take up of direct payments was supported further by the Carers and Disabled Children Act 2000, which extended the eligibility criteria to include carers, people with parental responsibility for disabled children and young disabled people. The commitment for social services to offer direct payments was legitimised with the introduction of the Health and Social Care Act, s. 57 2001, which placed a duty, as opposed to a power, on social services to offer a direct payment to those who met the eligibility criteria for community care services. This was also accompanied by performance indicators (PIs) which were imposed on social services departments and acted as a driver requiring local authorities to provide data on the take up of direct payments to the Department of Health. Direct payments recipients could become an independent employer and recruit a personal assistant (PA) or purchase care from a private independent organisation, but due to restrictions were unable to employ a family member who was living in the same household (Glasby and Littlechild 2009). Support from community organisations was available to offer support and advice in relation to employment and managing funds. Direct payments demonstrated that they could be beneficial to service users by not only providing them with choice but also an opportunity to develop skills in recruitment and management as an employer, reducing the pressure on families to provide informal care and therefore improving relationships. The use of direct payments could also promote emotional wellbeing as PAs could support service users more flexibly, enabling them to access the community as opposed to a focus on self-care or domestic tasks (Arksey and Baxter 2012). The success of direct payments was a key catalyst for the move to personalisation and they continue to be the main vehicle for facilitating personal budgets.

In exploring the origins of personalised services, one of the first commentators to use the term 'personalisation' in relation to social care was the writer Charles Leadbeater in a series of publications starting in 2004 for the government think-tank Demos. Leadbeater (2004: 81) suggests:

> Public service users should have a voice directly into the service as it is delivered. That voice will be unlocked also if they have a degree of choice over when, where, how and to what end a service is delivered. The aim of personalised services is not to provide the self interested, self gratification of consumerism but to build a sense of self actualisation, self realization, and self enhancement.

This viewpoint gathered momentum with the concept of individual budgets being first proposed within the Cabinet Office Strategy Unit (2005) report, *Improving the Life Chances of Disabled People*, which identified individual budgets as a key mechanism to increase choice. This was followed by the Green Paper *Independence, Well-being and Choice* (DH 2005), which set out an ambitious 10- to 15-year transformational vision for adult social care which included a 'wider use of direct payments and the piloting of individual budgets to stimulate the development of modern services delivered in the way people want' (2005: 14).

The radical proposed reforms in government policy were influenced by the work of Simon Duffy and an organisation named In Control, who worked in partnership with the government and organisations working with disabled people promoting a 'self-directed support' approach to social care (Duffy 2008). The new system of 'self-directed support' (SDS) sets out a seven-step process to enable the service user to gain more control and choice on how to use their individual budget to achieve their desired outcomes. In brief, the seven steps consist of: a supported self-assessment process; the allocation of an individual budget (IB); the development of a support plan to meet identified outcomes; the plan is then agreed by the local authority; the support plan is put into place; the person lives their life; and the plan is then reviewed (see Carr [2010a] for more detail on the processes of personalisation and self-directed support).

Self-directed support and individual budgets were tested out by the creation of pilot schemes within adult social care. Early pilots ran in 2003–2005 with six local authorities working with a group of 60 people with complex needs. Although the sample was small the positive outcomes were significant. Due to this success, In Control extended its membership in 2006 to interested authorities, with 122 local authorities joining In Control's programme and by July 2008 7000 people were in receipt of an individual budget (Duffy 2008). The initial pilot schemes also explored the possibilities for drawing on a range of funding streams, not just from the social care budget, to provide an integrated, holistic approach to meeting needs. This included funding streams from Access to Work, the Independent Living Fund, Supporting People and the Disabled Facilities Grant. One of the radical changes proposed within individual budgets was that they aimed to offer a much broader range of options for service users than direct payments. For example, they could allow people to consider gym membership instead of attending a day centre or pay family members and friends for the support they provided (Glendinning et al. 2008). The terms 'individual budgets' and 'personal budgets' are often an area of confusion and are used interchangeably, therefore it is important to understand how they differ. At their conception individual budgets aimed to integrate wider funding streams as outlined above. The government recognised that to achieve this aim significant policy and legislative reform would be required. The government decided this was not achievable at that time therefore in 2009 the title 'individual budget' was changed to a 'personal budget' as it is now only funded from a social care budget (Carr 2010a).

The aims of self-directed support (SDS) are not only to be used just as a process but as a vehicle to enable service users to change their relationship with the state, to become active citizens who are involved in the direction and development of their life, their community and services (Duffy 2010). Duffy's Professional Gift and Citizen models (2003) outlined below demonstrates the significant shift in thinking required to ensure SDS is understood. The left-hand side of Figure 5.1 presents the Professional Gift model, where the service user is seen as the 'needy' person, a passive recipient of care which is provided by the state and accessed via a gatekeeping professional. In contrast to this, the right-hand side of Figure 5.1 illustrates the Citizen model; here the service user holds a central role as an active citizen who is entitled to negotiate their care while being firmly anchored within their community.

Points for reflection

Consider the changing relationships outlined in Duffy's Citizen model. What do you think will be the benefits and challenges for:

- The service user?
- Social work?
- Community care services?

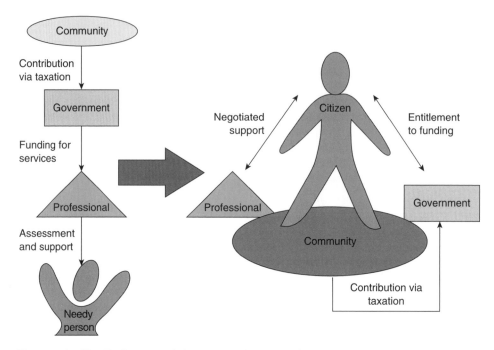

Figure 5.1　The Professional Gift model (left) and the Citizen model (right)

(Taken from www.centreforwelfarereform.org, a free on-line resource from The Centre of Welfare Reform Limited © Duffy 2003).

The changing relationship between the welfare state, social work and service users

While the personalisation agenda provides a distinct message to support service users to have more choice and autonomy (DH 2006; HM Government 2007), adult social care has arguably become increasingly controlled and regulated. The increased regulation of adult social care can be traced back to the New Right and neoliberal approaches which were central drivers for New Labour coming into office in 1997 (Needham 2007). A plethora of regulatory bodies were introduced to improve and standardise social work and social care with a view to controlling the 'bureau professionals' (Scourfield 2007). The move to increasing regulation is evidenced by the government's White Paper *Modernising Social Services: Promoting Independence, Improving Protection, Raising Standards* (DH 1998). The White Paper was identified as a forerunner in setting a climate of regulation and increased governance and highlights the New Right's impact on marketisation and managerialisation of the welfare system. The rationale for the modernisation of health and social services was in response to what the government described as 'too many examples of problems and failures in social services. As a result of these there is very low public confidence in our social services' (DH 1998, Executive summary). Neglect of vulnerable adults and children, inflexibility of service delivery and an inconsistency of care were identified as failings of social services. In terms of policy development, a significant step in progressing individual budgets was the local authority concordat *Putting People*

First: A Shared Vision and Commitment to the Transformation of Adult Social Care (HM Government 2007), which set out a three-year transformation agenda and outlined how every local authority in England would be supported and expected to undergo a whole system transformation. It recognised that although well intentioned, the NHS and Community Care Act 1990 'led to a system which can be over complex and too often fails to respond to people's needs and expectations' (HM Government 2007: 1). The concordat outlined a radical reform which aimed to,

> build on best practice and replace a paternalistic, reactive care of variable quality with a mainstream system focused on prevention, early intervention, enablement and high quality personally tailored services. (2007: 2)

The government continued to show their commitment to personalisation within the policy document *A Vision for Adult Social Care: Capable Communities and Active Citizens* (DH 2010b), which was underpinned by the sector partnership agreement Think Local, Act Personal (TLAP 2011). This document stated that everyone who is eligible for community support should be offered a personal budget by April 2013. The government's commitment to personal budgets was extended in the White Paper *Caring for Our Future: Reforming Care and Support* (DH, 2012), which requested local authorities to commission independent advice and support for service users and also increased the scope of personal budgets to include those living in residential care. Furthermore, the research undertaken by the Social Care Institute for Excellence (2011) highlighted that the independent sector had an important role to provide advice and advocacy to service users to enable them to benefit from personal budgets. There has also been rapid development of the technologies of personal budgets into other areas of policy, such as *NHS Personal Health Budgets* (DH 2009), although it is questioned whether there is enough robust evidence of the impact of personalisation to warrant this expansion (Needham and Glasby 2014).

The impact of these welfare reforms is not without criticism, with commentators expressing concern about the changing relationships with service users who may be construed as shifting from a passive recipient of prescribed services, as previously outlined in Duffy's Professional Gift model, to becoming an active citizen, arguably also a consumer, in choosing and purchasing their own services. Needham (2007) argues that consumerism has played a significant role in the reform of public services under New Labour and identifies two central opposing views within this debate. The supporters of the consumer-orientated approach who '[express] bewilderment that anyone, other than unapologetic paternalists or producerists could resist its penetration into public services', while critics 'see its common sense pretensions as a hegemonic project to erode the distinctive civic space of pubic services' (Needham 2007: 1). Spicker (2013) adds to this debate arguing that the marketisation of social care and the concept of individual purchasing power driving up quality and efficiency are flawed. For market forces to work in social care, there is a need for independent providers and competition from multiple purchasers. Service users living in potentially diverse geographical areas are not in a position to access a competitive market with multiple providers as the market is not yet developed. A central tenet of the personalisation agenda is for individualised approaches which aim to respond to individual needs and preferences. Spicker (2013) suggests that individual responsiveness is not always best and there is a place for generalised services, citing sheltered housing provision or meals on wheels as examples and argues that:

Without personalization the argument goes, services are liable to be mono-
lithic, unresponsive to need, forcing people to fit the mould. If a service is not
personal, it must be impersonal; if it is not responsive, it must be unresponsive;
and if it is not individually tailored, it must be ill-fitting. These are false
dichotomies. (Spicker 2013: 8)

A critical analysis of individualised approaches is called for as there is a need to
guard against the assumption that such an approach is always the best fit. There is
a fundamental concern that the individualistic approach to personal budgets may
weaken and dismantle the collective voice for community welfare services (Carey
2014; Ferguson 2007; Spicker 2013). Furthermore, the acceptance of neoliberal
political ideologies which underpin personalisation is in danger of taking us away
from the notion of citizenship and towards a state of consumerism (Lymbery 2012).
As local authorities transform their historical role of a provider to a commissioner
of services there is concern that the neoliberal market reforms and the fragmentation of services will create increasing problems in health and social care, particularly
for social work, as organisations become more disparate and disconnected and lose
the strength of a collective identity (Carey 2014). Furthermore, in a climate of austerity there is concern that local authorities are cutting the number of posts in adult
social work, which may undermine the ideals of personalisation by removing the
expert skills of social workers who can support the engagement of service users,
particularly those who are more vulnerable (Lymbery 2012).

Scourfield (2007) suggests that the promotion of individualised budgets as
benchmarks for choice and independence may camouflage another message, that
the state intends service users to become 'autonomous, managerial and enterprising
individuals' (2007: 108) and that the melding of user-centredness with themes of
independence, quality, achievement and self-regulation suggests that another transformation is under way. This transformation is not simply about the reconstruction
of citizens as consumers but the transformation of citizens into both managers and
entrepreneurs who are expected to use their business acumen to navigate the markets of social care. Scourfield (2007) argues that this is an example of how the
government has harnessed the emancipatory discourse connected to individualised
budgets to its modernisation agenda and is a measure of how the government has
utilised the 'person-centredness' approach to transfer responsibility away from the
government and back to the modern citizen. The relationship between the state and
citizen has been reconstructed and has resulted in the loss of local authorities as
separate organisational entities. Scourfield (2007: 107) argues that:

inherent in New Labour's project of modernization is the assumption that the
modern citizen should be both managerial and entrepreneurial. What were
once public responsibilities are being transferred to the individual.

The shift of responsibility from the state to the individual and the application of labels
such as consumer, customer and citizen and service user to people in receipt of services
is a central debate within the personalisation agenda. There is a body of work that
explores this argument in detail, see Needham (2007), Clarke and Newman (1997),
McLaughlin (2009) and Ferguson (2007). For the purpose of this chapter, elements of
these works are drawn upon to provide some explanation of these terms. McLaughlin

(2009) explores how we describe the relationship between those who provide services and those who receive them by examining the terms 'client' 'consumer', 'customer' 'service user' and 'expert by experience'. Each term brings with it a different lens which shapes our view of this relationship. McLaughlin argues that:

> the use of 'client' emphasizing passivity, and the use of 'customer' or 'consumer' suggest the managerialization and/or marketization of the social work relationship implying that the customer or consumer wishes were paramount. (2009: 1113)

The importance of language and how we attach labels to those in receipt of community care services is critical as it defines the expectations of that relationship. McLaughlin expands on this further and states that:

> The language we use labels individuals in different ways and, in doing so, acts as both a signifier and an external social control. Which ever label we use – 'service user', consumer, 'customer', 'client' or 'expert by experience' – it is descriptive not of a person, but of a relationship. (2009: 1114)

Simon Duffy, who is (at the time of writing) the director of the Centre of Welfare Reform, was a key architect in developing self-directed support (SDS) with the organisation In Control and argues that it was not designed to promote the marketisation of public services, but to support people who may have an impairment or disability to have more control over their lives (Duffy 2010). However, there have been expressed concerns about the poorly understood nature of personal budgets on a national level, as Glasby and Littlechild highlight:

> As personal budgets have become something of a hot topic, the biggest danger is that they get hijacked by people who do not understand them or who have other motives, allowing the old system to pay lip service to the concept while essentially recreating itself. (2009: 86)

Points for reflection

- Do you think the personalisation agenda provides equal access and benefits to all service user groups? What might the areas of challenge be and what can be done to address them?
- There are commentators who argue that the move to individualised care may dismantle collective services and undermine the role of the welfare state, what are your views on this?

Is choice a reality?

Choice was a key selling point in the New Right/neoliberal approaches underpinning New Labour's political agenda for social care and has been embraced by the Coalition government acting as a central thread throughout social care reforms with the introduction of direct payments (DH 1996) and individual and personal budgets (DH 2006). In terms of social policy, choice can be used to promote new flexible services for service provision. Stevens et al. (2011) draw on the work of Clarke et al. (2007) and Glendinning et al. (2008) to put forward the view that the ability for a person to choose who undertakes their care, and they emphasise personal care as an example, not only provides choice but 'in this light, choice is constructed as a means to overcome oppression and is related to concepts of autonomy, inclusion and rights and citizenship' (Stevens et al. 2011: 259). This view supports the model of citizenship put forward by Duffy (2010) that the notion of choice is complex and inherently bound to the realisation of citizenship.

The reality of providing equitable choices to a wide range of services users who have a multiplicity of complex needs and varying levels of support is challenging. This complexity is exacerbated by the need to address issues of power with both professionals and services that are governed by public bodies within a climate of marketisation, while also attempting to balance choice, autonomy and minimise risk (Stevens et al. 2011). The notion of choice and independence is complex. Rabiee (2013) argues that a narrow view of independence should be avoided as independence is not just about self-care but about the ability to make decisions about one's life and to achieve desired goals. Also, the binaries of dependence and independence should be replaced by the concept of 'interdependency', particularly given that a service user may be the carer as well as the cared for and that mutual dependence affects all human beings, not just disabled or older people.

A further central debate within the personalisation agenda is how we can ensure that those who are deemed vulnerable, isolated or lack capacity can realise choice and are not left behind in the marketisation of social care. Leece and Leece (2006) argue that there is evidence to suggest that direct payments, which are the main deployment of personal budgets, are taken up disproportionately by more educated, middle class and affluent people who have the business acumen to navigate the move from service users to employer status. They suggest that social workers are in danger of contributing to the creation of a 'two-tiered system' which may discriminate against those who are reliant on traditional services as they do not have the ability or desire to take on the responsibility of employing and organising their own care. Those with more robust social networks and social capital may be in a stronger position to engage with personalisation. For those without support this can bring about a further inequity as they may be denied the same opportunities (Stevens et al. 2011).

Points for reflection

- Think about how you may have experienced choice in your own life, what were the limitations to this?
- Do you think the personalisation agenda provides choice? If so in what way, and for whom?

Does personalisation work? And if so, for whom?

The Department of Health commissioned the Individual Budgets Evaluation Network (IBSEN) to undertake a wide-ranging evaluation of 13 IB pilot projects (Glendinning et al. 2008). The aim was to examine whether IBs provided better outcomes for adults eligible for social care, what was the impact of these changes on the workforce and also to identify any particular benefits or challenges for particular groups. The findings from the IBSEN evaluation were positive with those in receipt of IBs feeling overall that they had more control over their lives. The most positive outcomes were for people in mental health services, although it is recognised that this was a small sample group. However, further studies undertaken by MIND (2009) support this finding as service users accessing mental health services stated that IBs complemented a recovery model of care, as it promotes a strengths perspective and offers them more control and independence. People with sensory or physical disabilities also had positive outcomes but it is noted that this group had more experience and knowledge in using direct payments. There was a mixed response from people with learning disabilities and their carers from the evaluation as some found the process stressful but it was also noted that the principles of personalisation and person-centred approaches have their foundations based in learning disability services therefore they may not have found the process of IBs offering anything particularly new. More recent evaluations indicate that there is less evidence of benefits for older people using personal budgets and for them to meaningfully engage in the process they will require a higher level of support (Woolham and Benton 2013).

For carers, the introduction of IBs was not accompanied by supporting guidance on how their needs would be considered in this process. The IBSEN conducted a further associated study to explore the impact of IBs on carers, specifically examining how they were consulted and considered in the assessment and provision of services (Glendinning et al. 2009). Further analysis of these data demonstrated that there was a lack of consistency across the pilot sites as to how carers' needs were included in the assessment process. A concerning finding was that if a carer was providing support this often resulted in a reduction in the budget allocation for the service user as it was assessed that the carer was already meeting a particular need (Moran et al. 2012). However, despite this, carers found that the impact of IBs was positive, highlighting increased choice as a key improvement. As Moran et al. state:

> In comparison to carers of people in receipt of conventional services, carers of IB holders had significantly higher quality of life, were significantly more likely to be fully occupied in activities of their choice and carers of older people in the IB group were significantly more likely to report having a social life. (2012: 474)

Gray and Birrell (2013) draw on the work of Vickers et al. (2012) and Carr and Robbins (2009) to argue that the needs and views of Black and minority ethnic groups have not been explored within the research or evaluation of personal budgets and there is a lower take up of direct payments and personal budgets for marginalised groups. A lack of accessible information and clarity on how to access personal budgets, alongside a lack of community resources and difficulties in recruiting staff who could meet cultural and linguistic needs are cited as barriers to engagement.

The impact of personalisation for social work

The role and identity of professional social work within personalisation is contested (Jones 2014; Lymbery 2012; McGregor 2014). This has been fuelled by a raft of changes and reviews in social work education, all of which have aimed to improve the quality and status of social work as a profession (Croisdale-Appleby 2014; DH 2014a; DH 2014b; TCSW 2012). The underlying ethos of personalisation aims to reflect social work core values of self-determination, respect and promoting independence. The aim is that social work moves away from the professional social work 'expert' assessing the service user with much more focus on the skills and knowledge of the service user themselves in defining their needs and desired outcomes as part of a supported self-assessment process. *Putting People First* (HM Government 2007) and *Transforming Social Care* (DH 2008) outlined that social work would move away from the role of gatekeeper and assessor and have more of a role in advocacy and brokerage, supporting the service user to identify resources and to facilitate their choices. There is a conflicting dilemma as social workers endeavour to advocate for service users to receive appropriate care but also act as gatekeepers for local authority budgets (Scourfield 2007, 2008). Service users have expressed concerns about the ambiguous role of social workers within personalisation. Leece and Leece's (2011) study explored the views of service users and asked what role social work should take in supporting self-directed support. Respondents from the study questioned whether social workers can be truly unbiased and advocate for service users if social workers themselves are constrained and managed by the local authority. Furthermore, over half of the respondents questioned the value and usefulness of social workers and 'the powerful position that professionals occupy' (Leece and Leece 2011: 214). The need for an unbiased and independent brokerage role was identified and it was clear from the responses that social workers within the local authority did not have the freedom to provide this role. These views challenge the proposed role of social work put forward in government polices as advocates and brokers (HM Government 2007). As one respondent within Leece and Leece's study states:

> I would not want any interference from any social worker or support broker telling me how I should spend my money. This is again unwarranted interference from our 'Nanny State' type of government (Carol, Elders Forum). (2011: 214)

The findings also identified a different response from older people who suggested having a social worker involved in organising their care might be helpful. Although this study used a small sample the findings highlight the disparity in the expectations of social workers from service users in supporting personal budgets.

A further central debate within the personalisation agenda is how social work can ensure that those who are deemed vulnerable, isolated or lack capacity can realise choice and are not left behind in the marketisation of social care. Personal budgets can be accompanied by increased responsibility as service users become employers, managing their own support, which may be accompanied by increased stress. There is a dichotomy for social workers who value the ethos of individualised budgets but also struggle with the potential risks of abuse and stress to vulnerable services users who are responsible for managing their own care. This was identified in the early stages of the personalisation agenda by Clark and Spafford (2002: 253), who highlighted that 'the extra responsibility might pose increased stress for older people and informal carers if the care manager was not there to fall back on'.

The reality of providing equitable choices to a wide range of service users who have a multiplicity of complex needs is challenging and there is a body of work that critiques the benefits of personalisation and suggests that it is not a 'one size fits all' system (Moran et al. 2012; Newbronner et al. 2011; Woolham and Benton 2013; Spicker 2013). This complexity is exacerbated by the need to address issues of power with both professionals and services that are governed by public bodies within a climate of marketisation, while also attempting to balance choice, autonomy and minimise risk (Stevens et al. 2011). As personalisation promotes a culture of increased choice and autonomy, safeguarding adults increasingly requires the expert assessment skills of social workers to ensure that service users are involved where possible in the decision-making process (Carr 2010b; DH 2010; Lymbery 2012; SCIE 2011). It is recognised that safeguarding legislation is fragmented and there is an unresolved ambiguity over the accountability of risk (Mandelstam 2013; Spencer-Lane 2011). Finding a balance between empowerment and protection within personalisation is an ongoing challenge for social work as it strives to promote self-determination and meet a professional and legal duty to protect (Ellis 2007).

The above discussions aim to identify some of the challenges for adult social work in meeting a broad and diverse range of expectations within the personalisation agenda. The multi-faceted and often dichotomous role that social work is expected to fulfil in this new landscape is arguably difficult to reconcile as expectations are often juxtaposed at polar positions. Figure 5.2 developed by the author aims to summarise some of these complex dichotomies.

For adult social work to find its professional and organisational home within the personalisation agenda, it will need to find a way to reconcile these complex dichotomies. The implementation of personalisation has coincided with unprecedented cuts in social care. Although the introduction of IBs were thought to be cost-neutral there is now a fear that in the face of significant cuts the government may be turning the personalisation agenda into a 'wolf in sheep's clothing', dressed in the persuasive language of choice and control but utilised by local authorities as a tool to cut social care. Concerns are expressed that with local authorities having to cut social care by 33% by 2015 there may be a manipulation of the processes within personalisation to reduce budgets, impose increased control, and an opposition to creative support planning that goes against the norm (Duffy 2012). As Netten et al. state:

Social workers could be forgiven for thinking themselves maybe caught between a rock and a hard place in a policy climate that emphasizes improvements and outcomes (Department of Health 2010) and a financial climate that necessitates cuts in expenditure on social care (Audit Commission 2010). (Netten et al. 2012: 1557)

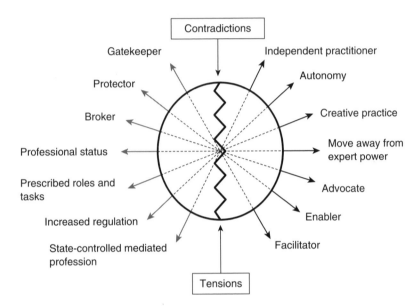

Figure 5.2   Adult social work in the context of personalisation: complex dichotomies and contradictions

Conclusion

In conclusion, this chapter has provided a broad overview of the origins and development of personalisation, charting its progression through legislation and policy frameworks. The impact of neoliberal approaches and the changing relationships between the welfare state, social work and service users has been discussed with a particular focus on the complex and dichotomous role social work is expected to fulfil. It is recognised that there is an expanding amount of literature which debates the impact of personalisation and a more comprehensive exploration of these discussions is beyond the scope of this chapter but it is hoped that it has provided an insight into some of these debates. Going forward, it is recognised that the purported values of personalisation, choice, independence, self-determination and social justice are not new to social work; they mirror social work's core values and are embedded in social work education. The challenge for social work is how to keep these values honest and meaningful in a climate of restricting criteria and unprecedented financial cuts to social care. It is hoped that the introduction of the Care Act 2014 (DH 2014c) will provide clarity as it embeds personalisation within a legal framework for the first time and places a duty on local authorities to provide a personal budget to all service users. The outcomes of these legislative changes are yet to be seen but it is hoped that they will provide some much needed clarity for adult social care.

Points for reflection

- How do you think the personalisation agenda will affect the role of social work?
- What are some of the opportunities for the profession?
- What are some of the challenges? And how do you think they can be addressed?

References

Arksey, H. and Baxter K. (2012) 'Exploring the temporal aspects of direct payments?', *British Journal of Social Work*, 42 (1): 147–164.

Cabinet Office Strategy Unit (2005) *Improving the Life Chances of Disabled People*. London: Cabinet Office.

Carey, M. (2014) 'The fragmentation of social work and social care: some ramifications and a critique', *British Journal of Social Work*, advanced access, 29 September, 1–17. doi10.1093/bjsw/bcu088.

Carr, S. (2010a) *Personalisation: A Rough Guide* (revised edn). London: Social Care Institute for Excellence.

Carr, S. (2010b) SCIE Report 36: *Enabling Risk, Ensuring Safety: Self-Directed Support and Personal Budgets*. London: Social Care Institute for Excellence.

Carr, S. and Robbins, D. (2009) *The Implementation of Individual Budgets Schemes in Adult Social Care*. London: Social Care Institute for Excellence.

Clark, H. and Spafford, J. (2002) 'Adapting to the culture of user control?', *Social Work Education*, 21 (2): 247–257.

Clarke, J. and Newman, J. (1997) *The Managerial State: Power, Politics and Ideology in the Remaking of Social Welfare*. London: Sage.

Clarke, J., Newman, L., Smith, N., Vidler, E. and Westmarland, L. (2007) *Creating Citizen-Consumers: Changing Publics and Changing Public Services*. London: Sage.

Croisdale-Appleby, D. (2014) *Re-visioning Social Work Education: An Independent Review* [Online]. Available at: www.gov.uk/government/uploads/system/uploads/attachment_data/file/285788/DCA_Accessible.pdf (accessed 10 October 2014).

Department of Health (DH) (1996) *Community Care (Direct Payments) Act*. London: DH.

Department of Health (DH) (1998) *Modernising Social Services: Promoting Independence, Improving Protection, Raising Standards*. London: DH.

Department of Health (DH) (2005) *Independence, Well-Being and Choice: Our Vision for the Future of Social Care for Adults in England, Cm 6499*. London: DH.

Department of Health (DH) (2006) *Our Health, Our Care, Our Say*. London: DH.

Department of Health (DH) (2008) *Transforming Social Care*, Local Authority Circular [Online]. Available at: www.cpa.org.uk/cpa/Transforming%20social%20care%20DH.pdf (accessed 22 July 2015).

Department of Health (DH) (2009) *Personal Health Budgets: First Steps*. London: DH.

Department of Health (DH) (2010a) *Personal Budgets for Older People – Making it Happen; Ensuring Personalisation and Safeguarding Work Hand in Hand*. London: DH.

Department of Health (DH) (2010b) *A Vision for Adult Social Care: Capable Communities and Active Citizens*. London: DH.

Department of Health (DH) (2012) *Caring for Our Future: Reforming Care and Support, Cm 8378*. London: The Stationery Office.

Department of Health (DH) (2014a) *Making the Education of Social Workers Consistently Effective: Report of Sir Martin Narey's Independent Review of the Education of Children's Social Workers* [Online]. Available at: www.gov.uk/government/uploads/system/uploads/attach ment_data/file/287756/Making_the_education_of_social_workers_consistently_effective. pdf (accessed 10 October 2014).

Department of Health (DH) (2014b) *Draft Knowledge and Skills Statement for Social Workers in Adult Services: A Consultation* [Online]. Available at: www.gov.uk/government/uploads/ system/uploads/attachment_data/file/362491/knowledge_and_skills_for_adult_social_ work_consultation.pdf (accessed 14 October 2014).

Department of Health (DH) (2014c) *Care Act 2014: Statutory Guidance for Implementation*. London: DH.

Duffy, S. (2003) *Keys to Citizenship*. London: Paradigm.

Duffy, S. (2008) *Personalisation in Social Care*. Sheffield: Centre of Welfare Reform. Available at: www.centreforwelfarereform.org/library/by-az/personalisation-in-social-care1.html (accessed 16 May 2013).

Duffy, S. (2010) 'The citizenship theory of social justice: Exploring the meaning of personali- sation for social work', *Journal of Social Work Practice, Psychotherapeutic Approaches in Health, Welfare and the Community*, 24 (3): 253–262.

Duffy, S. (2012) *Is Personalisation Dead?* London: Centre for Welfare Reform.

Ellis, K. (2007) 'Direct payments and social work practice: The significance of "street-level bureaucracy" in determining eligibility', *British Journal of Social Work*, 37: 405–422.

Ferguson, I. (2007) 'Increasing user choice or privatizing risk? The antinomies of personalisa- tion', *British Journal of Social Work*, 37: 387–403.

Ferguson I. (2008) *Reclaiming Social Work: Challenging Neo-Liberalism and Promoting Social Justice*. London: Sage.

Glasby, J. and Littlechild, R. (2009) *Direct Payments and Personal Budgets: Putting Personalisation into Practice*, 2nd edn. Bristol: Policy Press.

Glendinning, C., Arksey, H., Jones, K., Moran, N., Netten, A. and Rabiee, P. (2009) *The Individual Budgets Pilot Projects: Impact and Outcomes for Carers*. York: Social Policy Research Unit , University of York.

Glendinning, C., Challis, D., Fernandez, J., Jacobs, S., Jones, K., Knapp, M., Manthorpe, J., Moran, N., Netten, A., Stevens, M. and Wilberforce, M. (2008) *Evaluation of the Individual Budgets Pilot Programme: Final Report*. York: Social Policy Research Unit, University of York.

Gray, M. and Birrell, D. (2013) *Transforming Adult Social Care: Contemporary Policy and Practice*. Bristol: Policy Press.

HM Government (2007) *Putting People First: A Shared Vision and Commitment to the Transformation of Adult Social Care*. London: HM Government.

Jones, R. (2014) 'The best of times, the worst of times: Social work and its moment', *British Journal of Social Work*, 44 (3): 485–502.

Leadbeater , C. (2004) *Personalisation through Participation: A New Script for Public Services*. London: Demos.

Leece, D. and Leece, J. (2006) 'Direct payments: Creating a two-tiered system in social care?', *British Journal of Social Work*, 36: 1379–1393.

Leece, J. and Leece, D. (2011) 'Personalisation: perceptions of the role of social work in a world of brokers and budgets', *British Journal of Social Work*, 41: 204–223.

Lymbery, M. (2012) 'Social work and personalisation', *British Journal of Social Work*, 41: 204–203.

Mandelstam, M. (2013) *Safeguarding Vulnerable Adults and the Law,* 2nd edn. London: Jessica Kingsley.

McGregor, C. (2014) 'History as a resource for the future: A response to "best of times, worst of times: Social work and its moment"', *British Journal of Social Work* (advanced accessed) 3 May: 1–15. doi:10.1093/bjsw/bct197.

McLaughlin, H. (2009) 'What's in a name: "client", "patient", "customer", "consumer", "expert by experience", "service user"– what's next?', *British Journal of Social Work*, 39: 1101–1117.

MIND (2009) *Personalisation in Mental Health: Creating a Vision, Views of Personalisation, from People Who Use Mental Health Services.* London: MIND.

Moran, N., Arksey, H., Glendinning, C., Jones, K., Netten, A. and Rabiee, P. (2012) 'Personalisation and carers: Whose rights? Whose benefits?', *British Journal of Social Work*, 42: 461–479.

Needham, C. (2007) *The Reform of Public Services under New Labour: Narratives of Consumerism.* London: Palgrave.

Needham, C. (2011) 'Personalisation: 'From story-line to practice', *Social Policy & Administration*, 45 (1): 54–68.

Needham, C. and Glasby, J. (2014) *Debates in Personalisation.* Bristol: Policy Press.

Netten, A., Jones, K., Knapp, M., Fernandez, J.L., Challis, D., Glendinning, C., Jacobs, S., Manthorpe, J., Moran, N., Stevens, M. and Wilberforce, M. (2012) 'Personalisation through individual budgets: Does it work and for whom?', *British Journal of Social Work*, 42 (8): 1556–1573.

Newbronner, L., Chamberlain, R., Bosanquet, K., Bartlett, C., Sass, B. and Glendinning, C. (2011) *Keeping Personal Budgets Personal: Learning from the Experiences of Older People, People with Mental Health Problems and their Carers*, Adults' Services Report, 40. London: Social Care Institute for Excellence.

O'Brien, J. (1987) 'A guide to lifestyle planning: Using the activities catalogue to integrate services and natural support systems', in B. Wilcox and G.T. Bellamy (eds), *A Comprehensive Guide to the Activities Catalogue: An Alternative Curriculum for Youth and Adults with Severe Disabilities.* Baltimore, MD: Paul H. Brookes.

Rabiee, P. (2013) 'Exploring the relationships between choice and independence: Experiences of disabled and older people', *British Journal of Social Work*, 42: 461–479.

Scourfield, P. (2007) 'Social care and the modern citizen: Client, consumer, service user, manager and entrepreneur', *British Journal of Social Work*, 37: 107–122.

Scourfield, P. (2008) 'Going for brokerage: A task of "independent support" or social work?', *British Journal of Social Work* (advanced access). doi: 10.1093/bjsw/bcn141. Published 21 October.

Social Care Institute for Excellence (SCIE) (2011) Report 39, *Protecting Adults at Risk: London Multi-Agency Policy and Procedures to Safeguard Adults from Abuse.* London: SCIE.

Spencer-Lane, T. (2011) 'Reforming the legal framework for adult safeguarding: The Law Commission's final recommendations on adult social care', *Journal of Adult Protection*, 13 (5): 275–284.

Spicker, P. (2013) 'Personalisation falls short', *British Journal of Social Work*, 43: 1259–1275.

Stevens, M., Glendinning, C., Moran, N., Challis, D., Fernandez, J., Jacobs, S., Jones, K., Knapp, M., Manthrope A., Stevens, M. and Wilberforce, M. (2011) 'Assessing the role of increasing choice in English social care services', *Journal of Social Policy*, 40 (2): 257–274.

The College of Social Work (TCSW) (2012) *The Professional Capabilities Framework for Social Workers in England.* London: The College of Social Work.

Think Local, Act Personal (TLAP) (2011) *A Sector-wide Commitment to Moving Forward with Personalisation and Community Base Support*. London: TLAP.

Vickers , T., Craig, G. and Atkin, K. (2012) 'Addressing ethnicity in social care research', *Social Policy & Administration,* doi:10.111/j.1467-9515.2012.00851.x.

Wolfensberger, W. (1972) *The Principle of Normalization in Human Services*. Toronto: National Institute on Mental Retardation.

Woolham, J. and Benton, C. (2013) 'The costs and benefits of personal budgets for older people: Evidence from a single local authority', *British Journal of Social Work*, 43 (8): 1472–1491.

6

Mental Capacity and Social Policy

Stefan Brown

Introduction

This chapter explores the link between social policy and mental capacity. It focuses on England and Wales, where the Mental Capacity Act 2005 (MCA 2005) has had significant impact on health and social care practice. The merits of the approach taken by the MCA 2005, and how this contrasts with other approaches to capacity are examined. A core theme is the suggestion that the MCA 2005 attempts to occupy a neutral position, but it needs to be recognised that it is subject to prevailing values and ideas of the state and the social work profession. This chapter examines the role of the key players such as the state, which occupies a central role in formulating policy. However, policy developments in relation to mental capacity also allow for greater opportunities for services user and carer participation in decision-making. This chapter considers the role of transnational institutions like the European Court of Human Rights (ECHR) and policies, in particular the UN Convention on the Rights of Persons with Disabilities (UNCRPD), which pursue the human rights approach. These influences are contrasted with the pursuit of neoliberal policies which challenge ideas of building the rights of people who lack capacity.

Historically, there has been little consistency around how social care professionals have gone about making decisions for vulnerable service users. This was largely due to a lack of clear legal frameworks for assessing capacity. Attempts were made to address this in the late 1980s by Lord Mackay who invited the Law Commission to investigate and report on all areas of law which affect decisions about the personal, financial affairs of people who lack capacity. Subsequent to this report the Mental Capacity Act 2005 was introduced. The five key principles found in Section 1 of the Act are:

- A person must be assumed to have capacity unless it is established that he/she lacks capacity.
- A person is not to be treated as unable to make a decision unless all practicable steps to help him/her to do so have been taken without success.
- A person is not to be treated as unable to make a decision merely because he/she makes an unwise decision.
- An action taken, or decision made, under this Act for or on behalf of a person who lacks capacity must be done, or made, in his/her best interests.
- Before the action is taken, or the decision is made, regard must be had to whether the purpose for which it is needed can be as effectively achieved in a way that is less restrictive of the person's rights and freedom of action (HM Government 2005: 1).

Mental Capacity Act 2005 summary

The Act came into force in October 2007, covering England and Wales. It provides a statutory framework for supporting people to make decisions for themselves wherever possible as well as processes and safeguards for decision-making involving people who lack capacity to make their own decisions because of illness, injury or disability.

Mental capacity refers to a person's ability to make their own decision and, if this ability is hindered because of some impairment of the mind or brain, the MCA ensures the individual remains involved in any decision-making process and that decisions are based upon their best interests. (Jenkins 2012: 3)

Approaches to mental capacity

The MCA 2005 as a statutory framework has been credited as a policy that strengthened the rights of vulnerable groups (Boyle 2009; MacKenzie and Rogers 2013; Manthrope et al. 2008) who may lack capacity and has been recognised as providing greater autonomy for those who previously would not have been supported in making decisions for themselves. Three approaches to assessing mental capacity have been identified: outcome-based, status-based and functional.

Outcome-based approaches focus on the consequences of the decisions that an individual will make and premise that where decisions are made in stark contrast to conventional wisdom, their mental capacity should be questioned. Arguments supporting outcome-based approaches rely on justifying actions to prevent significant harm to an individual and have been criticised as undermining rights. The limitations to outcome-based approaches are significant and relate to the suppression of individual self-determination. Despite this notable limitation, the Law Commission in their report on law reform for mentally incapacitated adults noted that in practice many doctors employ an outcome approach (Law Commission 1995). Nearly 20 years since the Law Commission highlighted this, the practice prevails, as was evident in the findings of Williams et al. (2012) who found that under the MCA some practitioners would often base decisions about capacity on the suitability of the decision to the situation.

Status-based approaches are based on a qualifying factor such age or diagnosis as the grounds for a defining capacity. The status approach can lead to significant numbers of people being unnecessarily defined as lacking capacity without thorough exploration of the underlying issues. This then leads to an all or nothing approach to understanding capacity (Browning et al. 2014), which strips the individual of any sense of agency. Thus, a firm argument against status approaches is in the incompatibility with wider human rights for all citizens.

A *functional approach* is based on assessing an individual's ability at a given time and whether this ability meets the requirements of a specific decision. The MCA 2005 in current practice largely encompasses a functional approach. Adopting a functional approach presents progression from the outcome and status approaches, yet the drawbacks should not go unnoticed. One drawback is a lack of clarity around the threshold for capacity. O'Connor (2011) highlights the importance of thresholds in a literature review on provision of support for people with intellectual disability. She suggests that levels of capacity differ depending on one's relationship with others, noting the presence of trust and power as key issues. Other drawbacks related to the functional approach are the potential for stigmatising effects that could leave individuals with a problematised label of the circumstances (Donnelly 2009).

In relation to the three approaches to understanding capacity described above, the MCA fits a functional approach to mental capacity. A recognised strength of the MCA 2005 is the emphasis on individual decision-making through specifying the particular time of the decision, which supports opportunities for individuals to have decisions about their capacity reviewed. Despite promoting a functional approach the MCA (2005) also retains a strong element of a status approach. For example, the first part of the mental capacity test (MCA 2005 s. 2 (1) states that: 'A person lacks capacity if at the material time he is unable to make a decision for himself in relation to the matter because of impairment in, or disturbance of the functioning of the mind or the brain.' The Act also clearly states that a person's lack of capacity should not be established by merely referring to their age or a condition or aspect of their behaviour (HM Government 2005: 2).

This part of the MCA 2005 therefore can be interpreted as a type of diagnostic test which emphasises the presence of a condition that in many cases will be a diagnosis. It also recognises a procedural style (MacKenzie and Rogers 2013) by emphasising the completion of two stages prior to a conclusion of whether an individual has capacity to make a decision or not. However, the MCA 2005 also retains elements of a status approach in that a large number of conditions will by default meet the Section 2 criteria, making this part of the assessment more like a qualifying or 'status' test. Williams et al. (2012), for instance, found that for individuals who have dementia, professionals still use the diagnosis as an indicator for understanding whether the person has capacity. This has led to some like Bartlett (2012) to contend that it is inevitable' that an individual's mental disability will be relevant to any assessment of capacity. This suggests that there can be limited scope for those using the MCA to reverse discrimination towards individuals who need health and social care assistance whether within or outside the provision of the Act.

The section above reviewed three approaches to assessing mental capacity and concluded that the MCA 2005 primarily fits a functional approach, but also contains elements of the status approach. Table 6.1 summarises the strengths and limitations of the three approaches.

Table 6.1   Comparison of different approaches to mental capacity

Approach to understanding mental capacity	Emphasis for determining mental capacity	Examples	Limitations	Benefits
Status	Characteristics of the individual (diagnosis)	Practice prior to the MCA, some elements of the MCA	Assumption based on condition and characteristics	Ability to quickly support most vulnerable
Functional	Ability to carry out a set of determined tasks	MCA 2005	Interpretative Subject to bias	Universally agreed criteria
Outcome	Consequence of decision-making and risk	Practice prior to MCA and poor practice today	Suppress self-determination Paternalistic	Manage potential harm and safety

Points for reflection

- Considering the five key principles outlined earlier, which of them stand out the most?
- What are the implications of the three approaches to mental capacity for practice?

Autonomy, paternalism and MCA 2005

Central to the discussion of mental capacity are the concepts of autonomy and paternalism. Autonomy refers to the ability or right to decide one's own course of action and the freedom from interference from others, whereas paternalism refers to the practice where individuals with authority use their power to restrict the freedom of others. The emphasis on autonomy reflects a movement away from what was seen as paternalistic attitudes that marginalised individuals who did not have capacity (EDF 2009). Paternalistic approaches were characterised by an imbalance of power between services users and organisational and professional practices in health and social care. The campaigns of disability rights movements, both locally and internationally, focused policy-makers' attention on the importance of empowering service users. There is now a broader acceptance that the wishes of service users should be incorporated into decision-making frameworks at all levels. However, while paternalism is broadly recognised as having a negative impact, it is still evident in the use of the MCA 2005, particularly where decisions about mental capacity are still primarily made by professionals (Williams et al. 2012).

Autonomy is an idea within the MCA 2005 enables individuals to make decisions rather than have decisions made for them (Craigie 2013a). Autonomy to make decisions is presumed by the MCA 2005 and where capacity to make decisions is found to be absent, decisions have to be made within a supportive framework, known as Best Interests. This framework aims to ensure that decisions are suitable to the situation.

MacKenzie and Rogers (2013) note that concepts of self-governance and self-determination are embedded in the notion of autonomy. Self-governance can be understood in relation to internal ability to decide the course of action whereas self-determination emphasises external conditions which support one's decision (MacKenzie and Rogers 2013). Key aspects of autonomy from a philosophical perspective are freedom, competence and authenticity (Craigie 2013a). These aspects provide clues as to the typology of autonomy which is embedded in the MCA 2005.

Ideas of autonomy are embedded in Section 1 of the MCA 2005, principles 2 and 3:

2. A person is not to be treated as unable to make a decision unless all practicable steps to help him to do so have been taken without success;

3. A person is not to be treated as unable to make a decision merely because he makes an unwise decision;

These principles emphasise autonomy in terms of individuals being able to make their own independent decision, essentially autonomy is conceptualised as a form of independence in terms of the ability to make their own decision free from the control of other people. While independence can be of great benefit to service users, it is increasingly interpreted in welfare policy as self-reliance (Vernon and Qureshi 2000).

Despite there being some appeal towards independent decision making there is another way in which using the MCA 2005 can better understanding how to support autonomous decision-making. This is by embracing ideas of interdependence. Interdependence refers to decisions being made in reference to relationships with others. Interdependence has been recognised as central by some including Dhanda (2008), who notes that decisions are not made in isolation but in reference to other people. Including interdependence in the framework of supporting autonomous decision making can support a more relational approach reflecting the realities of a person's decision making network. Therefore, supporting the greater autonomy of individuals in decision-making under the MCA 2005 through promoting their independence alone can be considered a narrow conceptualisation of autonomy. Furthermore, this approach to autonomy relates to a broader set of ideas which assumes individuals to be competent agents and able to make positive decisions for themselves. It chimes with welfare approaches that increasingly require individuals to take responsibility and to negotiate their position in the complex market place by making self-empowering choices.

Mental capacity and the legal system

The implementation of the MCA 2005 has seen an expansion in the role of the legal system in the health and social care system. There was, for instance, a 6% increase in the volume of cases referred to the Court of Protection in 2012 (Ministry of Justice 2013). While most of the cases presented to the Court of Protection concerned property affairs, the MCA 2005 also gave the court more powers to receive applications relating to health and welfare matters (Ministry of

Justice 2013: Series 2013a). The increasing role of the legal system in mental capacity matters represents a transfer of governance from policy-makers directly to the legal system in the form of the Court of Protection (Craigie 2013a); a move that can be perceived as the government distancing itself from the politicised issues of rights and freedoms for those who lack capacity.

The increasing role of the legal system has in many ways benefited those who do not have mental capacity. It established a strengthening of the legal or civil rights for individuals by enhancing access to the courts and by the criminalisation of neglect and ill treatment of people who lack capacity (MCA 2005 s. 44). These developments have become important protections for adults subject to abuse. The Serious Case Reviews at Winterbourne View (2012) and Orchid View (2014) highlight the necessity of access to legal recourse where there are concerns about abuse. However, a continuing challenge is that access to the law is not universal, as the costs ascribed to accessing legal support can be substantial. While in many cases concerning the health and welfare of individuals attract legal aid, most cases concerning property and personal affairs are subject to costs often payable from the estate of the person lacking capacity.

Although the MCA 2005 has been operational since 2007 scrutiny has highlighted that there has been limited understanding about its implementation by welfare agencies and professionals (House of Lords 2014). Part of the problem here is that it can also limit service users' and carers' rights and their access to the law. Considering an aspect of the MCA 2005 known as deprivation of liberty, the case of LB *Hillingdon* v. *Steven Neary (2011) EWHC 1377 (COP)* is an example of how lack of information and awareness can limit access to justice (see panel). The lack of awareness of the legal rights and processes for deprivation of liberty impacted not only Steven and his father who cared for him, but also the local authority who were ordered by the Court of Protection to pay damages due to their failure to conduct an effective review, appoint an IMCA and refer the case to the Court of Protection in a timely manner.

Steven Neary case

In 2010 Steven Neary was an 18-year-old man with learning disabilities who lived with his father and was supported by a care package arranged by his local authority. Following a request for additional support from his father, Steven was admitted to a care home where he was deprived of his liberty for nearly a year without legal recourse. The local authority eventually authorised a deprivation of liberty, but the Court of Protection found that it failed to inform both Steven and his father of their rights and fulfil its public duty to refer the matter to the Court of Protection. The Court of Protection quashed the deprivation of liberty order and Steven was returned home to live with his father. Two years later (2012), the local authority was eventually required to pay costs of £35,000 by the Court of Protection.

For further details see: www.mentalhealthlaw.co.uk/Re_Steven_Neary;_LB_Hilling don_v_Steven_Neary_(2012)_MHLO_71_(COP)

Deprivation of liberty and rights

Individuals who lack mental capacity to make decisions should have access to the same rights as everyone else. Were lacking mental capacity to make a decision incorporated within the broader description of disability, there would be greater scope for understanding how the rights of people who lack capacity should be protected. Ensuring that equal access to rights for those with a disability is a central theme of the UN Convention on the Rights of Persons with Disability 2006 (UNCRPD), which was ratified by the UK government in 2009. The UNCRPD came about as a result of global recognition that disability was not sufficiently incorporated into the existing human rights framework (EDF 2009). In contrast to traditional approaches that arguably medicalise disability, the UNCRPD draws on a social rights perspective and sees disability as part of the human experience rather than a deficit (EDF 2009). Article 12 (2) of UNCRPD, for instance, states that the requirement of equality of recognition before the law for people with different types of disability is fundamental. Applying the principles of the UNCRPD to the MCA 2005 highlights some discrepancies.

A key discrepancy is that UNCRPD recognises the importance of an individual not only retaining a capacity to have rights, but also being given the opportunity to exercise those rights (MDAC 2013). A legal code that gives rights to those who lack mental capacity does not go far enough: it also needs to empower them to apply these rights (Bartlett 2012). The deficit in capacity to exercise rights in UK law was highlighted in the Supreme Court ruling in the cases of *P* v. *Cheshire West and Chester Council and P & Q* v. *Surrey County Council* (2014). The court drew attention to the fact that individuals who are deemed to lack capacity fall short of the same rights before the law as everyone else. The previous Court of Appeal decision in this case highlighted that an approach of 'relative normality' should be used based on an individual's treatment not being more restricted than anyone else with disabilities, but was overturned largely because it was believed to be incompatible with the European Convention of Human Rights and the UNCRPD (Bowen 2014).

The *P* v. *Cheshire West and Chester Council* and *P & Q* v. *Surrey County Council* (2014) United Kingdom Supreme Court 19 decisions went further to elucidate the role of the state through declaring that there is a public duty to people who the state has placed in supported living or private care settings. This undid the previous practice where the state was only required to address deprivation of liberty where someone had been placed in a care home or hospital. This emphasised the role of the state in retaining a public duty to protect the rights of individual under Article 5 of the European Convention of Human Rights. The implications of the Cheshire West decision are far reaching giving access to protection under the deprivation of liberty safeguards to a number of individuals who had previously fallen outside these safeguards (Bowen 2014). The ruling also draws attention to the issue of the responsibility of state in a mixed economy of care provision, where it can be argued that promoting individual responsibility for welfare cannot be a basis for the government relinquishing its duty to regulate and uphold the rights of citizens.

The Supreme Court decision raises concerns about the safeguards for those without legal capacity who access private domiciliary care and private residential care and support. Currently, people within these arrangements do not fall under the deprivation of liberty safeguards which secure rights from unlawful deprivation (*A Local Authority* v. *A (A Child) & Anor (2010)* [cited in Series 2014]). Although public authorities are not involved in the private arrangements, they have a role in setting the private care and support framework for many people (Bowen 2014). In a way similar to *P* v. *Chester West and Chester Council* and *P & Q* v. *Surrey County Council (2014)*, the state may have direct/indirect responsibility to safeguard the Article 5 rights of individuals in private arrangements.

In short, the MCA 2005 represents some progress in terms of developing the legal rights of individuals who may lack capacity; however, a broader rights perspective suggests that there are still gaps in providing equality of rights for those who lack capacity. Social rights for those who lack capacity encompass the rights to welfare services including homecare, residential support and welfare benefits. The state has attempted to strengthen the legal rights of individuals who have their legal capacity denied, but it has also weakened social rights. The trend in broader welfare policy adopted by successive governments throughout the 1980s until the present has been to curtail the social rights of those who lack legal capacity. Policies such as the NHS and Community Care Act 1990 have resulted in the decreasing role of the state in the provision of domiciliary and residential care and encouraged a greater role for private provision in these areas. The eligibility criteria and welfare entitlement changes under the Welfare Reform Act 2012 and the residualisation of welfare support for the most vulnerable (Ellis 2004) meant that many who lack capacity under MCA 2005 receive care and support in an increasingly individualised and market-based system.

The emphasis on individual responsibility has also seen increases in charging for welfare services, a growth in the role of the private providers and the rolling out of personalised care structures which promote consumerism. The promotion of consumerism can be seen as particularly effective as a mechanism for increasing the responsibilities of individuals in need of social care services. However, in terms of welfare services, consumerism redraws the relationship between health and social care organisations and the people who use their services (Newman and Vidler 2006) and presupposes that individuals are able to optimise services to achieve best outcomes for themselves. As noted by Clarke and Newman (2007), people are required to choose even where they do not understand that they are consumers. This approach is based on the presupposition of an ability to optimise choices and has been strongly questioned in relation to older people and people with dementia (MacDonald 2010), the two major groups of people in the population who are assessed as lacking mental capacity under MCA 2005. Consumerism therefore, instead of being empowering, may be ushering in further restrictions to the lives of those who lack legal capacity.

In summary, people who lack capacity under the MCA 2005 are impacted by broader welfare developments which have the effect of reducing the options available to them, by increasing procedural rights, but tending not to promote social citizenship.

Conclusion

This chapter has drawn on a number of themes which highlight that the MCA 2005 is complex and contains competing and contradictory matters and is subject to the influence of professionals, government and supranational policies and organisations. The MCA 2005 has effected positive changes, including: individualising capacity to decision specific matters and strengthening the rights of those who are deemed to not have legal capacity. However, at the same time, looking through the lens of broader welfare policy, we see that rights have been limited and there remain key gaps for some, e.g. deprivation of liberty in private settings where rights are still not being protected. Accordingly, the MCA 2005 falls short of offering a robust rights approach to supporting people who lack capacity.

The role of the state in relation to the MCA 2005 can be seen as part of its broader activities of determining the arrangements for health and social care services. This has shaped social care policy in line with neoliberal ideology, which has resulted in exposure of those subject to the MCA 2005 to the challenges of consumerism and marketised welfare. This amounts to individual social rights and broader citizenship being weakened for those who need substantial support in making the majority of their health and social care decisions.

The role of supranational organisations, such as the UN and European Court of Human Rights, has been pivotal in shaping the implementation of the MCA 2005. While they have had a significant influence over mental capacity policy, this has not always led to revisions in national policy. Furthermore, while these organisations articulate a strong rights agenda they also embrace ideas of individual economic and wealth accumulation that can lead to individual rights being placed above social rights. This can be unhelpful for those who lack capacity where the need for social empowerment and stronger social citizenship is key.

Current and more recent developments suggest that there will be some changes to MCA policy and practice, which could lead to strengthen the rights of those who lack legal capacity. The Supreme Court ruling in *P* v. *Chester West and Chester Council* and *P & Q* v. *Surrey County Council* (2014) has led to a broader definition of deprivation of liberty, and public authorities have had to reassess cases where deprivation of liberty was not believed to be an issue. Another development is the House of Lords Select Committee on the MCA's post-legislative scrutiny, which gave a significant endorsement for broadening the IMCA role in MCA 2005. If implemented the recommendations would enhance the rights of individuals who lack capacity by extending opportunities for supportive decision-making, as envisaged by the UNCRPD. Finally, the Care Act 2014, which is being introduced at the time of writing, seeks to reinforce the importance of the self-determination of service users through increasing advocacy support.

References

Bartlett, P. (2012) 'The United Nations Convention on the Rights of Persons with Disabilities and Mental Health Law', *Modern Law Review*, 75 (5): 752–778.

Bowen, P. (2014) '*A gilded cage is still a cage:*' *Some thoughts on the Supreme Court Judgement in P V Cheshire West and Chester Council and P and Q V Surrey County Council* [Online]. Available at: www.doughtystreet.co.uk/documents/uploaded-documents/DSC_Cheshire_West_Judgment_summary.pdf (accessed 22 July 2015).

Boyle, G. (2009) 'The Mental Capacity Act 2005: Deprivation of liberty safeguards and people with dementia: the implications for social care regulation', *Health and Social Care in the Community*, 17 (4): 415–422.

Browning, M., Bigby, C. and Douglas, J. (2014) 'Supportive decision-making: Understanding how its conceptual link to legal capacity is influencing the development of practice', *Research and Practice in Intellectual and Developmental Disabilities* [Online]. Available at: http://dx.doi.org/10.1080/23297018.2014.902726 (accessed 22 July 2015).

Clarke, J. and Newman, J. (2007) 'What's in a name?', *Cultural Studies*, 21 (4–5): 738–757.

Craigie, J. (2013a) 'Capacity, value neutrality and the ability to consider the future', *International Journal of Law in Context*, 9 (1): 4–19.

Craigie, J. (2013b) 'Introduction: Mental capacity and value neutrality', *International Journal of Law in Context*, 9 (1): 1–3.

Department of Constitutional Affairs (2007) *MCA Code of Practice*. London: The Stationery Office.

Dhanda, A. (2008) 'Constructing a new Human Rights lexicon: Convention on the Rights of Persons with Disabilities', *International Journal of Human Rights*, Issue 8 [Online]. Available at: www.surjournal.org/eng/conteudos/getArtigo8.php?artigo=8,artigo_dhanda.htm (accessed 22 July 2015).

Donnely, M. (2009) 'Capacity assessment under the Mental Capacity Act 2005: Delivering on the functional approach?', *Legal Studies*, 29 (3): 464–491.

Ellis, K. (2004) 'Promoting rights or avoiding litigation? The introduction of the Human Rights Act 1998 into adult social care in England', *European Journal of Social Work*, 7 (3): 321–340.

European Disability Forum (EDF) (2009) *Equal Recognition Before the Law and Equal Capacity to Act: Understanding and Implementing Article 12 of the UN Convention on Rights of Persons with Disabilities*. Brussells: EDF.

HM Government (2005) *Mental Capacity Act 2005*. London: The Stationery Office.

House of Lords (HL) (2014) *Post-Legislative Committee on the Mental Capacity Act 2005*. London: The Stationery Office.

Jenkins, K. (2012) *Mental Capacity and the Mental Capacity Act 2005: A Literature Review*. London: Mental Health Foundation.

Law Commission (1995) *Mental Incapacity. Item 9 of the Fourth Programme of Law Reform: Mentally Incapacitated Adults*. London: HMSO.

MacKenzie, C. and Rogers, W. (2013) 'Autonomy, vulnerability and capacity: A philosophical appraisal of the Mental Capacity Act', *International Journal of Law in Context*, 9 (1): 37–52.

MacDonald, A. (2010) 'The impact of the MCA on decision-making and approaches to assessing risk', *British Journal of Social Work*, 40 (4): 1229–1246.

Manthorpe, J., Stanley, N. and Rappaport, J. (2008) 'The Mental Capacity Act 2005 and its influences on Social Work Practice: Debate and Synthesis', *Practice: Social Work in Action*, 20 (3): 151–162.

Mental Disability Advocacy Centre (MDAC) (2013) *Legal Capacity in Europe: A Call to Action to Governments and the EU*. Budapest: MDAC.

Ministry of Justice (2013) *Court Statistics Quarterly: January to March 2012, Ministry of Justice Statistic Bulletin*. London: National Statistics.

Newman, J. and Vidler, E. (2006) 'Discriminating customers, responsible patients, empowered users: Consumerism and the modernisation of health care', *Journal of Social Policy*, 35 (2): 193–209.

O'Connor, J. (2011) *Literature Review on Provision of Appropriate and Accessible Support to People with an Intellectual Disability Who are Experiencing Crisis Pregnancy*. Dublin: National Disability Authority and Crisis Pregnancy Agency.

Series, L. (2013a) *What is Mental Capacity?* Blog: Small Places [Online]. Available at: http://thesmallplaces.wordpress.com/2011/06/06/what-is-mental-capacity/ (accessed 20 May 2014).

Series, L. (2013b) *Is the Mental Capacity Act too Paternalistic?* Blog: Small Places [Online]. Available at: http://thesmallplaces.wordpress.com/2011/06/06/is-the-mental-capacity-act-2005-too-paternalistic/ (accessed 22 July 2015).

Series, L. (2014) *The Acid Test*. Blog: Small Places [Online[. Available at: http://thesmallplaces.wordpress.com/2014/03/20/the-acid-test/ (accessed 20 May 2014).

Vernon, A. and Qureshi, H. (2000) 'Community care and independence: Self-sufficiency or empowerment?', *Critical Social Policy,* 20 (2): 225–276.

Williams, G. Boyle, M., Jepson, M., Swift, P., Williamson, T. and Heslop, P. (2012) *Making Best Interest Decisions: People and Processes*. London: Mental Health Foundation.

Legal cases

A Local Authority v. *A (A Child) & Anor (2010)*

LB Hillingdon v. *Steven Neary (2011) EWHC 1377 (COP)*

P v. *Cheshire West and Chester Council and P & Q* v. *Surrey County Council* (2014) UKSC 19

HL v. *UK 45508/99 (2004) ECtHR 471*

7

Social Welfare Policy in Racialised Contexts

Frank Keating

This chapter explores the relationship between 'race', ethnicity and policy to provide an analysis of social welfare and racialisation. According to Barot and Bird (2001: 601) racialisation 'is a process that ascribes physical and cultural differences to individuals and groups'. A Critical Race Theory (CRT) perspective is utilised to examine and understand the complexities of welfare policy in a racialised society such as the UK. CRT argues that racism is a real and lived experience for racialised groups such as Black and minority ethnic groups (BME); it is endemic and demands political action across all sectors (Delgado and Stefancic 2001). Taking a historical perspective, the chapter provides an overview and critique of key events of racism in the development of social welfare policy in the UK. It suggests ways in which welfare policy could be transformed to meet the needs and wellbeing of minority ethnic communities. This is a very large topic and the aim in this chapter is not to provide a detailed account, but to offer an overview to help orient the readers to key aspects of the racialised context of social welfare. For example, other issues such as ethnic matching also require attention, but are beyond the scope of this chapter.

When thinking about issues of 'race', culture and ethnicity in the UK context, it is clear that social policy in general and welfare policy in particular undermined the potential for wellbeing for BME (Williams and Johnson 2010). 'Race' and multiculture are among the most politicised areas of policy-making. A clear example is the recent media scare stories about immigration and the pressure on welfare services that are being used as a smoke screen to underfunding (Bradshaw 2012). However, the evidence shows that there are fewer welfare claims from migrants, instead, there has been a net benefit to the UK economy (Vargas-Silva 2014). Another example is the debate on what Muslim women should and should not wear in a western context.

The case of a 16-year-old pupil who was barred from wearing a *niqab* (a veil that only shows her eyes) to school (Sanghani 2014) comes to mind.

Clarification of concepts

The discourse on 'race' and its associated concepts are complex and it is important to clarify what these mean (Dominelli 2008). A discourse, according to Fook (2002: 3), refers to 'the way in which we make meanings of and construct our world through the language we use (verbal and non-verbal) to communicate about it'. In relation to 'race', Garner (2010: ix) suggests that it involves 'historical and multi-faceted sets of social relations'. 'Race' as construct in the terms of this chapter is treated as a pseudo-scientific construct that has been used to create artificial boundaries between groups and will be enclosed in inverted commas (Singh 2013). It has to be acknowledged that this is a difficult construct to define, because there is no clarity or consensus as to what it means (Garner 2010). Questions arise as to whether it pertains to skin colour, hair type, nose shapes or genetic differences. Bloch et al. (2013: 14), for instance, defines 'race' as: 'a set of ideas and institutional practices that help to shape wider sets of social, political and cultural relations'.

However, it is difficult to pin down 'race' to a single meaning as it takes on a wealth of different meanings in different contexts. Garner (2010) suggests that, instead of attempting to define 'race', it is more important to consider how its use and the meanings ascribed to it make access to resources easier for some groups and more difficult for others. However, 'race' acknowledges that racism based on skin colour and ethnic origin is real, endemic and pervasive. 'Race' as a construct has been mobilised in two ways. Law (2010) suggests that it has been used on the one hand to colonise and dominate groups of people (e.g. in parts of Africa, India and South America), while at the same time it has been mobilised to resist, challenge and revolt against racial (racist) domination. Ethnicity and culture are two constructs that are closely intertwined with the concept of 'race' but are equally contested due to the multidimensional and overlapping nature of these concepts. Ethnicity and culture share similar markers such as language, shared beliefs and group identity (Pilkington 2003). Ethnicity 'refers to the differentiation of groups of people who have shared cultural meanings, memories and descent, produced through social interaction' (Law 2010: 77). It is linked to birth place, a common language, a shared religion, collective culture and a shared history (Chattoo and Atkin 2012; Law 2010). Definitions of culture abound, but in essence it relates to language, beliefs, traditions and norms of groups (Chattoo and Atkin 2012). These constructs are dynamic and changing and should not be viewed as fixed, static or unchanging.

These dimensions of the human experience are often considered to only belong to BME groups, but this chapter takes the view that everyone has a culture and ethnic identity. The issue is: the extent to which people identify with and embrace these ideas and how they construe their identity in relation to other markers of identity such as gender, class, sexuality, age and ability. Chattoo and Atkin (2012) suggest that we need to adopt a critical and analytical stance to these concepts and in particular reflect on how they inform and shape the discourse on welfare.

Points for reflection

What are the differences between 'race', 'ethnicity' and 'culture'? How do these ideas apply to you?

Why are 'race', racism and racial inequality important?

The aim here is not to present BME communities in a negative light: these communities have a wealth of strengths and capabilities that are often undermined by the material, social and political conditions they experience. Racial inequalities exist and persist across all axes and indicators of social and economic need and the examples are numerous (Williams and Johnson 2010). Inequality and unequal treatment are evident in all categories of welfare provision, such as, for example, child and family welfare, informal care and mental health. Three examples are cited below to illustrate this experience.

Research evidence indicates that a disproportionate number of BME children are more likely to be subject to child protection plans and are often (and ultimately) placed in care (DfE 2014). Statistics for 2013 indicated that 16% of looked after children are from Black and mixed backgrounds and yet they only make up 5% of the total population of children in England. These statistics have to be considered and understood against the backdrop that BME families face similar challenges to other families, but they may experience additional stress due to poverty, poor housing, unemployment and racial discrimination.

The over-representation of BME people in mental health statistics is another striking example of racial inequality. The Chief Medical Officer's report in 2014 showed that individuals from BME groups are five times more likely to be given a diagnosis of schizophrenia and less likely to be offered psychological and more socially oriented approaches to treatment (Davies 2014). Pathways to care for these groups are adversarial, i.e. they usually come into contact with mental health services via the police or criminal justice system – the norm is for people to be referred via their general practitioner (GP).

A further example of racial inequality relates to BME carers, who face significant challenges in accessing support services. These include lack of information about support services, communication issues, lack of culturally appropriate services and a lack of understanding of how to support them. Their situation is compounded by the stereotypical views, i.e. 'that they look after their own', that are commonly held by professionals (IRISS 2010). Stereotypical views and attitudes such as these can therefore lead to formulaic assumptions about how their needs should be met.

A defining feature of racial inequalities in welfare is that these have persisted over a number of years and seem to be intractable. The situation therefore demands a continued focus on the negative impact of inequalities on the health and wellbeing of BME communities and the need for 'the creation of a welfare society – one in which the well-being of all is central and in which welfare arrangements are owned, shaped and co-produced with the active engagement of all citizens' (Williams and Johnson 2010: 2).

Welfare theory and 'race'

A key premise of this chapter is that the social policy arena does not know what it thinks or should think about 'race' and ethnicity: there is no shared agenda and no policy on 'race' and ethnicity. Policies on race equality abound, but there is a lack of policy to provide guidance on how to deal with the contested and tricky constructs of 'race', ethnicity and culture.

Prior to understanding how issues of 'race', ethnicity and culture have been addressed (or not) in welfare policy it is useful to review how these have been theorised in welfare theory in general. Williams (1987) provided an informative critique of four different perspectives on welfare theory. A brief summary is offered here, but the reader is encouraged to read this classic paper. The four perspectives are: anti-collectivism, social reformism, political economy of welfare and feminism. First, anti-collectivism promoted the freedom of the market and individualism, which meant that discrimination at an individual level could be over-ridden. Second, social reformism emphasised pragmatism and took certain things such as the division of labour and family for granted. 'Race' was marginalised because proponents of this perspective advocated that everyone should be treated equally, regardless of existing inequality. Third, the political economy of welfare perspective specifically offered a critique of welfare and the welfare state in its analysis based on class, capital and the state. Again, we note the absence of 'race' from this discourse. Fourth, feminist theorists critiqued how women were construed in welfare terms, but failed to highlight how Black women were exploited or how the critiques of patriarchy does not apply to Black women in the same way they do for White women. A theme that runs through all these perspectives is the fact that even though critiques of welfare were offered, 'race' and racism were absent from the discourse.

It is against this background that I suggest that an exploration of social policy in racialised contexts needs to be considered along three axes, i.e. 'race', immigration and racial equality.

Three axes (tri-axial analysis)

Discourse on 'race'

Starting from the *discourse on 'race'*, there is overall a lack of consensus about its meaning in a western context. Theorists view it as a social construct which has deep social consequences. Yet, when one considers how 'race' is construed and understood in the policy context, it is clear that it is not always viewed as a social construct, but rather a fixed entity in people's identity. 'Race' has become essentialised (Delgado and Stefancic 2001), meaning that it became based on a belief that this is the sole defining characteristic of BME groups and who they are (an approach that has been discredited but has resurfaced with the rise of multiculturalism). In practice, the focus or emphasis in 'race' discourse was the importance of understanding the culture of and traditions of BME groups – a practice seen as the pinnacle of cultural competence. For example, policy directives in relation to child and family welfare require respect for the child's 'race', culture and ethnicity. However, the fundamental principles underpinning any decision seem to be those of welfare and not 'race' or culture (Williams and Johnson 2010). On the other hand, in situations where the focus is solely on 'race' or culture, the needs of the child can be overlooked. This was clearly demonstrated in the case of Victoria Climbié, a young Black girl who was abused by her aunt and her partner (Laming 2003) and subsequently died. Professionals failed to identify the abuse as the actions of the aunt were located in a cultural context. This is an example of essentialising, where certain characteristics such as culture were seen as fixed in some groups thus creating a 'them' versus 'us' divide. The heterogeneous nature of culture across and within BME communities and the fact that identities are multi-faceted were completely overlooked or misunderstood. Moreover, a narrow focus on culture means that the harsher aspects and the devastating effects of racism and discrimination can easily be ignored.

The essentialising of culture has led to developments in culturally appropriate service responses. However, these responses have been mainly relegated to dietary needs and more latterly religious needs (less so spiritual needs) – the mantra of 'safaris, samosas and steel bands' come to mind here. It should thus come as no surprise when BME service users report much lower satisfaction rates with health and social care services.

Another dimension of the discourse on 'race' is the othering of BME groups. This is when groups are measured against a hegemonic ideal (i.e. White) and subsequently ascribed inferior status. In the classic paper referred to in an earlier section, Williams (1987) traces three aspects of policy development to illustrate how BME people have been 'othered' and marginalised. Williams (1987) argued that social imperialism, nationalism and immigration control were practised through subordination of class interests to those of nation and empire. Entitlement to benefits was linked to nationality as could be seen in the Old Age Pensions Act 1908. Black workers were kept in lower paid jobs and denied access to benefits, which meant lower social expenditure and inevitably a stratified workforce based on the erroneous belief that they could only work at unskilled levels. In situations where Black people were in receipt of welfare services, these where characterised by control rather than care and support. These communities were blamed for their deprivation because of their ways of living and their culture. Evidence of the control and harsher treatment of BME people is nowhere as stark as in the field of mental health care. The disparities in the treatment of BME people compared to the White population have persisted over centuries and can be seen in higher rates of diagnosis, higher rates of hospital admission and higher rates of seclusion and restraint (Davies 2014).

Racism and challenges to it are closely linked to the discourses on 'race'. Anti-racism (discussed below) involved movements to oppose and challenge racism. In particular it started with challenges to scientific racism, a practice to classify racial types and create racial hierarchies that led to stereotypical views that Black people had smaller brains than White people. For example, studies in the US in the early 19th century were measuring the size of the brains of different groups (craniology) and found that there were differences and concluded that these differences indicate that Black people are less intelligent than White people (Law 2010). The first major challenge to scientific racism was in 1950 when UNESCO organised a world panel of experts to announce that there was no scientific basis for 'race'. Craniology was refuted in 1983 when the sculls used in the earlier studies were re-examined by a scientist named Gould, who found no basis for the previous conclusions (Law 2010).

Discourse on immigration

The *discourse on immigration* is similarly fraught. On the one hand, Britain wants to be seen as welcoming and inclusive and this is reflected in policy such as the concept that health care is free to all at the point of access. However, when the notion of 'a British identity' is threatened, immigrants are viewed with suspicion and hatred that can often lead to violence. The infamous 'Rivers of Blood' speech made in 1968 by Enoch Powell is one such example. Powell, an MP and former government minister, made a speech to the West Midlands area Conservative Political Centre in which he was critical of Commonwealth immigration and anti-discrimination legislation. He argued in this speech that if Britain opened its doors to immigrants there would be violence and bloodshed and called for stricter controls on immigration. Islamophobia is another example – practices such as forced marriages, wearing the *niqab* and radical Islamism have become enmeshed in the current discourse on immigration. The anti-immigration sentiment can be seen in the Home Office's pilot scheme in 2013 to stop illegal immigration. The scheme entailed adverts on London busses that said: 'Go home or face arrest'. The scheme was challenged and subsequently withdrawn, but what is interesting to note is that the Prime Minister considered it acceptable to use such techniques to fuel a fear of illegal immigrants.

It has been argued that there is no such phenomenon as a 'National British Identity' (Fanshaw and Sriskandaraja 2010), and therefore, by implication, welfare need cannot be homogenised. However, the current discourse on 'race' and ethnicity is still very much focused on the notion of Britishness – citizenship ceremonies were introduced for immigrants who apply for citizenship. Community cohesion policies were also introduced to promote greater integration of minority groups (Cantle 2008).

A common thread that runs through immigration policy is to control and reduce the ability of migrants from the New Commonwealth (Asia and Africa) to enter the UK. This pattern can be traced back to the Aliens Act 1905, which was specifically aimed at Jewish immigrants from Eastern Europe. It brought tighter controls and restriction from benefits and was extended in 1919 to stipulate that all Jews were expected to carry identity cards. Another strategy was to keep Black people ignorant of their rights to out-of-work benefits (Fryer 1984). Other examples are the Immigrants Act 1968 and the Immigration Act 1971, and even the latest Immigration Act 2014, which prevents illegal immigrants from accessing and using public resources in the UK and makes it easier to remove people with no right of abode (Home Office 2014). The arguments are linked due the fact that immigration is about a right to citizenship whereas welfare is concerned with entitlements to resources. Social citizenship has been the traditional basis for access to welfare services and a critique that points to the fact that political citizenship excludes those in need (Williams and Johnson 2010). The discourse about citizenship and welfare is peppered with common myths that BME groups and migrants are a strain on welfare resources. Yet, evidence shows that immigration is economically beneficial to national states (Finney and Simpson 2009). Immigrants from outside the EU do not rely on public resources – instead they contribute to public revenue through direct taxation, are younger and therefore more likely to be economically active and make less demand on public resources to which they have recourse such as health care. It is interesting to note that there were similar arguments in the 1980s that ignored the fact that immigration was to bring skilled people to run welfare services and without them welfare would collapse (Bloch et al. 2013; Williams 1987). The policy of recruiting care and social work staff from out-side the EU has continued until the current economic crisis. This section illustrates the close alignment of welfare and immigration policies, and has argued that as long as this continues, the entrenched inequalities for BME groups will persist.

Discourse on racial equality

Equality and diversity have been embraced in the *discourse on racial equality*, but with contradictory or conflicting standpoints. On the one hand it is progressive, while on the other it is regressive. *Race equality, equality of opportunity* and *valuing diversity* became desirable goals policy objectives. They are progressive in the sense that these policies were aimed at reducing racial inequality and promot-ing race equality in public services. Yet, they are regressive in that at the same time as developing policies on equality a range of anti-immigration policies were introduced.

Points for reflection

Pause for moment and note down what you think the terms 'race equality', 'equality of opportunity' and 'valuing diversity' mean.

Employment practices designed to increase diversity in the workforce were seen to be an appropriate course of action to promote racial equality. It became acceptable to list racial/ethnic background as a 'qualification' for jobs in health and social care. This was enshrined in a scheme of funding under Section 11 (s. 11) of the 1966 Local Government Act) where ethnic minority status was seen as an advantageous characteristic/qualification for certain positions. However, these practices did not yield major economic benefits for BME workers in the health and social care sectors. BME staff were (and are mainly) employed in junior positions with little access to power and decision-making and were often the subject of disciplinary investiga-tions. More recent initiatives, such as the Department of Health's 'Delivering Race Equality' (DRE) for mental health (DH 2005) were a progressive move to address the racial disparities in mental health. With the advent of the Race Relations

(Amendment) Act 2000, racial equality, equality of opportunity and valuing diversity was extended to service delivery. Race equality initiatives sought to achieve equal outcomes for different groups.

Developments and policy initiatives such as these described here were progressive, but it has to be noted that at the same time the 1997 Labour government introduced a range of anti-immigration laws, which can be seen as regressive in relation to promoting race equality. A common theme that ran through these Acts of Parliament is the issue of access and entitlement to welfare benefits, thus establishing a link between welfare and immigration (Bloch et al. 2013). Ideas of race equality have been displaced by equality of opportunity and valuing diversity, which focus on equal processes meaning that everyone should be given the same chances or opportunities. Valuing diversity and equality of opportunity in service delivery is underpinned by stereotypical views. Think here about views that some groups prefer to 'look after their own', underlying a sweeping assumption that carers in these communities did not need support. Other stereotypical views, such as that older people will be looked after by their community or that the 'shame' of having a disabled child should be kept in the community, are deemed to be acceptable explanations for the limited uptake of services.

Policy responses to race equality and diversity

The aims of policy development to achieve racial equality can be categorised into four main themes: cultural deficiency, assimilation, multiculturalism and anti-racism. A common feature in policy responses to racial inequalities is the seemingly circular nature of the discourse – there seems to be a constant return to the notion of assimilation and 'taking on' of British identity or 'fitting in'. For example, one local authority in London cut spending on translated leaflets and providing interpreters on the basis that this discouraged BME groups from learning English and taking on a British Identity.

Cultural deficit approaches are premised on the standpoint that BME cultures are inferior to that of indigenous, i.e. White groups. Difficulties experienced by BME communities in relation to health and social care were located in their ethnic and cultural traditions and seen as deviant, which means that these experiences were pathologised (Lawrence 1982). For example, beliefs that Black parenting was inferior resulted in an over-representation of African Caribbean children in care (Pennie and Best 1990). It is interesting to note that these ideas still permeate the discourse, as can be seen in current debates on the practice of female genital mutilation in the UK.

Assimilationist ideas are premised on the idea that immigrants will progress if they adopt a 'British Identity', lifestyle and values. They are also informed by the viewpoint that the difficulties that BME communities experience are due to the fact that they refuse to adopt British customs. The aim of such policy was to assist these communities to integrate with other groups and specialist provision was seen as working against assimilation. The 1965 and 1968 Race Relations laws were aimed at stabilising social relations (Bloch et al. 2013). Provisions were made for policy intervention in housing and school education, and additional funding for teaching English in localities with significant migrant populations. However, assimilationist ideas failed to reduce racial and structural inequalities faced by BME communities and were discredited, with funding under Section 11 of the 1966 Local Government Act – the provision for local authorities to provide services for 'persons belonging to ethnic minorities whose language or customs differ from those of the rest of the community' – discontinued in 1999, and it was accepted that a shift in policy was required. Politicians at the time of the original legislation in the 1960s, such as Roy Jenkins who was the Home Secretary, argued for an integrative approach to cultural difference – hence the multiculturalism project that promoted accepting cultural difference.

Multiculturalism/culturalist embraced the notion that 'different cultures associated with migration were deemed needing to be recognised and understood amongst the majority culture' (Bloch et al. 2013: 13). Cultural diversity was promoted as a positive feature of society and an aspect of society to be celebrated. This led to the focus on cultural sensitivity and competence – learning about other cultures, the provision of interpreters and developing culturally sensitive and competent approaches were promoted. However, Atkin and Chattoo (2007) argue that the multicultural project did not address issues of power and institutional racism and this critique gave rise to the challenges from anti-racism.

The 1980s was seen as an 'extraordinary policy moment in which the politics of dissent, "race" social justice, social change and, community campaigns converged and became entangled' (Bloch et al. 2013: 31; see also Bartoli 2013; Bhatti-Sinclair 2011). Ethnic monitoring was introduced, race advisors, race units, race committees, racial harassment policies became established. This signalled a shift from the culturalist and assimilationist approaches that had prevailed to *anti-racism* and illustrates how the ideas of 'race' were mobilised as a site of resistance. However, the idea of 'race' became essentialised in its prioritisation over other social categories and unfortunately stood outside other social movements – the disability rights movement notably comes to mind here, a movement in which the voices of Black disabled people were not present (Stuart 2012).

This section has reviewed the different axes from which we can analyse 'race' and welfare policy. How we construe and understand issues pertaining to 'race', immigration and racial equality are vital to an appreciation of how welfare policy developed in the UK. The discussion has also illustrated the complexity of the issues and how the ideas of British Identity permeate the discourses on 'race'.

Points for reflection

- Institutional racism is the collective failure of an institution to provide appropriate and professional services to people because of their colour.
- Individual racism is overt or covert discrimination against people at a personal level because of their colour.

Learning point: Can you think about any organisation and examples of institutional practices that exclude or disadvantage people on the basis of their skin colour?

The modernisation project and 'race'

Modernisation of the traditional welfare state, which started with the Thatcher government, aimed at reducing state involvement in the provision of welfare services and at increasing the economic efficiency of public services. Suffice it to say that these developments did not bring benefits or positive results for already marginalised BME groups. Glimmers of hope resurfaced with two significant markers, i.e. the Stephen Lawrence Inquiry and New Labour taking office in 1997. The Stephen Lawrence Inquiry was launched after the racist murder of a young Black man in South London in 1993. Stephen was an A-level student who planned to go on to train as an architect. One evening, when he was on his way home with a friend, he was assaulted by a group/gang of young White men. He tried to run away, but collapsed and died as a result of the attack. His family had a long struggle to get the Metropolitan Police to investigate their son's murder and had to cope with police ineptitude. An inquiry was instituted and led by Sir William Macpherson, a senior judge, with a report launched in 1999. The inquiry's major finding was that there is institutional racism (see Points for reflection on p. 118) in the police force (and by implication other public services). The Race Relations Act 1976 was amended to make it a duty of all public services to combat racism in both employment practices and service delivery. The newly elected Labour government embraced a policy of collectivism and social citizenship, which augured promise for BME communities. This implied a paradigm shift from universalist approaches to welfare to a more collectivist approach, where individuals and communities could determine their own aspirations and needs thus leading to a more inclusive society. The Social Exclusion Unit was established to work towards reducing social inequality and promoting greater inclusion for marginalised groups. The modernisation agenda now focused on partnership working with the state taking on the role of regulator by setting up National Frameworks for service delivery. Each of these National Service Frameworks highlighted the need to respond to cultural diversity and challenge discrimination based on the grounds of ethnicity, belief or religion. As laudable as all these policy initiatives were, the anti-immigration sentiment prevailed and the government also passed four pieces of immigration legislation.

A further significant development was the resurgence of assimilationist ideas. The Parek Report published in 2000 set out an ambitious agenda for change. However, it was misinterpreted as an attack on the idea of Britishness (Mclaughlin and Neal 2004) and its recommendations were never taken up.

Assimilationist ideas were remodelled into an integrationist and cohesion agenda – implicitly blaming BME communities for not integrating with mainstream society and by further implication locating the source or causes of inequality within these communities; interestingly, this seemed to be a 'masked' return to the cultural deficit approach that was prevalent in the 1960 and 1970s. The shift from single frame equalities legislation such as the Race Relations (Amendment) Act 2000 and the Disability Discrimination Act 1995 towards a generic equalities framework was introduced with the Equalities Act 2010. The discourse changed from the meritocratic idea of 'equality of opportunity' to fairness, i.e. no group was to be singled out for special treatment or favouritism and that there should be equal outcomes for all (DCLG 2011).

It is clear from the discussion above that the complexities around providing welfare in a racialised context remain unresolved. The final sections of this chapter consider the contributions of the Black Voluntary sector to welfare and some suggestions for transforming welfare.

Challenges from the margins – the Black Voluntary sector

Given the failings of the welfare state and the way in which BME people are construed in social policy, Black groups have organised separately to provide welfare and support services in their communities. One such example is the Colonial Peoples' Defence Committee that organised welfare support for Black seamen in 1948 (Barbery et al. 2000). These organisations offer useful critiques of the Eurocentric nature of service models and provision, but operated and continue to exist at the margins of welfare service with insecure funding, not helped by the short-term nature of contracts (Fernando and Keating 2009; Williams and Johnson 2010). There has been to date no large-scale evaluation of services in the Black Voluntary sector and the intelligence in this sector has not been incorporated into mainstream ideas of welfare. This marginalisation of the BME voluntary sector limits opportunities for providing appropriate support in mainstream services. Personalisation is a current development in adult social care that seems to offer potential for individualised support, i.e. support that is focused on welfare in a racialised context. However, the scope for this is undermined by current cuts in welfare.

Transforming welfare

As a way forward this chapter suggests that we adopt a social constructionist approach informed by Critical Race Theory (CRT) and intersectionality. Constructionism argues that humans make sense of their experiences by creating a model of the social world and how it functions or operates (Teater 2014). CRT was introduced in the US as a counter-argument to the positivistic and liberal discourse on civil rights (Crenshaw 1991; Delgado and Stefancic 2001). In essence it argues that racism is endemic, it is real (lived experience), that Black people embody multiple identities (ethnicity is one dimension of BME identities) and that White power and privilege is maintained and sustained by law and policy. Combining these ideas helps us understand that policy needs to take account of how people construct their reality and acknowledge that such constructions may include racism and discrimination. Policy needs to be based on approaches that are formulated according to the experiences of BME groups and the strategy for welfare must be informed by needs as articulated by these communities.

Moreover, if we accept that 'race' intersects with other dimensions of identity and disadvantage we can overcome essentialist approaches to policy and service delivery. Issues of 'race', racialisation and racism are inherent dimensions of the fabric of British society and the policy agenda needs to engage constructively with these discourses.

Conclusion

This chapter reviewed the complex terrain of social policy in racialised contexts over the last century. It explored how the idea of a 'British Identity' permeates the discourse on welfare policy and entitlement to welfare resources. Discourses around 'race', immigration and racial equality have been considered to provide some insights into policy responses in these arenas. Addressing these issues in a single book chapter is an ambitious project, and readers who want to purse the issues introduced in this chapter are encouraged to read Bloch et al. (2013), Craig et al. (2012) and Williams and Johnson (2010).

Points for reflection

- What have you learnt about 'race', racism and welfare policy?
- How can this understanding be used to inform your social work practice?

References

Atkin, K. and Chattoo, S. (2007) 'The dilemmas of providing welfare in an ethnically diverse state: Seeking reconciliation in the role of a "reflexive practitioner"', *Policy and Politics*, 35 (3): 377–393.

Barbery, P., McHugh, J. and Tyldesley, M. (2000) *Encyclopaedia of British and Irish Political Organizations*. London: Bookcraft Ltd.

Barot, R. and Bird, J. (2001) 'Racialization: The genealogy of a concept', *Ethnic and Racial Studies*, 24 (4): 601–618.

Bartoli, A. (ed.) (2013) *Anti-Racism in Social Work Practice*. St Albans: Critical Publishing.

Bhatti-Sinclair, K. (2011) *Anti-Racist Practice in Social Work*. Basingstoke: Palgrave Macmillan.

Bloch, A., Neal, S. and Solomos, J. (2013) *Race, Multiculture & Social Policy*. Basingstoke: Palgrave MacMillan.

Bradshaw, J. (2012) *Mustn't Grumble: Immigration, Health and Health Use in the UK and Germany*. London: Centre for Economic Performance.

Cantle, T. (2008) *Community Cohesion: A New Framework for Race and Diversity*. Basingstoke: Palgrave Macmillan.

Chattoo, S. and Atkin, K. (2012) 'Race, ethnicity and social policy: Theoretical concepts and the limitations of current approaches to welfare', in C. Craig, K. Atkin, S. Chattoo and R. Flynn (eds), *Understanding 'Race' and Ethnicity: Theory, History, Policy and Practice*. Bristol: Policy Press, pp. 19–40.

Craig, C., Atkin, K., Chattoo, S. and Flynn, R. (eds) (2012) *Understanding 'Race' and Ethnicity: Theory, History, Policy and Practice*. Bristol: Policy Press.

Crenshaw, K. (1991) 'Mapping the margins: Intersectionality, identity politics, and violence against women of color', *Stanford Law Review*, 43 (6): 1241–1299.

Davies, S.C. (2014) *Annual Report of the Chief Medical Officer 2013: Public Mental Health Priorities*. London: Department of Health.

Delgado, R. and Stefancic, J. (2001) *Critical Race Theory: An Introduction*. New York: New York University Press.

Department for Communities and Local Government (DCLG) (2011) *Citizenship Survey: Community Spirit Topic Report, England*. London: DCLG.

Department for Education (DfE) (2014) *Children Looked After in England*. London: DfE.

Department of Health (DH) (2005) *Delivering Race Equality in Mental Health Care: An Action Plan for Reform Inside and Outside Services*. London: DH.

Dominelli, L. (2008) *Anti-Racist Social Work*, 3rd edn. Basingstoke: Palgrave Macmillan.

Fanshaw, S. and Sriskandaraja, D. (2010) *You Can't Put Me in a Box: Superdiversity and the End of Identity Politics in Britain*. London: Institute for Policy Research.

Fernando, S. and Keating, F. (eds) (2009) *Mental Health in a Mulit-Ethnic Society: A Handbook*. London: Taylor & Francis.

Finney, N. and Simpson, L. (2009) *Sleepwalking into Segregation? Challenging the Myths about Race and Racism*. Bristol: Policy Press.

Fook, J. (2002) *Critical Social Work: Theory and Practice*. London: Sage.

Fryer, P. (1984) *Staying Power*. London: Pluto Press.

Garner, S. (2010) *Racisms: An Introduction*. London: Sage Publications.

Home Office (2014) *Immigration Act, 2014*. London: Home Office.

Institute for Research and Innovation in Social Services (IRISS) (2010) *Improving Support for Black and Minority Ethnic (BME) Carers*. Edinburgh: IRISS.

Laming, H. (2003) *The Victoria Climbie Enquiry*. London: The Stationery Office.

Law, I. (2010) *Racism and Ethnicity: Global Debates, Dilemmas, Directions*. Harlow: Longman.

Lawrence, E. (1982) 'In the abundance of water the fool is thirsty: Sociology and Black "pathology"', in Centre for Contemporary Cultural Studies (ed.), *The Empire Strikes Back*. London: Hutchinson.

McLaughlin, E. and Neal, S. (2004) 'Misrepresenting the multicutural nation', *Policy Studies*, 25 (3): 155–175.

Pennie, P. and Best, F. (1990) *How the Black Family is Pathologised by the Social Service Systems*. London: Association of Black Social Workers and Allied Professionals (ABSWAP).

Pilkington, A. (2003) *Racial Disadvantage and Ethnic Diversity in Britain*. London: Sage.

Sanghani, R. (2014) 'Feminism, fashion and religion: Why Muslim women choose to wear the veil', *The Daily Telegraph*, 14 September. Available at: www.telegraph.co.uk/women/womens-life/11120588/Muslim-women-reveal-why-they-wear-the-veil-burqa-school-debate.html

Singh, S. (2013) 'Anti-Racist social work education', in A. Bartoli (ed.), *Anti-Racism in Social Work Practice*. St Albans: Critical Publishing, pp. 25–47.

Stuart, O.W. (2012) 'Not invited to the party?', in G. Craig, K. Atkin, S. Chattoo and R. Flynn (eds), *Understanding 'Race' and Ethnicity*. Bristol: Policy Press.

Teater, B. (2014) *An Introduction to Applying Social Work Theories and Methods*, 2nd edn. Maidenhead: Open University Press.

Vargas-Silva, C. (2014) *The Fiscal Impact of Immigration in the UK*. Oxford: Migration Observatory.

Williams, C. and Johnson, M. (2010) *Race And Ethnicity in a Welfare Society*. Maidenhead: Open University Press.

Williams, F. (1987) 'Racism and the Discipline of social policy: A critique of welfare theory', *Critical Social Policy*, 7: 4–29.

8

International Social Work: Understanding Social Work within Social Policy Systems

Tony Evans and Fabian Kessl

Introduction

Social work and social policy are closely interlinked, and because of this it can be difficult to disentangle shifts and changes in one's own policy context of practice, and identify their effect on the way social work is understood and is assumed to operate. One of the challenges is to stand back, question 'natural' changes and recognise underlying political and economic ideas and choices affecting these developments. This, we want to argue, is where international comparison can be of particular value. Comparing social work in different countries helps identify similarities and differences in the ways in which social work is practised and, in the process of comparison, we can also uncover how social work is, to a large extent, the product of national concerns and priorities (and cultural hegemony).

Social work with adults in Norway, for instance, tends to focus on assessment of unemployment benefits and (increasingly) the development of return to employment programmes; whereas in the UK adult social work is more concerned with the provision and rationing of care services and, to some extent, therapeutic social care work with adults (Brodtkorb and Evans in press). In relation to social work with children and young people, English social work is very much focused on child protection, risk management and minimisation, whereas from the perspective of German social work, which despite the influence of an increasingly risk-averse policy culture retains a strong tradition of social pedagogy and associated ideas of nurturing citizens and positive risk-taking, this approach looks quite alien (Bain and Evans 2013). At the same time international comparison can also help us identify similar strategies and concepts across social work in the wake of the transformation of the welfare state since the mid-1970s, and again in response to the financial crisis post-2008. By comparing how different welfare systems have responded to the neoliberal turn – ideas shifting risk to individuals, emphasising market solutions and individuals' responsibility for their own welfare and making public support more onerous and punitive – we can get a clearer sense of responses in different settings and how these reflect different circumstances, priorities and concerns, rather than simply seeing the transformation as irresistible and inevitable.

One of the major debates in social policy over the last few decades has been the question whether or not welfare policies and welfare states will converge under the pressure of neoliberal policies and economic globalisation. From a neoliberal perspective it is seen as inevitable that welfare states will collapse under their own weight – as welfare states grow they become more expensive and overburden narrowly economic-minded and self-interested taxpayers. In response to this argument, Regime Theory, developed by Esping-Andersen (1990), points out that, despite economic globalisation, there continue to be significant differences between welfare states, and that many welfare states strive to provide more than the bare minimum to their citizens. Welfare systems, it is argued, reflect different patterns of social and political responses in different countries and different choices about the degree to which social policy seeks to take fundamental aspects of human activity out of the market and establish them as citizen rights in advanced capitalist states.

In the first part of this chapter, we outline the main features of Regime Theory as an approach to understanding welfare states and consider how the theory has been used to explore different approaches to social work across Europe, setting out Esping-Andersen's framework and Lorenz's (2000) use of it to examine different regimes of social work and consider the strengths and limitations of this approach. While Regime Theory has a number of aspects to commend it in helping us understand the interaction of social work and social policy and diversity in social work, we argue that it is limited by its own focus on material relations and disregard for the emotional and reciprocal relations between individuals, families and groups. Furthermore, the relationship between social work and social policy is not simply one-way – social work is a creation of the broader policy context and an agent of social policy; and it is also an institution within the welfare state, which encounters the practical implications of policy (see Böhnisch 1982; Jordan 2000), such as benefit changes and tightening eligibility criteria, and using this experience challenges and can oppose the assumptions and prescriptions evident in social policy. In the final section of the chapter we consider the impact of these debates for understanding social work (both as a creation of social policy and as a welfare institution) and how we can set out a tentative framework to compare and contrast social work internationally.

What is Regime Theory? Citizens, markets and welfare

Over the past 20 years, an extensive literature has developed in social policy which looks at how welfare systems differ in advanced capitalist societies – which different services are offered, how these services are organised and what the underlying notions are of the roles and responsibilities of citizens. This literature is known under the collective term of Regime Theory and is based on the original work of the Danish welfare theorist Gøsta Esping-Andersen.

Esping-Andersen (2002) was interested in the relationship between welfare systems and social stratification. He argued that welfare systems do not simply respond to self-evident needs, they are also political and ethical projects which directly affect society: 'the welfare state is not just a mechanism that intervenes in, and possibly corrects, the structure of inequality; it is, in its own right, a system of stratification. It is an active force in the ordering of social relations' (2002: 165). His work was strongly influenced by Marshall's idea of citizenship (1963) in that he saw the welfare state as centrally concerned with the realisation of social rights that remove a person from dependence on their market position (what they earn and what they can afford to pay) to be able to 'share to the full the social heritage and to live the life of a civilised being according to the standards prevailing in the society' (Marshall 1963: 74). This is the genesis of Esping-Andersen's idea of decommodification, the idea that 'a service is rendered as a matter of right, and when a person can maintain a livelihood without reliance on the market' (1990: 22).

Esping-Andersen saw the key characteristics of welfare systems as the quality of social rights, the nature of social stratification and the relationship between state, market and family (1990: 169). He argued that when you compare welfare states you find different patterns and clusters of welfare systems that reflect different social priorities and social commitments towards their citizens. Some welfare systems, for instance, emphasise minimal support based on means-testing; others emphasise access to social support based on employment status; while in others state social support is universal and generous.

Esping-Andersen's original work distinguished three types of welfare regime: liberal, exemplified by the United States; corporate-statist regimes exemplified by Germany; and a primarily Scandinavian social-democratic regime.

Liberal regimes are characterised by the sanctity of the market. The state's relationship to the market is passive: welfare guarantees minimum benefits as a safety net. Beyond this, if people want more generous provision, they should make their own arrangements for their welfare through savings, insurance, etc. Behind this is the belief that the state cannot do as well as the market; it is by definition less efficient and effective. State welfare beyond the minimum level is believed to undermine the incentive to work and use of initiative. Benefits then tend to be minimal, at a basic level of sufficiency, and access to these minimal state services tends to be restricted by means-testing and strict entitlement rules. The market's 'invisible hand' is seen to be the appropriate mode of income distribution. This is reflected in significant income inequality and a highly stratified society.

Corporatist-statist regimes tend to be socially conservative. Markets are the primary means of income distribution but they are also restrained by concern about social stability. Social rights are important but they tend to be attached to employment status – particularly the role of male breadwinner. There is a strong emphasis on the family and civil institutions, particularly the church, in welfare as providers of social services. This is reflected in the idea of 'subsidiarity', the notion that the state should not interfere in the family except out of necessity. The role of the state is to augment family and community support, not to replace them; and while social benefits are generous, particularly when compared with liberal regimes, they are not intended to alter the basic structure of society by addressing inequality.

The third type of welfare regime identified by Esping-Andersen is *social-dem-ocratic*. This regime is essentially concerned with promoting equality. Benefits are universal and generous in order to reduce income inequality. There is more scepti-cism about the market as a mechanism of income distribution and service delivery, with a positive role being ascribed to the state in the provision of welfare and support for families – for instance, to enable women, who have traditionally been restricted by socially imposed caring responsibilities, to enter the labour market through the social provision of child care.

Points for reflection

Esping-Andersen's analysis relates to social policy systems across the advanced capitalist economies of Europe, North America and Australasia. Thinking about these three pat-terns of social policy regimes – liberal, corporatist-statist and social-democratic – which form of regime do you think best describes the policy context within which you practise?

Regime Theory is not simply descriptive. It challenges the neoliberal assumption that the welfare state must collapse under its own weight. Esping-Andersen points out that this assumption is an ideological assertion that is not borne out in fact: 'Paradoxically, the opposite is true. Anti-welfare-state sentiments [since the 1980s] have generally been weakest where welfare spending has been heaviest and vice versa' (1990: 33). The welfare state, he argues, is not simply an economic phenom-enon; it is also a political and cultural achievement. Welfare regimes reflect the success – or failure – of politics as a process through which coalitions of social and economic interests are forged and maintained:

> the liberal, residualist welfare states found in the United States, Canada and, increasingly, Britain, depend on the loyalties of numerically weak, and often politically residual, social stratum. In this sense, the class coalitions in which the three welfare-state regime-types were founded, explain not only that past evolution but also their future prospects. (Esping-Andersen 1990: 33)

Regime Theory and social work

An interesting aspect of this literature in relation to social work has been its use to examine different approaches to social work in different countries by relating prac-tice to the cultures, politics and focus of different welfare systems (e.g. Lorenz 2006). We now want to consider this approach to international comparison in terms of how far it helps us to understand our own social work practices within the policy context and to consider the exchange of ideas and expertise in social work across different regimes/countries.

Regime Theory has been used as a framework in the international comparison of social work. Lorenz (2006), for instance, has used Regime Theory to examine approaches to social work in Europe, linking different ideas of social work with different policy regimes. In corporate-statist social work regimes – Germany, for instance – the state tends to take an overview of social services, but the significant providers of social welfare are non-state actors. The goal and purpose of welfare services is to maintain a stable society. In contrast, in a liberal social work regime, such as the UK, the focus is on meeting the basic needs of people in poverty and the social control of deviance. The mandate for social service provision is not inclusive, nor is it universal; rather services tend to be provided on a reactive, targeted and residual basis. Service provision is often characterised by restrictive thresholds and eligibility criteria. The role of professional staff is to ration public resources and broker contributions from non-state providers. In the Scandinavian social-democratic regimes, social services have a much more proactive and universalistic role. The role of social welfare is to promote equality. Service provision tends to be universal, extensive and of high quality. Social care professionals are an integral part of welfare services, most often provided by the state.

Change, politics and regimes

Esping-Andersen's original work looked at welfare regimes in the advanced capitalist economies of Northern Europe, North America and Australasia. There have been two broad responses to this by policy commentators. The first has been to build on Esping-Andersen's three original types adding categories to identify further welfare state clusters and social policy regimes. For instance Leibfried (1993) augments Esping-Andersen's original three regimes with a fourth, the Latin Rim regime, which he associates with Iberia, Italy and Greece.

The second response takes a more critical approach to the principles used to categorise social policy regimes. The corporate-statist welfare regime model, for instance, has been criticised as a residual category, because the 'main models' – social-democratic and liberal – are based on two real-life welfare states, Sweden and the US, set up as 'ideal types' (e.g. Rieger 1998: 75ff.). Nevertheless, particular criticism has been focused on the Esping-Andersen analysis of liberal welfare regimes. He equated these with the Anglo-Saxon world and a neoliberal worldview. However, he has been criticised for lumping all Anglo-Saxon welfare systems into one category – seeing them simply as minor variations of the US welfare model – and ignoring significant internal differences within this regime cluster. Castles and Mitchell (1992), for instance, have argued that the welfare systems in the UK, Australia, New Zealand, Canada and the USA are significantly different and to see them as the same is misleading.

However, these critical developments also share the fundamental insight of Regime Theory, i.e. that welfare states are not simply economically determined but that they also reflect political and social coalition building. In most political systems the idea of coalitions suggests stability and the centre ground – paradoxically the fragility of shifting of coalition governments often leaves the system of public administration free to continue without sustained political interference. However, in first-past-the-post centralised parliamentary systems such as in the UK, political parties can take control of government without achieving majority support in society (Ipsos-MORI 2010), welfare regimes may be more liable to dramatic shift and change.

This, for instance, is part of the explanation for the fundamental shift in the UK from the 1980s onwards, where the social welfare system has been transformed in line with neoliberal ideas and commitments. In contrast, in Germany, there is a strong decentralised model of politics towards consensus and to avoid extreme shifts in policy. This, though, is not to say that change does not occur. Recently, there has been a shift in child protection policy with a new federal law (Federal Child Protection Law in 2012 – '*Bundeskinderschutzgesetz*') imposing a child protection agenda on local services reflecting a more punitive state approach.

We also need to be aware that policy regimes and processes of change within them are not always uniform or consistent. In the UK, for instance, despite the evident advance of the neoliberal agenda, the National Health Service continues to be a universal service and free at the point of access (DH 2013). In Germany, though, access to health is based on an insurance system with a growing socio-economic divide between basic public health insurance and private insurance provision (Gerlinger 2004; see also Bauer et al. 2008).

Welfare regimes are created, sustained and change in ways that cannot simply be explained in terms of market economics. As we shall see in the next section, they also exist through policy choices, political manoeuvres and underlying assumptions about the responsibilities of citizens, the role of the state and the state's relationship with wider society.

Care and control

Welfare states tend to be characterised as either democratising institutions that care for citizens or as more or less subtle systems of social control.

Democratising accounts of the development of welfare states, such as Marshall's influential analysis of social citizenship and welfare (1963) – which was a key influence on Esping-Andersen's work (1990) – identify welfare services as the culmination of a historical process of realising a social and democratic idea of citizenship. From this perspective welfare states can be defined as societies focused on increasing individual freedom and collective protection (Kaufmann 1997: 29). From this perspective welfare systems aim to open spaces for the empowerment and self-determination of citizens (Vobruba 1991: 34), and welfare agencies, such as social work, reflect the state's commitment to the 'democratisation' of capitalism.

An alternative account of the development of welfare agencies emphasises their role as agents of social control (Donzelot 1979). This is the idea of welfare as a form of moral regulation concerned with disciplining populations in line with customary ideas of normality. The inculcation and imposition of these norms to regulate and control behaviour so that it conforms to expectations of normal behaviour – 'normalisation' – is seen as the fundamental activity of welfare agencies. In contrast to the empowering motives that underpin the social-democratic account of the development of the welfare state, this disciplinary account sees welfare as a functional response to the requirements of industrialisation. Neo-Marxists, like Lenhardt and Offe (1977), have developed this idea to present welfare as a means of pacifying the population under capitalism.

These two perspectives reflect the main theoretical positions in welfare state research. However, neither 'democratisation' nor 'normalisation' accounts alone provide a convincing account of the development and contemporary operation of welfare states. In social work theory this insight is reflected in the idea of both the coming together of solidarity *and* control in practice, and the continuing tension and contradiction between these two ideas (see Böhnisch and Lösch 1973). It is important to recall Lessenich's (2003: 90, own translation) observation that rather than these positions being fixed and opposing categories there is more often a 'continuum of different models of how solidarity in welfare states is constructed'. Lessenich recommends that we should adopt an 'open categorisation' which allows for more flexible, dynamic and fluid analysis – which can move beyond understanding welfare states simply in terms of either a mechanism of redistribution or a system of social regulation.

Regulating care

Understanding regimes as political and cultural entities entails not only looking at how they organise services but also at the assumptions they embody and enforce about (public and private) welfare responsibilities. Over the past 40 years, a telling critique of welfare state policy, which has been particularly influential in social work, has been developed by feminist scholars, who have pointed out that policy-makers and commentators have tended to take for granted caring as a private familial transaction and characterised it as beyond policy (e.g. Finch and Groves 1980).

Regime Theory has been criticised for its lack of attention to the gendered roles ascribed to citizens within welfare regimes around the notions of the male breadwinner and the female homemaker and carer (Lewis 1992). Lister (1994), for instance, argues that Regime Theory has not taken sufficient account of the overwhelming burden of care placed on women – and that 'care' is the basic principle by which welfare systems should be assessed. (This criticism could, of course, be extended to take account of different cultural contexts and stereotypes that are often applied in policy and service provision to minority ethnic groups, e.g. 'they look after their own'.)

Daly and Lewis (2000) argue that the idea of 'care' – particularly what societies assume about, and how they organise and support, care across the life course – is central to welfare systems and should be basic to our understanding of welfare regimes. In Scandinavia, for instance, they point out that care tends to be collectivised, in order to remove caring from within the family context. In Mediterranean countries care tends to be seen as the private responsibility of the family. In corporatist regimes attitudes to care are varied. In some societies, such as Germany, assistance is provided to families in their caring responsibilities across the life span via the voluntary sector. In France, by contrast, social provision supports child care and is highly collectivised, but this is not the case in care for adults. While in the UK a strong distinction has been made between care for children, where the state is reluctant to intervene directly, and care for older people, where there is a greater recognition of the role of collective provision.

Daly and Lewis (2000) argue that to understand the centrality and complexity of care within modern welfare systems we need to recognise three dimensions of care:

- All care involves labour, whether paid or unpaid, formal or informal, and the state has a role in valorising what is seen as care labour.
- Care exists within human relations and the state has a role in influencing the norms of care – who is expected to do what for whom – that underpin these relationships.
- Care costs – not just economically but also emotionally – and the state plays a role in determining how these costs are distributed between individuals within families and between families and the broader society.

Daly and Lewis (2000) argue that care is an increasingly acknowledged issue in the analysis of welfare states because previous assumptions about the role of women as carers are no longer viable. In advanced capitalist societies over the past few decades women have been entering the labour market at increasing rates and policy-makers are having to confront this fact alongside increasing demand for care as the population ages and many states seek to retrench welfare services.

The arguments of Lessenich (2003) and of Daly and Lewis (2000) point to the need to extend our understanding of welfare regimes beyond just the relationship between citizens and the labour market to include consideration of the regulation of the 'reproduction of labour' and recognising care as a form of labour. This broader understanding of welfare regimes provides, we would argue, a more fruitful way to approach and understand the role of the welfare state, and in relation to our concern in this chapter with social work, it also provides a richer perspective from which to recognise the tensions and contradictions within welfare states and to understand the dynamic context in which welfare agencies such as social work operate. In the final part of this chapter, we want to explore these observations further by considering more closely how we can understand social work as a welfare state actor and the different aspects of social work which can be identified and compared and contrasted in social work practices across social policy regimes.

Points for reflection

Donna Chung's chapter in this book (Chapter 9) looks at the development of policy towards domestic violence in the UK and Australia. Think about Regime Theory and feminist critiques of the theory in relation to the changing role of the state and its intervention in families. How can these ideas help you understand the development of policy towards domestic violence in both countries?

Social work – in its international setting and local contexts

There is an attempt to capture the nature of social work in the international statement that sets out the role and function of professional social work (see the International Federation of Social Workers [IFSW] and the International Association of Schools of Social Work [IASSW] 'Code of Ethics' (IFSW/IASSW 2012)). In the statement, social work is characterised as a universal public service and also an agency of socialisation, which is concerned with both solidarity (for strangers) and (social) control maintaining standards of normality in given national welfare systems.

Despite these general observations, though, it is difficult to identify a fixed unified entity called 'social work' across the globe; beyond general statements, empirically social work looks different in different countries. This analysis suggests that social work needs to be understood as an institution, a profession, within a welfare state system. It is difficult – particularly in international comparisons – to specify social work in terms of a particular set of tasks within welfare states. Perhaps because of social work's concern with the operation of welfare as a system within a state, it is often confronted with gaps or problems in services, and in addressing these it develops in particular ways and develops (different) particular responsibilities, interests and so on within the policy context. Looking at the profession in this way allows us to see that it not only has specific welfare functions and concerns, but also that it reflects wider social influences that structure the ways in which it is organised (Lessenich 2012: 82ff.).

Social work, for instance, looks quite different from 'traditional' professions such as medicine and the law – because it tends to be more bureaucratised and professional discretion is more circumscribed by organisational rules and procedures (Evans 2013). However, the role of social work tends to be more fluid than the role of other welfare professions. Medicine and nursing are concerned with health; teachers are concerned with education. If we try to pin social work down to an equivalent domain – some say 'problems in living' (Böhnisch and Schefold 1985), 'care' (see Brückner 2004) or others say 'social justice' (see Schrödter 2007) or 'human rights' – it does not seem to work. If we think of 'caring', for instance, how can social work be systematically distinguished from the other caring professions, such as nursing? Similarly, how can social work claim 'social justice' or 'human rights' as its exclusive domain in contrast to other social professions, and politicians and social movements in general?

But if we focus on social work at a very general level of analysis we can see that social work is: a practice, intervening in a planned way to support people in their everyday lives where there are problems or where there are likely to be problems in the future (prevention); and as a public project managing the gap between the promises of welfare and social justice, and the realities of people's day-to-day existence. However, what this means in practice is closely related to the idea of social work itself as an actor within the welfare state. In its concern with how society enables people to be social citizens, social work is implicated in how the current regulation system (see Jessop 2002) and organisational and professional aspect of the system work together (Kessl 2013). In turn, the relationship of social work to social policy helps us to understand how we can talk about social work as an international profession while recognising that the profession reflects local differences in its operation.

Dimensions of difference and similarity in social work practice

Local institutional settings frame social work and both enable and constrain practice. This means that any international comparison of social work needs to recognise that social work as a professional formation has to be understood within its particular political, policy and organisational context: German social work, for instance, has a strong tradition of being publicly regulated (strong state), but delivered by quasi-state organisations, such as the religious organisations – Catholic and Protestant – political parties such as the Social Democrats and specialist welfare organisations such as the Red Cross (*Wohlfahrtsverbände*). English social work has been closely associated with services provided by local government and continues to be a profession associated with local government. Recently, however, while social work continues to be a profession predominantly found within local public bodies there are moves to shift to a system where social work is commissioned from market and quasi-market bodies such as social enterprises and small-scale professional partnerships (DoE 2012; SCIE 2013).

The challenge in comparing social work in an international context is: how do we make sense of diversity without either reducing the idea of social work to an abstract generalisation or just giving up on any attempt to make connections between social work across boundaries? Understanding social work in relation to its policy context reflects one way of reconciling this tension. However, there is a danger in this approach that it can end up over-emphasising both the uniformity of welfare institutions within welfare states and difference between welfare regimes, seeing social work within a particular regime setting as simply a reflection of the principles of that regime and as quite different from social work in any other regimes. While it would be a mistake to ignore the significant top-down pressure that dominant policy arrangements in particular policy contexts can have on the organisation and purpose of social work this is not the whole story. The shape and operation of welfare institutions such as social work are not simply determined by top-down pressures; rather, they reflect the cross-cutting influences of a range of pressures and are best understood, as Kaufmann (1997) and Donzelot (1979) suggest, as multidimensional.

Dimensions of social work

Accordingly, we need to recognise that social work is both the same and different in different countries. It shares common dimensions and tensions but also has to respond to these in different social, political and policy contexts in quite different ways. This can be seen in the range of dimensions that characterise social work/ social policy relations.

One way of thinking about the welfare state is as a commitment by society to ensure a certain level of social and political participation for all its members (Marshall 1963). Social work, then, is involved in using social policy to assist citizens; it makes systems work for individuals. If we think, for example, of caring or of social justice not just as attitudes but also as areas of concern, this helps towards understanding what social work is about. Social work's concern is with nurturing, supporting, enabling people as social actors and as citizens. It bridges the personal and the political – it is concerned with welfare as a response to the way people are categorised as being vulnerable, deviant or (potentially) problematic. Recognising this is to recognise the strong and fundamental link between social work and social policy, but also the different, more concrete nature of the connection between social work and service users (in comparison to the more general and abstract link between social policy and the population). Public assistance for families, for instance, has tended to be reframed by policy-makers in the UK and to some extent too Northern and Western Europe, as a policy for 'troubled families'. This reframing has set the context within which social workers and families have to work – but at the same time practitioners, working directly with families, can see that issues such as poverty are not simply private problems, they are also public issues (Mills 1959), which need to be highlighted and challenged.

Social work, as an aspect of welfare policy, can be understood as an agent of public regulation. It is a welfare institution that categorises people as good or bad (parents, carers, etc.), as being educable or in-educable, as being eligible or ineligible for support. Social policy tends to focus on social positions – systems, structures and so on – whereas social work tends to start from individual experiences and dispositions: this could be called the service or pedagogical dimension of the welfare state. Social work intervenes at the level of everyday life, while social policy tries to influence the circumstances that influence how people operate in their everyday lives. The result is that social work often has to operate at the margins of the policy system and has to engage with the tension between private problems and public issues in the relationship between social work and policy.

One aspect of this is where social work interventions simply 'make do and mend' to disguise or mitigate the damaging and disruptive effects of dysfunctional policy. This, for instance, is the case when social work is not operating as a different, complementary part of the welfare state, but as a substitution for an adequate welfare policy. If somebody is living on the streets after losing their job or has also lost their flat as a result of the extremely high rent in a large European city, such as London or Munich, this person needs material support to pay the rent in the short term, help to find a cheaper flat and support to get a new job. But in the absence of resources to provide this support, all that social work can do is to offer counselling – to cope with the distress and to encourage the person to manage their situation 'more effectively'. In the absence of an adequate social security system social work can step into maintain a difficult situation, but in the continued absence of adequate resources counselling people to 'cope' masks inadequate welfare provision.

Another aspect of this is where social work redefines or manipulates complex individual needs into a simple production process to better conform to policy-driven systems. In the transformation of the welfare state since the late 1970s in almost all welfare states (for example in the UK: Thatcherism, New Labour, Big Society) the relationship between social policy and social work has fundamentally changed. Welfare agencies have been reformed to re-educate citizens. Classically this can be seen in 'workfare' policies that link unemployment benefits with conditions to comply with work preparation requirements. Welfare is bound to individual obligations, which are instilled through educational programmes of the 'enabling state', or child welfare is remodelled as child protection, where parents are blamed and find themselves in parenting programmes rather than in receipt of support to address poverty.

Social work also seeks to fill the gaps social policy often leaves – either before policy has recognised them or where policy tries to force individuals into inflexible categories. Paradoxically, in casting social work in this role, society has also created one of its most constant critics. Social work not only deals with problems in society but also has to work with the problems created by policy and is often driven to critique politics when confronted 'by the constantly emerging damage' (Mollenhauer 1964/1993: 21, own translation) social work encounters and in the process craft spaces for resistance.

Points for reflection

Earlier chapters in this book have looked at the changing relationship between social policy and social work since the latter part of the 20th century. Drawing on the idea of the dimensions of social work outlined above, review an area of social work and social policy discussed in an earlier chapter.

Conclusion

In this chapter, we have looked at how international comparison can help us understand the relationship between social work and social policy. Thinking internationally requires us to consider the different ways in which social work and social policy are understood and how policy and practice interact in different ways in different settings. The value of international comparisons is that it can help us see that what we often take for granted as common sense is neither inevitable nor the only way to see policy and practice.

In comparing social policy and social work, Regime Theory offers a helpful starting point. Regime Theory challenges the assumption that social policy is simply determined by economic forces. Policy, it argues, also reflects political choices. Welfare policy in the UK, for instance, used to bear comparison more with Scandinavian welfare states than with American minimalist welfare. However, while the UK has taken a more neoliberal road to welfare, this is much less the case in Scandinavian countries. The decision to move away from social welfare in the UK was driven by political choices that framed (and themselves contributed to) economic circumstances (Stedman-Jones 2012).

However, we also argued that Regime Theory – which focuses on the relationship between citizens and labour markets – is too narrow to capture the whole policy context of social work. We need to expand our understanding of social policy to include insights from critical theory about the ways in which the state and its welfare institutions regulate interpersonal relationships, particularly caring relationships.

This broader sense of the social policy framework enables us to see that the influence of policy on practice is not simply a one-way process in which policy makes practice necessarily either benign or malign. International comparison helps us to see that social work has an ambivalent relationship to policy that needs to be understood in its context. Local policy has a significant effect on how social work is understood and how social workers can practise; but policy itself is the accretion of disjointed initiatives – it is seldom a clear and coherent set of ideas, but rather is often confused, incoherent and full of contradictions. In this context, social work may reflect dominant policy or stand in opposition to it; and it often has to find a way of negotiating the tensions between advancing social justice, ameliorating problems and regulating behaviour.

Social work can be understood as having a similar identity grounded in its relationship with social policy; and this relationship is central to understanding why social work is also different in different countries. International comparison can show us how social work can have shared and different concerns, and how social work can do things differently in different settings. It can help us understand how these different areas of focus and forms of practice reflect particular responses in particular policy contexts. By understanding what lies behind these differences, we can learn from each other about different ways of doing social work, the setting in which different approaches work, and the assumptions which social work and social policy make about each other.

References

Bain, K. and Evans, T. (2013) *The Internationalisation of English Social Work: The Migration of German Social Work Practitioners and Ideas to England*. London: Royal Holloway, University of London (RHUL).

Bauer U., Bittlingmayer, U.H. and Richter, M. (eds) (2008) *Health Inequalities. Determinanten und Mechanismen gesundheitlicher Ungleichheit*. Wiesbaden, VS.

Böhnisch, L. (1982) *Der Sozialstaat und seine Pädagogik: sozialpolitische Anleitungen zur Sozialarbeit*. Neuwied and Darmstadt: Luchterhand.

Böhnisch, L. and Lösch, H. (1973) 'Das Handlungsverständnis des Sozialarbeiters und seine institutionelle Determination', in H.-U. Otto and S. Schneider (eds), *Gesellschaftliche Perspektiven der Sozialarbeit*. Band 2, Neuwied: Luchterhand, pp. S. 21–40.

Böhnisch, L. and Schefold, W. (1985) Lebensbewältigung: soziale und pädagogische Verständigungen an den Grenzen der Wohlfahrtsgesellschaft. Weinheim and München: Juventa.

Brodtkorb, E. and Evans, T. (in press) 'Adult social care – Exploring the Norwegian and English approaches', in F. Kessl, W. Lorenz, H.-U. Otto and S. White (eds), *European Social Work – A Compendium*. Leverkusen: Barbara Budrich.

Brückner, M. (2004) 'Changing Europe and the relevance of care and the caring professions', *Social Work & Society*, 2 (1). Available at: https: //www.socwork.de/Brueckner2004.pdf (accessed 22 July 2015).

Castles, F. and Mitchell, D. (1992) 'Identifying welfare state regimes: The links between politics, instruments and outcomes', *Governance*, 5: 1–26

Daly, M. and Lewis, J. (2000) 'The concept of social care and the analysis of contemporary welfare states', *British Journal of Sociology*, 51 (2): 281–298.

Department of Education (DoE) (2012) *Research Briefing: Evaluation of Social Work Practices*. London: Department of Education. Available at: www.gov.uk/government/uploads/system/uploads/attachment_data/file/197523/DFE-RB233_Research_brief.pdf (accessed 22 July 2015).

Donzelot, J. (1979) *The Policing of Families*. New York: Random House.

Esping-Andersen, G. (1990) *The Three Worlds of Welfare Capitalism*. London: Polity Press.

Esping-Andersen, G. (2002) *Why We Need a New Welfare State*. Oxford: Oxford University Press.

Evans, T. (2013) 'Organisational rules and discretion in adult social work', *British Journal of Social Work*, 43 (4): 739–758.

Finch, J. and Groves, D. (1980) 'Community care and the family: A case for equal opportunities?', *Journal of Social Policy*, 9: 487–511

Gerlinger, T. (2004) 'Privatisierung – Liberalisierung – Re-Regulierung: Konturen des Umbaus des Gesundheitssystems', *WSI-Mitteilungen*, 57 (9): 501–506.

International Federation of Social Workers (IFSW) and the International Association of Schools of Social Work (IASSW) (2012) *Statement of Ethical Principles* [Online]. Available at: http://ifsw.org/policies/statement-of-ethical-principles/ (accessed 26 August 2014).

Ipsos-MORI (2010) *How Britain Voted Since October 1974* [Online]. Available at: www.ipsos-mori.com/researchpublications/researcharchive/poll.aspx?oItemID=101 (accessed 26 August 2014).

Jessop, B. (2002) *The Future of the Capitalist State*. Cambridge: Polity.

Jordan, B. (2000) *Social Work and the Third Way: Tough Love as Social Policy*. London: Sage.

Kaufmann, F.-X. (1997) *Herausforderungen des Sozialstaats*. Frankfurt am Main: Suhrkamp.

Kessl, F. (2013) *Soziale Arbeit in der Transformation des Sozialen. Eine Ortsbestimmung.* Wiesbaden: Springer VS.

Leibfried, S. (1993) 'Towards a European welfare state?', in C. Jones (ed.), *New Perspectives on the Welfare State in Europe*. London: Routledge.

Lenhardt, G. and Offe, C. (1977) 'Staatstheorie und Sozialpolitik. Politisch-soziologische Erklärungsansätze für Funktionen und Innovationsprozesse der Sozialpolitik', in C. Ferber (ed.), *Soziologie und Sozialpolitik*. Opladen: Westdeutscher Verlag, pp. 98–127.

Lessenich, S. (2003) 'Schluss: Wohlfahrtsstaatliche Semantiken – Politik im Wohlfahrtsstaat', in S. Lessenich (ed.), *Wohlfahrtsstaatliche Grundbegriffe: historische und aktuelle Diskurse*, Frankfurt am Main and New York, Campus, pp. 419–426.

Lessenich, S. (2012) *Theorien des Sozialstaats. Zur Einführung*. Hamburg: Junius.

Lewis, J. (1992) 'Gender and the development of welfare regimes', *Journal of European Social Policy*, 2: 159–73.

Lister, R. (1994) '"She has other duties": Women, citizenship and social security', in S. Baldwin and J. Falkingham (eds), *Social Security and Social Change: New Challenges to the Beveridge Model*. New York: Harvester Wheatsheaf, pp. 31–44.

Lorenz, W. (2006) *Perspectives on European Social Work: From the Birth of the Nation State to the impact of Globalisation*. Opladen and Farmington Hills: Barbara Budrich.

Marshall, T.H. (1963) 'Citizenship and social class', in *Sociology at the Crossroads and Other Essays*. London: Heinemann.

Mills, C.W. (1959) *The Sociological Imagination*. New York and London: Oxford University Press.

Mollenhauer, K. (1964/1993) *Einführung in die Sozialpädagogik: Probleme und Begriffe der Jugendhilfe*. Weinheim and Basel: Beltz.

Rieger, E. (1998) Soziologische Theorie und Sozialpolitik im entwickelten Wohlfahrtsstaat', in S. Lessenich and I. Ostner (eds), *Welten des Wohlfahrtskapitalismus*. Frankfurt am Main and New York: Campus, pp. 59–89.

Schrödter, M. (2007) 'Soziale Arbeit als Gerechtigkeitsprofession. Zur Gewährleistung von Verwirklichungschancen', *Neue Praxis*, 37 (1): 3–28.

Social Care Institute of Excellence (SCIE) (2013) *Social Work Practice Pilots and Pioneers in Social Work For Adults*. London: SCIE.

Stedman-Jones, D. (2012) *Masters of the Universe*. Princeton, NJ: Princeton University Press.

Vobruba, G. (1991) *Jenseits der sozialen Fragen: Modernisierung und Transformation von Gesellschaftssystemen*. Frankfurt am Main: Suhrkamp.

9

Domestic Violence: UK and Australian Developments

Donna Chung

Introduction

It is easy to take for granted current domestic violence policies and services. However, these responses have only evolved in the past 40 years, as a direct result of second-wave feminists making domestic violence a political concern over the preceding decades. In this chapter, the policy and practice developments of the UK and Australia are compared. These two democracies have differing systems of government, however domestic violence policies and practice are remarkably similar. The reasons for the similarities and the major policy and practice responses are examined. Some contemporary issues confronting efforts to end domestic violence are presented and ideas outlined about how policy approaches to domestic violence require reorienting.

A short note on domestic violence as a social policy problem

As Bacchi (2009) and other academics have argued, social policy exists to respond to 'known' social problems of concern to the state because they are understood to affect significant numbers of the population. This is not an objective process nor is there a rational set of policy tasks to be undertaken to respond to the problem (Murray and Powell 2011). How the social problem is understood, the number and range of people affected, the political processes and actors and dominant ideologies and discourses all impact on policy and programmes. In examining social policy responses to domestic violence this is relevant because it is not the responsibility of a single government department but of a number of departments which can vary in their understanding of the problem, the culture and discourses within the departments and potential responses. In the following section how domestic violence became a social policy problem demonstrates the beginnings of this process.

The emergence of domestic violence as a social policy concern

Initially, domestic violence was understood as the use of physical violence by a male against his female partner. This understanding did not indicate its causes or breadth. Therefore it provided little guidance for intervention. In the 1960s, second-wave feminists in western nations were increasingly aware of the extent to which then married women were subjected to violence and abuse from male partners in the home. Domestic violence was seen as a private matter between the couple and not something subject to state, community or family 'interference'. Feminists' concern about domestic violence was part of a broader political agenda about promoting change to stop all forms of male violence against women including rape, sexual harassment and discrimination and childhood sexual abuse (Murray and Powell 2011).

Prior to second-wave feminism, biological and medical explanations of domestic violence dominated which individualised and pathologised women victims and male perpetrators and did not consider structural inequalities as influential in explaining domestic violence (Gelles 1976). This individualised understanding meant there was no need for national policies but rather just for improved talking therapies for people seen as capable of change. In contrast, feminists argued domestic violence was a consequence of women's oppression within a patriarchal society. Women's experiences of domestic violence were not based on them being masochists or other personality traits, but that a patriarchal society gave men personal and public power over women. This was evident in various institutions that prevented and stigmatised women who attempted to leave relationships. Furthermore, this acted to silence women about their private experiences of violence from men (Breckenridge and Laing 1999; Burton et al. 1998).

Domestic violence[1] remains a contested political issue, its history reflects an evolving definition as knowledge has increased. As with much policy development, a case has to be made for its prevalence to promote action. In the UK and Australia efforts have gone into establishing the extent of domestic violence to demonstrate its costs to individuals, governments, the community and the private sector. National studies in both countries indicate that at some time across their lifetime, one in four or one in five women will be subjected to male violence (COAG 2013; HM Government 2010). This has provided a continuing rationale for responding to domestic violence.

Domestic violence is part of a wider field of violence against women which encapsulates multiple forms of violence including sexual assault and rape, sexual harassment, gender-based discrimination, harmful cultural practices perpetrated on females and sexual exploitation of women. UK and Australia are signatories to the United Nations Convention on the Elimination of All Forms of Discrimination Against Women (CEDAW), of which eliminating violence against women is an element. The UN conceptualises violence against women as a human rights violation. This has set the scene for the respective national governments' domestic violence policies. Under conservative national governments the definitions have become more 'gender' neutral, implying domestic violence is not necessarily or always a result of gendered inequality. Whereas feminists would argue that domestic violence is predominantly an act of maintaining gender inequality and oppression.

Currently, both national governments locate their policies within a framework of violence against women. The UK has produced a policy entitled *A Call to End Violence against Women and Girls* (HM Government 2010) and in Australia, *The National Plan to Reduce Violence against Women and their Children* (COAG 2013). Both national policies contain aspects concerning domestic violence. In terms of language the UK title is more specifically focused on gender.

The UK policy does not provide a specific definition of domestic violence, rather it draws on the United Nations (1993) definition (HM Government 2010: 1):

> The United Nations (UN) Declaration (1993) on the elimination of violence against women to guide our work across all government departments: 'Any act of gender-based violence that results in, or is likely to result in, physical, sexual or psychological harm or suffering to women, including threats of such acts, coercion or arbitrary deprivation of liberty, whether occurring in public or in private life'.

The Australian policy includes a specific definition domestic violence:

> Domestic violence refers to acts of violence that occur between people who have, or have had, an intimate relationship. While there is no single definition, the central element of domestic violence is an ongoing pattern of behaviour aimed at controlling a partner through fear, for example by using behaviour which is violent and threatening. In most cases, the violent behaviour is part of a range of tactics to exercise power and control over women and their children, and can be both criminal and non-criminal.
>
> Domestic violence includes physical, sexual, emotional and psychological abuse. (COAG 2013: 2)

The following section presents how policy developments in domestic violence have evolved.

Points for reflection

Before domestic violence responses are discussed, consider your current knowledge about domestic violence services by thinking about the following scenario. A friend of yours knows you are studying social work so thinks you might be able to help, she discloses her partner is verbally abusive and at times physically abusive and threatening. She wants to know who you think might be helpful to speak with about this and find

(Continued)

(Continued)

out about her legal rights as well as what she might be able to do. Write down what you think you might say in this situation where you have been put on the spot. Having done this, what questions does this now raise for you about what you would need to find out about domestic violence responses if the situation arose again?

Domestic violence policy strategies

Three areas of policy and programme development which have formed the basis of much work to end domestic violence are discussed. These are legislative reform and law enforcement, homelessness and housing and partnership working and coordinated responses.

Legislative reform and law enforcement

A key platform for demonstrating the seriousness and unacceptability of domestic violence was to emphasise that it was a crime, described by feminists as 'criminal assault in the home' (Hamner et al. 1989). This strategy to address domestic violence had two main elements: legislative reform and improving law enforcement responses. These strategies were predicated on the assumption assaults in the home were not taken seriously by law enforcement as criminal acts, reflecting community attitudes about the gravity of the offence; whereas when an assault occurred in public between non-intimates, law enforcement and the courts took it seriously, indicated by people being charged with assault. This 'naming' strategy highlighted the double standard for women assaulted by partners (Hester 2006; Scutt 1995).

In terms of law enforcement, domestic violence policing reforms have included: domestic violence training, specialist officers and units in the police force and detailed regulations about how to respond including undertaking risk assessments, promoting safety, referrals to support services and 'pro-arrest' approaches, whereby if there is evidence a criminal act has taken place then the perpetrator should be arrested (Laing et al. 2013; Walklate 2008). This has led to changes in how police are expected to respond to domestic violence incidents. There are now protocols in place and greater emphasis on victim safety. Policing during this time has also involved greater partnership working with other local agencies in order to intervene more effectively. This includes attending local multi-agency fora and attending case conferences. While police responses still vary, there have been a number of efforts to improve domestic violence responses by police in both the UK and Australia.

There have been changes to civil, family and criminal laws. Early legislative change involved the introduction of civil restraining or protection orders that prevent perpetrators being in the vicinity and making contact with the victim(s). These were introduced in the UK through the Domestic Violence and Matrimonial Proceedings Act 1976. In Australia there is similar legislation.[2, 3] In both nations this has been the main legal intervention to protect women and children from further domestic violence. This civil law remedy is focused on the need for the person(s) to be protected (Benitez et al. 2010). It is not within the criminal law realm of the perpetrator being charged with assault for domestic violence. The intention was that such orders enabled women to seek protection via the courts.

Time has shown, however, that it is often very difficult for women to go to court and have orders put in place for reasons including: courts are mostly a foreign and intimidating environment; victims fear it may increase the violence; and they fear seeing and facing the perpetrator in the court and surrounds. While they are the major legal response to domestic violence, there has also been long-standing criticism that civil restraining orders are not effective deterrents as men have frequently breached their orders with little or no consequence. For perpetrators subject to an intervention order deterrence has relied heavily on the fear of the consequences of breaching the order (Douglas 2007). Men least likely to comply with orders include those who have prior criminal histories (particularly those including violence) and/or who are considered high risk due to the level of controlling behaviour exhibited (Laing et al. 2013). This is an important point because while they are civil law court orders, a breach in conditions, e.g. making contact with the victim, is a criminal offence (Douglas 2007). The consequences for breaching the order can be serious, but if policing of breaches is inconsistent then women's safety remains compromised and their confidence in the law is eroded, so they may not even seek future protection.

Specialist domestic violence courts are another development introduced. The organisation of domestic violence courts varies across jurisdictions, some are diversionary and others are inclusive of sentencing when guilty of a domestic violence related offence. Key aspects of importance with regard to domestic violence courts are that they should provide a safe and appropriate space for victims when they are attending court, they receive information that is easily understood and they have the option for someone to support them in court and explain afterwards what will happen. Magistrates with expertise in domestic violence who hear the cases is a key feature, and court staff and processes that are safety focused. It is important to have referral and accountability processes so that men are assessed and referred to programmes for domestic violence as soon as possible. Courts working in partnership with agencies delivering services in the community can provide valuable coordinated responses.

This brief discussion of law enforcement and law reform has included the key responses to domestic violence. In short, the civil law protection orders and the criminalisation of domestic violence have been the main emphases in the UK and Australia to respond to domestic violence. Police responses to domestic violence have been subject to change over the past 30 years to better take account of the danger and the impact on those affected. While legal and law enforcement is not universally used in domestic violence, it has provided a major platform for change and saved lives.

Points for reflection

Imagine you are working with a woman who has decided she needs help leaving her house and finding somewhere to live as she can no longer stay with her abusive partner. What sort of information might you need about her circumstances? Conduct an internet search to identify information and support services that might be able to help. Would it make any difference to her options if she had two small children that also had to be accommodated? Why/why not? What does this suggest about housing services?

In both nations, leaving the family home is the main means by which women and accompanying children escape domestic violence.[4] Consequently, the earliest responses to domestic violence were women's refuges; the first opened in 1971 in England and 1974 in Australia. There are now two national bodies representing the refuge sector in the UK, Women's Aid and REFUGE. The Women's Aid Federation was established in 1974 involving 40 refuges across England. Women's Aid has provided a coordinating point for political and social action to raise awareness and improve responses. REFUGE established the first refuge in 1971 and has also been advocating for the rights of women and children. Women's refuges remain a pivotal service response as domestic violence is a major reason for women's homelessness.

National data about domestic violence and homelessness are generated from homelessness and social housing services providing information on their service usage. In the UK, women's refuges and related services are funded under the Supporting People Programme; in Australia, the same types of services are funded under the National Partnership Agreement on Homelessness. The Supporting People statistics show in 2011–2012, 11.3% of homelessness service use was due to 'people at risk of domestic violence'; in Australia, domestic or family violence was the most commonly reported reason for accessing homelessness services at 26%, and especially among female service users (36%). As a direct result of violence and abuse, the majority of people seeking homeless services in Australia are female (59%) (AIHW 2012).

The necessity for women to leave the family home and effectively become homeless in order to try and live free of violence has led to many women being caught in long periods of transition, uncertainty and loss of income (Spinney and Blandy 2011; Chung et al. 2000; Murray 2002, 2008; Theobald 2011). Exposure to domestic violence has a legacy of poverty, homelessness and uncertain futures for its victims, all of which compound to further disadvantage women. As Murray (2008) eloquently argues, the unhelpful 'common sense' response of the community 'Well why doesn't she just leave?' completely ignores concerns such as where can she go, how will she get there, how will she afford it, how will she transport anything she owns? Murray (2008: 67) notes reasons other than the physical aspects, such as 'financial dependence on their partner, their lack of knowledge of or access to appropriate support services to assist them or their fear of what their partner may do to them if they did leave'. Other reasons include the cultural significance of marriage and coupledom and the stigmatising isolation being outside these arrangements; a belief in children living with their fathers 'even if there are problems'; and continuing love and feelings for a male partner who women hope will change.

When women do try to leave they are often confronted with being unable to access refuge accommodation as demand has always outstripped supply. For example, in 2012, Women's Aid (2012) estimated that 27,900 women were unable to access the first refuge where they sought help. Of those women who are able to access refuges they might remain there for long periods as they are unable to access safe, affordable, stable and appropriate housing. While lack of affordable housing is an international problem, the gendered dimension for women can be a further burden as they may have insecure income, dependent children and often suffer the traumatic effects of violence which impact on their health.

Over a decade ago, I undertook my first research project on domestic violence and homelessness. I am still struck by how this quote from a woman with two children still captures the reality of many (Chung et al. 2000: i):

> Why do we women live in refuges when the perpetrators live in the comfort to which they are accustomed? Why must we three eke out a living on a pension of $330 per week of which $130 goes in rent while my husband lives on his salary of $750 per week of which $85 goes on the mortgage and lives alone in a four bedroom, two bathroom house?

Unsurprisingly, many women return to the family home at least once to see if things can improve (Chung et al. 2000; Murray 2008). For many women, they are homeless on a number of occasions before finally leaving. The injustice of the situation is striking whereby a woman has been a victim of crime yet she is expected to leave home while the perpetrator of the crime remains in the home. Spinney and Blandy (2011: 16) explain the unintended consequences of having a refuge system:

> Domestic and family violence refuges have played a pivotal role both in Australia and internationally in keeping women and children safe, and in empowering and enabling them to restart their lives. However, an unintended impact of this has been to 'normalise' the situation where women and children were the ones who were expected to become homeless in order to leave a violent relationship. This became the dominant perspective for over 30 years, and has coloured how policy responses to domestic and family violence have been developed during that time.

Intervention types have expanded beyond the high security refuge model to have outreach approaches whereby women living with their partners are provided with support and safety planning. This gives women a connection for support so some can make a more planned exit from the home. Both governments have introduced initiatives where the perpetrator is removed from the home and the woman (and children) remain. These initiatives are known variously as Safe at Home and Sanctuary (Spinney 2012). The programmes are not intended to replace refuges, nor are they a universal option, but are viewed as a means of preventing some women's and children's homelessness (Spinney and Blandy 2011).

Programme participation commonly has a number of criteria such as:

- The woman wishes to remain in her home.[5]
- The woman can financially afford to remain in the home.
- Safety planning occurs which assesses the woman is safe to remain.
- A restraining order or similar is in place so that the perpetrator has to remain away from the property.
- Support services will continue to be in place to provide support and assess woman's safety (Brady 2012).

The programmes have a number of agencies working in partnership. These include police and justice services to ensure intervention and exclusion orders are in place and consistent responses to breaches which do not jeopardise victim safety. There are support and housing services working with women to engage in safety planning and support so they remain safe. Risk assessment is critical to ensure safety is not compromised. One important component is having the locks changed and safety upgraded. This has often been prohibitive due to cost for women, however this element should not form a stand-alone programme as it cannot take account of safety comprehensively. Spinney (2012) found partnership working between agencies was the bedrock of programmes. She argues an understanding of domestic violence dynamics, risks and a consistent response are central for all agency partners.

Since the refuges of the 1970s, there has been considerable development: refuges have expanded into national networks, outreach and Sanctuary programmes are available alongside policy development by mainstream government organisations in policing, courts, housing and social services. With more agencies involved the necessity of partnership working and coordinated responses is central so that important information is shared and situations comprehensively assessed and interventions planned. In the following section the growing emphasis on partnership working is examined.

Partnership working and coordinated responses to domestic violence

Services working together to reduce possible duplication, minimise gaps and promote consistency has been asserted since the 1970s in social policy. For example, Lord Laming's UK reports are reflective of a long history of similar concerns in both nations. Domestic violence policy and practice is not unique in trying to attain this end.

One dynamic of domestic violence is the number of people affected by any one situation, and consequently, a number of agencies can be involved. Women victims may access various support, statutory and legal services, responses to men using violence include the police, courts and men's programmes, as well as services for children. This prompted practitioners to identify how they could better coordinate. Often this began as individual practitioners discussing how to improve things for victims and overcome barriers in service delivery. Contemporary partnership working was driven by bottom-up developments from practice. Barriers then included agencies' confidentiality policies prohibiting active multi-agency case discussions (and still do in some instances), variation in agencies' assessments to identify domestic violence risk and differing understandings of domestic violence and how to best intervene.

Points for reflection

Lord Laming's words below while referring to children and young people, are equally relevant for the protection of women and children living with domestic violence.

Despite considerable progress in interagency working, often driven by Local Safeguarding Children Boards and multi-agency teams who strive to help children and young people, there remain significant problems in the day-to-day reality of working across organisational boundaries and cultures, sharing information to protect children and a lack of feedback when professionals raise concerns about a child. Joint working between children's social workers, youth workers, schools, early years, police and health too often depends on the commitment of individual staff and sometimes this happens despite, rather than because of, the organisational arrangements. (2009: 10–11)

As a social worker working with schools, teachers are concerned and frustrated about the behaviour of two six- and eight-year-old siblings – they exhibit both aggressive and withdrawn behaviour and do not socialise with their peers. You think they may be living with domestic violence, your interviews with the children confirm this as they describe their mother being assaulted to you. The mother and father do not have regular contact with the teachers. You are concerned for the mother's and children's safety. What would you plan to do as you know nothing about the parents, and the mother may already be seeking help? What would be your next steps and what do you think might be the challenges you would face in partnership working with a range of services in this situation?

There are some common approaches to partnership or coordinated[6] domestic violence practice in the UK and Australia. The most influential model, developed by Ellen Pence in Duluth in North America,[7] has provided guidance for UK and Australian developments (Shepard and Pence 1999). Some key tenets are:

- Core set of agencies participating (statutory, voluntary, specialist and mainstream agencies).
- Localised geographical basis.
- Agreed understanding of domestic violence and good practice to promote women's and children's safety.
- Protocols and procedures between agencies for information sharing, common risk assessment and agreed joint actions in response to high risk.
- Improving partnerships requires constant review and feedback.

Other models of practice include the UK developed Multi-Agency Risk Assessment Conference (MARAC) which operates in various local authorities. It is similar to Duluth concerning multi-agency working, information sharing, agreed actions and accountability between agencies. In some areas only families identified as being at high risk are subjects of MARAC and in other areas it targets a wider group.[8] The aim of coordinated responses is to stop further violence, and prevent escalation and fatalities (Laing et al. 2013).

Partnership working and coordinated responses to domestic violence have become the accepted basis for service development to provide comprehensive and consistent responses. The majority of coordinated responses are focused on crisis and early points of contact; as we move further to the medium- and long-term needs of those affected the levels of support and coordination taper, as is common with many social and health services. National policy directives signify the importance of responding to domestic violence and support coordinated responses. However, on a daily basis the complex dynamics of domestic violence and the wide range of potential service providers to engage in a coordinated response make the outcomes of partnership working a continuing work in progress.

Some contemporary challenges in responding to domestic violence as a social policy problem

There has been a considerable growth in domestic violence knowledge as policy and practice has developed. In this final section, some aspects about the diversity of women experiencing domestic violence are considered to stimulate critical thinking about how policy and practice need to extend in the future.

Domestic violence affects all groups within society, however some groups are notably absent or disproportionally small in number among those accessing domestic violence services. Practitioners and researchers are increasingly aware of how the diversity of women's social locations, experiences and subsequent needs shapes service use. Early responses to diversity were focused on Black, minority ethnic, refugee and Indigenous populations of women. This has led to specialist services for some of these groups of women as it was recognised that they had unique additional needs that could not be met by mainstream services (for example, Southall Black Sisters in England, refuges for South Asian women in the UK and Aboriginal women's refuges in Australia), as well as specialist bi-cultural workers within mainstream services who can support women from particular cultural backgrounds. There is a policy shift away from funding such specialist services and a preference for mainstream services to be inclusive,[9] this however overlooks the specialist knowledge of workers and agencies and the practices that have evolved to address specific needs.

Populations of women whose presence is small among service users include women with disabilities, mid-aged and older women and women in same-sex relationships. Other groups of women who have found it difficult to access domestic violence services are women experiencing a multiplicity of concerns which include poverty, substance misuse and mental ill-health (Laing et al. 2013).

The first study of domestic violence and disabled women in England and Wales highlighted the urgency for the domestic violence and disability sectors to work more closely together (Hague et al. 2010). The research confirmed a high prevalence of violence against disabled women from partners, family members or carers (in the home and institutions), and showed how the circumstances of disabled women 'hid' the violence from others or how people overlooked or were unaware of the abuse. For example, women without oral communication reported not being able to tell people about the abuse, others were often trapped in their homes so had little chance to seek help. The difficulties in accessing appropriate support services for safety and protection demonstrate the significance of all social workers and other professionals being aware of domestic violence and able to identify and respond to risk.

In relation to mid-aged and older women, data indicate women 45 years and over represent fewer that 20% of all females accessing refuge services (AIHW 2012). This contrasts with demographic trends of an increasing ageing population. Research has shown a number of older women did not define their situations as domestic violence; some women but considered remaining married very important; while others reported pressure from adult children to remain in the relationship and that leaving would split family loyalties (Morgan and Disney 2001). Research has found that older women may be financially unable to leave the relationship as they have no money of their own; some were unaware of support services; health and other professionals never screened for domestic violence; and others reported that they would not be comfortable using refuge services which predominantly house younger women with children (Straka and Montiminy 2006). Band-Winterstein and Eisikovits (2009) importantly note that while statistics indicate that older couples 'age out' of violence, the empirical data with older people show this to be inaccurate with violence continuing into old age. All authors argue the importance of a specialist response which cuts across social services and older people's services and includes an understanding of domestic violence and the unique situation of older people who may remain in their relationships (Band-Winterstein and Eisikovits. 2009; Morgan and Disney 2001; Straka and Montiminy 2006).

There are some specialised services established to deal with areas such as domestic violence and substance misuse, however the services are small in number. Therefore to have their needs met many women have to access multiple services across a complex service system with differing eligibility criteria, remits, service types, availability and costs making navigation of these difficult at best and impossible at worst. Unfortunately, women's lives cannot be simply 'case managed' into their component parts, e.g. substance misuse by one service, parenting support by another and domestic violence by another, because what makes needs complex is the interacting and intersecting of all these elements. Therefore it is about how do services support women 'at these intersections'. For the social worker this means that they need a working knowledge of how to support people confronting these complexities not just knowledge about one area and skills in case management.

Conclusion

Domestic violence policy and practice has come a long way from its early traditions. It is a case study in how activists can influence state actors to progress social policy. Some of the early services remain important although they are changing as knowledge grows and are not in their original form. It was important for domestic violence to become a priority of the mainstream agencies in order to aid women's safety and protection. However, it was never intended that this be at the expense of specialist services and practice. At the moment both coexist in the UK and Australia, however smaller specialist services are finding it increasingly difficult to survive with contracting out which can favour large mainstream services. The UK and Australia currently have very similar policy and practice and there are similar challenges. To address the complexity of domestic violence and diversities of women victims requires a reorientation to a wider evidence base to inform social policy-making alongside the capacity to develop policy across departments. This has the potential to develop programmes and practice based on responding to the complexity. In practice, this would support a combined approach with mainstream services where there is a high level of awareness and consistent first-line response, practitioners with contemporary knowledge about domestic violence and specialist services and practitioners able to respond to the needs of victims.

Notes

1. Domestic violence is also known as 'intimate partner violence' and 'family violence'.
2. Such orders are known variously as protection orders, domestic violence orders, intervention order and so on, all with the same intent.
3. As the vast majority of perpetrators of domestic violence are male and interventions are currently directed towards men, the term 'him' has been used.
4. Domestic violence is the second most common reason for accessing homeless services in the UK and the most common reason in Australia.
5. Not all people wish to remain in their homes as they may find continuing to live in the house where they have experienced the violence distressing and traumatising.
6. The terms 'partnership' and 'coordinated approaches' are used interchangeably in the literature. In essence, the approach is aimed at multiple agencies and workers cooperating and sharing information in the assessment and support of individuals and families affected by domestic violence. For example, the structures of coordination include information sharing so that all involved have full information to make assessments, joint assessments and case conferences as well as high risk protocols associated with the need to respond promptly and comprehensively where there is a risk to safety.
7. Often referred to as the Duluth model.
8. For more information on MARAC, see: www.caada.org.uk/marac/Information_about_MARACs.html
9. This is not to suggest that mainstream services were not racially and culturally inclusive in their service access and support previously, but it was not their specific remit to develop expertise in such areas.

References

Australian Institute of Health and Welfare (AIHW) (2012) *Specialist Homelessness Services 2011–12*. Cat. No. HOU 267. Canberra: AIHW.

Bacchi, C. (2009) *Analysing Policy: What's the Problem Represented to Be?* French's Forest, NSW: Pearson Education Australia.

Band-Winterstein, T. and Eisikovits, Z. (2009) '"Aging out"' of violence: The multiple faces of intimate violence over the life span', *Qualitative Health Research*, 19 (2): 164–180.

Benitez, C., McNiel, D. and Binder, R. (2010) 'Do protection orders protect?', *Journal of American Academy of Psychiatry and the Law,* 38 (3): 376–385.

Brady, C. (2012) 'Rush safe at home program: Staying housed and safe', *Parity*, 25 (9): 46–47.

Breckenridge, J. and Laing, L. (1999) *Challenging Silence: Innovative Responses to Sexual and Domestic Violence.* St Leonards: Allen & Unwin.

Burton, S., Regan, L. and Kelly, L. (1998) *Supporting Women and Challenging Men: Lessons from the Domestic Violence Intervention Project.* Bristol: Policy Press.

Chung, D., Kennedy, R., O'Brien, B. and Wendt, S. (2000) *Home Safe Home: The Link between Domestic and Family Violence and Women's Homelessness.* Canberra: Department of Social Services, Australian Government.

Council of Australian Governments (COAG) (2013) *The National Plan to Reduce Violence against Women and their Children.* Canberra: COAG.

Douglas, H. (2007) 'Not a crime like any other: Sentencing breaches of domestic violence', *Criminal Law Journal*, 31: 200–233.

Gelles, R. (1976) 'Abused wives: Why do they stay?', *Journal of Marriage and the Family,* 38 (4): 659–668.

Hague, G., Thiara, R., Mullender, A. and Magowan, P. (2010) *Making the Links: Disabled Women and Domestic Violence Final Report.* Bristol: Women's Aid Federation, UK.

Hamner, J., Radford, J. and Stanko, E. (1989) *Women, Policing and Male Violence.* London: Routledge.

Hester, M. (2006) 'Making it through the Criminal Justice System: Attrition and domestic violence', *Social Policy and Society*, 5: 79–90.

HM Government (2010) *A Call to End Violence against Women and Girls.* London: The Stationery Office.

Laing, L., Humphreys, C. and Cavanagh, K. (2013) *Social Work and Domestic Violence: Developing Critical and Reflective Practice.* London: Sage.

Laming, H. (2009) *The Protection of Children in England: A Progress Report.* London: House of Commons.

Morgan, E. and Disney, H. (2001) *Two Lives – Two Worlds: Older People and Domestic Violence*, Partnerships Against Domestic Violence. Canberra: Commonwealth of Australia.

Murray, S. (2002) *More than Refuge: Changing Responses to Domestic Violence.* Perth: University of Western Australia Press.

Murray, S. (2008) '"Why doesn't she just leave?" Belonging, disruption and domestic violence', *Women's Studies International Forum*, 31 (1): 65–72

Murray, S. and Powell, A. (2011) *Domestic Violence: Australian Public Policy.* Melbourne: Australian Scholarly Publishing.

Scutt, J. (1995) 'Judicial bias or legal bias? Battery, women and the law', *Journal of Australian Studies*, 19 (43): 130–143.

Shepard, M.F. and Pence, E.L. (1999) *Coordinating Community Responses to Domestic Violence: Lessons from Duluth and Beyond.* London: Sage.

Spinney, A. (2012) *Home and Safe? Policy and Practice Innovations to Prevent Women and Children who have Experienced Domestic and Family Violence from Becoming Homeless.* Australian Housing and Urban Research Institute Swinburne Research Centre AHURI Final Report No. 196.

Spinney, A. and Blandy, S. (2011) 'Homelessness prevention for women and children who have experienced domestic and family violence: innovations in policy and practice', AHURI Positioning Paper No. 140, Australian Housing and Urban Research Institute (AHURI), Melbourne.

Straka, S.M. and Montminy, L. (2006) 'Responding to the needs of older women experiencing domestic violence', *Violence Against Women,* 12 (3): 251–267.

Theobald, J. (2011) 'A History of the Victorian Women's Domestic Violence Services Movement: 1974–2005'. PhD Thesis, RMIT University, Melbourne.

Walklate, S. (2008) 'What is to be done about violence against women? Gender, violence, cosmopolitanism and the law', *British Journal of Criminology*, 48 (1): 39–54.

Women's Aid (2012) *Cuts in Refuge Services Putting Vulnerable Women and Children at Risk.* 27 Nov 2012. Available at: www.womensaid.org.uk/domestic-violence-press-information.asp?itemid=2944&itemTitle=Cuts+in+refuge+services+putting+vulnerable+women+and+children+at+risk&section=0001000100150001&sectionTitle=Press+releases (accessed 29 July 2015).

10

Local Policy in a Global Context: Regimes of Risk in Mental Health Policy and Practice – The Case of Community Treatment Orders

Hannah Jobling

Introduction

It has long been argued that the rise of risk and an associated emphasis on methods of control have been the key trends in UK mental health policy and practice over the past two decades (Campbell et al. 2006; Kemshall 2002). Most recently in England,[1] the Mental Health Act 2007 became a focal point for debate about the place of coercion in mental health practice, with critics concluding that the Act was a lost opportunity for a more enlightened approach to mental health care (Daw 2007) and a 'doggedly authoritarian' piece of legislation (Pilgrim and Ramon 2009: 278) primarily concerned with public safety. Much valuable work has been done on tracing the legal, historical, cultural and institutional roots of the Mental Health Act, in order to understand how it developed in the face of significant opposition by professional and service user groups (see Daw 2007; Fennell 2005; Pilgrim 2007; Pilgrim and Ramon 2009; Prins 2008).

In this chapter, those accounts of the mental health policy-making process will be extended, using the concept of policy transfer as the framework for discussion of a contentious aspect of the Mental Health Act, the inclusion of community treatment orders (CTOs). Broadly summarised, policy transfer refers to the process 'in which knowledge about policies, administrative arrangements, institutions, etc. in one time and/or place is used in the development of polices, administrative arrangements and institutions in another time and/or place' (Dolowitz and Marsh

1996: 344). CTOs provide a good illustration of this process as their implementation has grown rapidly in the last 25 years, becoming embedded in the mental
health policy regimes of a wide range of countries.

The first section of the chapter gives an overview of what CTOs are, how they
have evolved over the years and how they fit into a wider discourse of risk management in mental health. The second section describes further the concept of policy
transfer before applying it to how CTOs came to exist in England. The third section concentrates on the meaning of this policy transfer for policy and practice, by
comparing the different ways CTOs have been enacted internationally. The chapter
concludes by considering what implications the form CTOs have taken 'locally' in
England may have for mental health practitioners in general and social workers in
particular.

Community treatment orders: Definitions and development

CTOs give mental health professionals the power to impose conditions on how
certain service users live in the community, particularly in regard to medical treatment, and provide a mechanism for detention and treatment enforcement if these
conditions are not met or if the service user's mental health has deteriorated to
the extent that they are deemed to be a risk to the health and safety of themselves
or others. Modern mental health services, both in the community and in hospital,
have always contained elements of compulsion and coercion, which can be seen
as forming a continuum, from informal persuasion through to formally mandated
hospital treatment (Monahan et al. 2001). However, a distinction can be made
between the undefined and discretionary use of treatment pressure in the community and the legislatively defined role of CTOs. As Churchill et al. (2007: 20)
state, CTOs are qualitatively different from what has gone before in the countries
where they have been implemented because they 'enforce community treatment
outside (and independently) of the hospital, contain specific mechanisms for
enforcement and/or revocation and are authorised by *statute*' (original emphasis).
Opinion on CTOs is strongly divided, with opponents fearing that an extension
of compulsion into the community may result in unnecessary coercion, a loss of
liberty and rights for service users, and the neglect of alternative, less coercive
methods of engagement (Brophy and McDermott 2003; Geller et al. 2006; May
et al. 2003; Mental Health Alliance 2007; Pilgrim 2007). Conversely, supporters
of CTOs argue that they will help to engage service users who are hard to reach
and/or considered a risk, facilitate community-focused care, reduce rates and
length of detention, encourage better treatment, improve clinical outcomes and
promote recovery (Lawton-Smith et al. 2008; Munetz and Frese 2001; O'Reilly
2006). Social workers in England play a significant role in CTO implementation
as both Approved Mental Health Professionals and care coordinators, including:
advising service users and carers on what the CTO means and what their rights
are; monitoring service users who are on CTOs; providing a social perspective in
key decisions such as recall of a service user to hospital; and generating social

circumstances reports for tribunals. Their roles overlap with that of other social workers who have a broader remit such as facilitating and enabling access to statutory social care and support recovery and inclusion through partnership working with service users and communities.

International policy development

Internationally, CTOs have taken a number of different forms over the last 40 years. Ironically, given the human rights protestations they now engender, CTOs were initially developed as part of the patient rights movement in the USA during the 1960s and 1970s, as a way of maximising individual liberty by minimising involuntary hospitalisation (Hiday 2003). This 'first wave' of CTOs have been classified as 'least restrictive' (Churchill et al. 2007), as they effectively allowed for compulsory community care under the same legal criteria as compulsory inpatient care, thus creating an alternative to detention. However, 'least restrictive' CTOs were little used as it became evident that it was politically and practically unviable to treat people in the community who met the risk criteria for detention in hospital.

In response to these constraints on their use, a new kind of CTO, the 'preventative' CTO, became prevalent from the 1980s (Churchill et al. 2007). Preventative CTOs have lower thresholds for use, and instead of being an alternative to inpatient detention, became a way of compulsorily treating individuals in the community either following their release from hospital, or before they reached the threshold for involuntary treatment. Preventative CTOs thus have different legislative criteria from involuntary inpatient treatment and are often aimed at specifically targeted individuals, usually those defined as 'revolving door' patients who have a history of non-compliance and who go through rapid and continuous cycles of release from hospital, deterioration and re-detainment. In this sense, preventative CTOs are more explicitly concerned with risk management both for the individual and for society rather than the earlier aim of promoting civil liberty (Hiday 2003). It is this type of CTO that has become most widespread and formed the foundation for the development of CTOs as they are used currently.

There is no definitive list of where preventative CTOs have been enacted, but a review of the literature suggests that they are in place in around 70 jurisdictions, including in most US states by 1994 (Torrey and Kaplan 1995), in all Australian states by 1999 (Power 1999), Israel in 1991 (Bar et al. 1998), New Zealand in 1992, Canada in 1994, Scotland in 2005, almost all US states by 2006 (Churchill et al. 2007) and England and Wales in 2008. CTOs then, arrived in two sequential phases, the 1990s and the mid-2000s, and seem predominantly to be enacted in countries with similar cultural backgrounds, and in the case of the Commonwealth countries, legal heritage. Less widely reported is their use in secondary English-speaking European countries; Norway has had preventative CTOs in place since the 1960s, but became a rare example of a state revising the law to enable least restrictive CTOs in 2001 and Sweden legislated for CTOs in 2008 (Sjostrom et al. 2011). Switzerland and the Netherlands have also been reported to have CTOs (Dawson 2005; Kortrijk et al. 2010).

Policy drivers

CTOs are complex policy interventions which encompass a shifting range of legal and medical mechanisms dependent on the cultural and societal norms of the jurisdiction in which they are enacted. A signifier of this is the wide range of terms used to refer to CTOs dependent on country, including involuntary outpatient treatment, mandated outpatient commitment and compulsory community care, to name a few. However, despite differences between countries, it is still possible to highlight broad trends that have instigated what Brophy and McDermott (2003: 86) term a 'domino effect' in the global spread of compulsory community care. The expansion of CTOs in developed countries has arisen from an array of interacting factors, including the process of deinstitutionalisation, the increased focus on risk and community safety in mental health services, and the continuing dominance of a neurobiological discourse, which emphasises the use of drug treatment as a 'solution' to mental disorder. CTOs can thus be described as a consequence of the burgeoning movement towards community care in the last 50 years, combined with the perceived need to maintain some form of control through treatment over individuals deemed as posing a risk to themselves or others (Brophy 2009).

Deinstitutionalisation refers to the process in a number of western societies from the 1960s onwards, whereby the focus of mental health care moved from the 'total institution' of the asylum (Goffman 1961) to care in the community, driven by a combination of the growth of patient rights movements, the advent of anti-psychotic medication and the rising costs associated with inpatient care. While community care has provided many people with a better quality of life (Leff 1997), it has also been critiqued for letting down those service users who have characteristics that mean they struggle to survive in society and consequently have been left 'rotting with their rights on' (Appelbaum and Gutheil 1979; Novella 2010). Thus, particularly in countries such as the US where health care is more fragmented, CTOs have been positioned as a way of obligating services to provide quality care (Wagner et al. 2003).

As well as concerns about service users being abandoned to their fate, community care has become associated with public fears about insufficiently controlled individuals presenting a risk of harm to the community at large. Rose (2002a) describes how in this regard the focus of the debate has shifted over the years since the 1980s. Increasingly, instead of service failure being discussed in terms of the 'plight' of service users, it is now 'posed in terms of the failure of assessment, prediction, and management of risky individuals and the minimisation of risk to the community' (Rose 2002a: 216). CTOs as a tool for regular monitoring and medication compliance can thus be seen as a response to public concerns, most obviously in the North American practice of naming their introduction after the victim of homicide by a mentally disordered individual (for example, Brian's Law in Ontario, Kendra's Law in New York and Laura's Law in Florida). Sjostrom et al. (2011) describe how in Sweden, a number of high profile incidents in 2003 (including the death of a government minister), although not acted on by government at the time in terms of introducing more compulsory measures, did resurface in parliamentary discussion five years later, when CTOs were debated with reference to dangerousness being the primary concern. A similar narrative was evident in England, beginning in 1998 when the then Secretary of State for Health Frank Dobson proclaimed that 'community care has failed' (Dobson 1998). As with Sweden, the US and Canada, a spate of much reported homicides committed by individuals[2] in contact with mental health services provided impetus for policy reform, with the Home Office as well as the Department of Health shaping policy based on public safety. Institutional and external constraints including a sustained process of revision by the House of Lords and fierce opposition from pressure groups in response to consultation, meant it took nine years for the legislation to be passed. Despite these pressures, the position of the government remained consistent over time, as a Department of Health official was reported as saying, 'it was trench warfare' but 'there was never any wavering … [against] the stakeholders' position' (Cairney 2009: 681), including with the unpopular inclusion of CTOs. As the then Minister for Health Services Rosie Winterton made clear, the argument for CTOs was closely linked to risk:

> There are 1,300 suicides every year and 50 homicides by people who have been in contact with mental health services. We believe that supervised community treatment is vital to helping patient continue to take treatment when they leave hospital and to enable clinicians to take rapid action if relapse is on the horizon. (HC Hansard, Vol 461, col 1193, June 18, 2007)

However, it would be simplistic to suggest an overriding concern with risk was the sole driver behind policy-making on CTOs. CTOs have also been associated with a somewhat paternalistic version of the recovery approach in mental health, where it has been surmised they can act to provide a secure foundation for individuals to operate from and to encourage self-efficacy. Dawson (2009: 29) argues that this understanding of CTOs as enabling self-direction and choice is philosophically grounded in the concept of positive liberty, which he defines as 'our capacity for self-governance … our ability to set goals and have some chance of meeting them, and to maintain important relationships, without being dominated by internal constraints that prevent this occurring'. The framing of CTOs as a conduit for individual growth is most evident in Munetz and Frese's (2001) assertion that CTOs are reconcilable with the recovery model and indeed, can act as an opportunity for individuals to become well enough to start the recovery process. Sjostrom et al. (2011: 425) comment that even though adverse incidents provided the 'window' for CTOs to be introduced in Sweden, 'where the official rationale for the policy was eventually spelled out, it is striking to observe how reducing risk was pushed to the background by an agenda oriented towards treatment and rehabilitation'. Similarly in England, in parliamentary debate about CTOs, they were defended with recourse to rehabilitation:

> Supervised community treatment is a new, modern and effective way to manage the treatment of patients with serious mental health problems. It will allow patients, so far as possible, to live normal lives in the community. This will reduce the risk of social exclusion and stigma associated with detention in hospital for long periods of time or with repeated hospital admissions. (House of Commons Library 2007: 21)

Perhaps this disparity in stated policy aims reflects the need for policy to be 'sold' to different audiences, in this case both the public in regard to risk management and the professionals who will be implementing it in terms of clinical and social out-comes. However, underpinning the dual discourse on additional compulsory powers in the community is a characterisation of community mental health services as dif-ferentiating 'low risk' individuals who are 'empowered' to become responsible, autonomous and self-regulating members of society from 'high risk' individuals who require external regulation (Kemshall 2002). As Rose (1996: 12) emphasises, 'profes-sionals now are not so much required to cure as to teach the skills of coping, to inculcate the responsibility to cope, to identify failures of coping, to restore to the individual the capacity to cope'. If this is not possible, then the generation and shar-ing of risk knowledge through professional networks of communication and surveillance enact 'circuits of exclusion' in which the threat that 'high risk' individu-als pose within the 'territory of the community' is managed (Rose 1999: 262). Policies, programmes and interventions that develop to meet this requirement are, by their nature, preventative in their aims and objectives.

Within this framework, CTOs can be viewed as a mechanism which contains both inclusionary and exclusionary facets. CTOs enable the reformation of individ-uals and their conduct if possible, but also allow for control and separation of the individual from society and the application of sanctions, should this enterprise fail. Behaviour control in this sense is concerned with a more abstract conceptualisation of risk, where prudent individuals are expected to make their own way in society while complying with complex rules and requirements, or as Rose (2002b: 19) puts it in regard to mental health, '"play the game" of community care'. However, CTOs can also be viewed in a more concrete way as a preventative 'early detection' system for events yet to occur. Moreover, the defining characteristic of the CTO as a preventative community intervention means that it can be used for a broad range of risk-related reasons, including early intervention and thus encompass a large number of service users.

Policy transfer and CTOs

Delineating the possible policy drivers for CTOs helps us to understand how differ-ent countries may develop a similar rationale for the use of CTOs. This is necessary to contextualise policy-making, because as Hall (1993) suggests, the role of ideas and ideology needs to be accounted for in policy formation as the normative struc-ture that is taken for granted by the general policy-making community, but which nevertheless shapes what are viewed as policy problems to be solved. However, how these drivers led to the particular implementation of CTOs in England, rather than, for instance, the reinforcement of existing similar community provisions is less obvi-ous. Policy transfer may help to provide at least part of the explanation, although as will become evident, it is not a straightforward concept to apply to the policy-making process. This is partly because policy transfer was developed by Dolowitz and Marsh (1996) as a loose concept encompassing a wide range of activities, actors and ideas. As Evans (2009) describes, policy transfer can take many different theo-retical forms, including 'bandwagoning', social learning, convergence, diffusion, emulation and lesson-drawing. Evans (2009: 244) goes on to argue that to make the study of policy transfer meaningful, it should be limited to the analysis of 'action-oriented intentional learning: That which takes place consciously and results in policy action,' thus focusing on the actions of agents of transfer.

Demonstrating a causal process in policy transfer can be difficult, and involves disproving the hypothesis that similar policies in different jurisdictions are simply a result of unintentional policy convergence, for example, policy as a response to broad cultural shifts (Jones 2006). Taking the policy-making process as a whole, it would also be simplistic to suggest that policy transfer is the only factor at play in reform; Smith (2004) found dialectic movement between external and domestic influences in his study of climate policy, and Hudson and Lowe (2009) emphasise how policy transfer interrelates with institutions and policy networks to shape policy. Furthermore, Dolowitz (2009) suggests that it is important in the analysis of policy transfer to clarify whether the process has incorporated simple forms of learning such as copying of a policy or more complex learning such as the reformation and translation of concepts to a local context. In this way, he infers that structural constraints need to be considered alongside agency. Given the many issues that can arise when attempting to present policy transfer as an explanatory model, it is perhaps better to think of it as an 'analogical model' which adds to our understanding of policy development in particular domains, enabling new theories of change to be explored (Jones 2006: 33). In this regard, both Dolowitz and Marsh (2000) and Evans and Davies (1999) have outlined questions that are helpful to delineate the policy transfer process, and which will be used in this chapter in an amalgamated form to trace the policy transfer journey of CTOs in England.

Who are the agents of policy transfer?

Conceptions of agents of transfer emphasise pluralist governance, and the role of policy networks. Agents can therefore originate from a broad group of actors, from 'state players' such as politicians and bureaucrats, to policy entrepreneurs, academics, pressure groups, national, trans- and supra-international organisations (Stone 1999). Cairney's (2009: 681) research, which involved key informant interviews with those who played a part in the development of the Mental Health Act for England, concludes that there was 'often low ministerial interest, but consistently high commitment' to the core provisions, suggesting that elected officials were integral to keeping CTOs on the agenda. In this, they gained support from 'epistemic communities' (Haas 1992), a term that denotes 'communities … comprised of natural and social scientists or individuals from any discipline or profession with authoritative claims to policy relevant knowledge' who share similar beliefs and values (Evans 2009: 252). From the parliamentary debates and submissions to the Joint Committee on the Draft Mental Health Bill (House of Lords 2005a), it is evident that international experts informed government thinking on CTOs. Perhaps most interestingly, the opposition at the time expressed cynicism at the government's use of a 'predictable dozen' experts to regularly brief in a positive manner about CTOs, including researchers from the USA who had conducted favourable studies on CTOs (HC Hansard, Vol 461, col 1188, June 18, 2007).

Why do actors engage in policy transfer?

The lesson-drawing analogy used in policy transfer suggests a rational process of identifying policy problems, looking elsewhere to find solutions, before adapting said solutions to the local context (Dolowitz 2009). Certainly, CTOs were introduced during a time when the discourse of evidence-based policy was at its height, with the Cabinet Office (1999) proclaiming government 'must produce policies that really deal with problems; that are forward looking and shaped by evidence rather than a response to short-term pressures; that tackle causes not symptoms'. In this light, overseas experts and their research findings were playing a key role in providing technical advice in a policy area where little local knowledge could be drawn upon. An alternative reading, however, as intimated in the parliamentary debates, is that such evidence can help political actors legitimise change, by presenting 'policy lessons from abroad ... as politically neutral truths' (Robertson 1991: 55). Policy transfer therefore becomes more rhetorical rather than transformative (Dolowitz 2009). It is notable in the case of CTOs that the Department of Health commissioned a wide-ranging review of the international use of CTOs (Churchill et al. 2007), which concluded that there was little evidence to support either positive or negative outcomes for CTOs. That the government did not appear to incorporate any negative lesson-drawing from these findings suggests that their choice of expert advice was at least partly driven by political expediency. As Wolff (2002) argues in her analysis of the English mental health reform agenda, the policy problem – the purported failure of community care – was leading to policy solutions that were designed to mitigate political rather than actual risk. She goes on to suggest the government was managing the risk of 'error-in-judgement' by deploying experts to support their view, and the risks of 'ineffectiveness' and 'inactivity' by taking a 'shotgun approach' where in the absence of certainty about answers to the problem of 'troublesome' individuals in the community, a number of different initiatives, including CTOs, were going to be implemented at once in the hope that one of them would work. This can be characterised as defensive policy-making, where the government is seen to be trying all means possible to limit risk, even if certain strategies fail. The reasons why policy transfer is called upon, therefore, stems in the first instance from how policy problems are framed.

What conclusions can be drawn from the nature and extent of policy transfer?

Taking the nature of policy transfer first, Evans and Davies (1999) distinguish between 'soft' transfers, such as ideas, ideologies and attitudes and 'hard' transfers, such as tangible programmes and instruments. Dolowitz (2009) holds a slightly different perspective, arguing that 'hard' policy transfers are associated with voluntaristic, rationalist approaches to learning, whereas 'soft' transfers are more common, because the policy-making process is likely to be conditional on factors such as cultural biases, institutional frameworks and ideological predispositions that limit both what knowledge policy-makers recognise and what they can implement in the prevailing system. While CTOs are a commonly recognised policy instrument, the form they can take differs widely and an analysis of their characteristics in different jurisdictions would be necessary in order to infer a 'hard' programme transfer. Even so, from parliamentary speeches, we can see that proponents of CTOs used examples from a range of different policy regimes, and so perhaps the idea of what problems CTOs could solve mattered more than the mechanics of what they entailed. By taking this approach the link between policy form and outcome is downplayed, where 'policy objectives may be borrowed but the form of implementation, the tools and procedures adopted in various locales may result in quite different outcomes' (Stone 1999: 56). Indeed, if we move on to the second part of the question, the extent of policy transfer, CTOs can be seen as an example of policy hybridisation whereby elements of programmes from other regimes are combined to produce a culturally relevant policy, as opposed to direct copying or emulation (Evans 2009). An examination of the countries most called upon in English debates – the USA, Canada, Scotland, New Zealand and Australia – supports the common assertion that similar systems tend to be drawn upon in policy transfer to the neglect of others (Peck and Theodore 2010).

How good is the evidence to support a claim of policy transfer?

Bennett (1997) suggests that policy transfer can be surmised if it can be demonstrated that policy-makers are aware of the policy being used elsewhere and it can be shown that this knowledge was used in domestic policy debates. The discussion so far has highlighted instances that suggest both these tests were met in regards to CTOs. More specifically, alongside the utilisation of experts, two further themes are evident in the parliamentary debates: first, the use of other countries' experiences to highlight the liberal nature of the proposed regime in England; as Rosie Winterton stated (incorrectly): 'It is only in Canada that it is necessary for a patient to be detained before going on to a CTO. Even in those circumstances, the detention need not take place immediately beforehand, as it must under our proposals' (HC Hansard, Vol 461, col 1190, June 18, 2007). Second, that if so many other jurisdictions are using them, despite evidence to the contrary, they must be doing something right, as Lord Warner, a Minister of State in the Department of Health at the time argued: 'Whatever the detailed reservations about particular studies, they do not set aside ... the clear positives I have mentioned. It is perhaps significant that other countries have not ceased using CTOs, and have continued to see benefits in using them' (HL Hansard, January 2007). The use of an international context thus positioned CTOs as a modern, normative and reasonable response to community care.

It is easier to evaluate how good the evidence for transfer is than it is to analyse the ensuing question of the evidence for non-transfer, for example if elements of a programme have been derived from domestic history rather than from overseas lessons. Pathway dependency can act as a constraint on policy transfer, as 'policy makers are inheritors before they are choosers ... new programs cannot be constructed on greenfield sites ... they must be introduced into a policy environment dense with past commitments' (Rose 1993: 78). In the case of CTOs, their evolution in England can be traced back to the late 1980s when the Royal College of Psychiatrists proposed introducing CTOs and the Conservative government legislated for supervised discharge in 1995 as a watered down response, widely believed to lack the level of compulsion necessary to ensure adherence to treatment (Holloway 1996). When CTOs resurfaced in the late 1990s to address this issue, they were substantially different to what eventually became legislation; essentially the original CTOs allowed for the clinician to choose whether to compulsorily treat an individual in the community or in hospital and were called 'non-resident' and 'resident' orders to reflect this. Sustained lobbying on the practical and more importantly, ethical consequences of forced community treatment led to the revised 'compromise' version we see now. What this policy narrative demonstrates is that the shape of CTOs has been partly determined by an overarching and consistent concern in domestic mental health policy-making with what balance needs to be taken in regard to rights and risk. However, where that balance lies is open to external influence; the European Convention on Human Rights was cited by opponents to the original CTOs, and as the government would have been aware due to their review of legislation elsewhere, 'The line that emerges from the study of ... statutes ... as the Rubicon that should *not* be crossed, is the authorisation of "forced medication" in community settings' (Dawson 2005: 149, original emphasis). It is by studying the pathways of policies therefore, that the intersections between local and global influences can be illuminated.

By using these questions to analyse the policy transfer of CTOs we can see that alongside state actors, other key agents included members of 'epistemic communities', drafted in to fill gaps in policy knowledge and more significantly to support the prevailing policy narrative. This secondary purpose suggests that CTOs, despite their tangible nature, represent more of a 'soft' transfer, with the ideas behind their use being more important than their actual form. In turn, their use could be constituted as a synthesising of different policy regimes that are similar enough to enable the adaptation of CTOs to a domestic context. It is not always easy to evidence whether policy transfer actually takes place, but by undertaking a reading of parliamentary debate and policy history, it is possible to come to an understanding of both how experiences elsewhere influence policy, and how this influence is delimited by local structural factors. Bennett's tests (1997), however, should not be taken at face value; a further way of thinking through policy transfer in regard to CTOs involves moving beyond discourse to exploring the actual similarities and differences between policy regimes.

Policy regimes compared

In a helpful paper, Dawson (2006) used the metaphor of 'fault-lines' in order to contrast the divergent treatment of key concepts in CTO legislation across countries. He mentions, among others, the principles of capacity and reciprocity, and the prerequisites for use of a CTO. Additional differences that can be considered are how risk is dealt with and what oversight of the system exists. Taking forward the point that English policy-makers paid most attention to the experiences of Canada, the USA, Australia, New Zealand and Scotland,[3] this section will compare those countries in reference to the above concepts. Table 10.1 provides an overview of the analysis.

Table 10.1 A framework for assessing the differences between CTO policy regimes

| | Capacity clause? | Risk level | Reciprocity clause? | Constraints on discretion | |
				Conditions for use	Judicial approval
England	No	Low	No	Weak	No
Victoria, Australia	No	Low	No	Weak	No
New Zealand	No	Medium	No	Weak	No
Western Australia	No	Medium	No	Weak	No
New South Wales, Australia	No	Low	Yes	Medium	Yes
Scotland	Yes	Medium	Yes	Weak	Yes
Saskatchewan, Canada	Yes	Medium	Yes	Medium	No
Ontario, Canada	Yes	High	Yes	Medium	No
USA	Yes	High	Yes	Strong	Yes

Capacity

Capacity refers to the ability of individuals to make informed decisions about their treatment (Appelbaum 1998). The inclusion of capacity criteria in CTO legislation tends to reflect a general approach to capacity in mental health in that particular country. For instance, in the USA and Canada only those individuals deemed without capacity can be treated without their consent in hospital, and the same principle applies to whether CTOs can be imposed. This aligns mental health law with the ethical principles of autonomy and competence held in general health care, and consequently 'removes the suggestion that the law discriminates against mentally disordered people when it applies less favourable rules to their psychiatric treatment' (Dawson 2006: 486). However, including a strong capacity clause may preclude a preventative, longitudinal approach to treatment, which can take account of the fluctuating nature of mental health (Fistein et al. 2009). Hence, the recently reformulated mental health legislation in Scotland (2003) has included a lower threshold for capacity, which goes some way to meeting both clinical 'best interest' principles and the principle of autonomy, as it requires that a patient's decision-making ability must be 'significantly impaired' due to their mental disorder before any formal use of compulsion, including CTOs, takes place. In this sense, Scottish and English mental health law have diverged, with the English government explicitly stating it did not see the merit of including a capacity clause in the new Act on the basis that it may enable individuals who pose a risk but nonetheless maintain capacity, to refuse treatment (DH 2005). English law is most similar to Australasian statutes, where criteria for CTOs are based on the presence of mental disorder and an associated risk of harm, with no mention of capacity.

Risk

In North America, the threshold is set high for risk, with probability of 'dangerousness' and risk of 'serious harm' featuring widely, and a number of states requiring evidence of previous violence to initiate a CTO. The criterion for what constitutes risk in English mental health law, including for CTOs, is broad and largely undefined, referring to whether an individual poses a risk to the 'health and safety' of themselves or others. Fistein et al. (2009: 152) argue that when no capacity test is adopted, a stringent risk test should be adopted to counterbalance its absence, and vice versa. This would 'avoid overly paternalistic treatment of people who are able to make their own decisions' while protecting against potential serious harm. The flexible criterion for risk in the new Act, combined with the lack of a capacity test, sets a worryingly low threshold for compulsion. Indeed, the new Act is placed near the bottom of the table rating autonomy in mental health legislation in Commonwealth countries. As has been noted (Lawton-Smith 2005) in some jurisdictions such as in Australia, a 'low-risk-no-capacity' CTO regime may have contributed to an increasing and defensive use of community compulsion, and there are concerns a similar process is occurring in England (Care Quality Commission 2010).

Reciprocity

One way of justifying the use of compulsion in the community is to include a reciprocity clause in legislation, so the individual who is subject to a CTO would at least gain some benefit from their status (Wales and Hiday 2006). The principle of reciprocity can be incorporated into CTO criteria through the inclusion of arrangements for outpatient care and social support. CTOs therefore become contracts that work both ways, by binding services to provide quality care as well as compelling individuals to engage. The USA, Canada and Scotland have the strongest duties imposed on services to provide care and support, whereas Australasian jurisdictions implement weaker criteria with no reciprocal arrangements specified, aside from New South Wales (Churchill et al. 2007). In Scotland, there is a duty placed upon clinicians to inform a tribunal if services as per the care plan are not being delivered, and the tribunal can revoke the CTO on this basis, although even with this procedure in place, it is questionable how much it is being implemented (Royal College of Psychiatrists 2009). In England, when the legislation was in process, the Parliamentary Committee that oversaw the Bill argued that the Scottish model should be followed and services should be guaranteed to those on a CTO as an obligation, so that extended compulsion could not be imposed without an associated level of care (House of Lords 2005b). However, there is not a direct reference to provision of community services in the CTO criteria, and the government argued that it was not necessary in an Act for which the prime purpose is to enforce treatment without consent (DH 2005). In further support of their approach, the government stated that those on a CTO would in any case be entitled to Section 117 aftercare services, which place a duty on health and local authorities to provide an appropriate level of free support and accommodation to discharged patients. However, it has become clear over the years that the provision of Section 117 aftercare is not consistently applied and legal challenges have suggested that health and local authorities have a large amount of discretion in deciding what counts as appropriate, given resource limitations (Bartlett and Sandland 2007). It is for precisely this reason that Dawson (2006) suggests jurisdictions such as New Zealand have weak and carefully drafted duties of care for service providers in CTO legislation, in order to avoid liability should they fail to provide services. By making changes to mental health law in terms of compulsion but not service obligations, it appears that England has followed suit.

Discretion

Discretion in the case of CTOs refers to the ability of a mental health practitioner to make judgements on when to use them and how to use them. The legislation on CTOs can constrain or enable this in two ways: first, by the number and type of conditions that have to be met before a CTO can be used; and, second, through the level of oversight that CTOs are subject to. Preconditions include risk and capacity criteria as already described, but also whether an individual must have a history of hospitalisation and/or has been given the opportunity to engage voluntarily. In Canada and the USA, CTO legislation generally stipulates that a person has to have been detained for a certain period of time, or number of occasions in the past two years and in addition, most US states include a clause that individuals must have been given the chance to participate of their own accord. Similar provision is made in New South Wales, but the rest of the Australasian jurisdictions and Scotland do not mention hospitalisation or prior engagement at all in their legislation. The criteria for English CTOs also leave considerable room for clinician discretion. As Peay (2003: 118) states, mental health law in England operates through a system of *parens patriae* in that it is 'highly reliant on the judgement of the practitioners who are required to apply it' and it appears that the new legislation maintained this tradition. This is particularly evident in the lack of specific criteria for identifying which individuals should be made subject to CTOs, beyond stating that a person must have been subject to a Section 3 or 37 immediately prior to the CTO. It is noteworthy that despite reassurances that CTOs were aimed at a small, targeted group of 'revolving door' service users, the government overturned amendments to the legislation attempted in the House of Lords which would have ensured CTOs could not be applied to a broader group, stating that 'it would immediately risk excluding patients who might benefit ... and would fetter clinical judgment' (HL Hansard, Vol 693, col 842, July 2, 2007). In terms of oversight, only a few of the jurisdictions (New South Wales, Scotland and the USA) require that practitioners must apply to a court with evidence in order to secure a CTO. While England has a rather complex framework for legal oversight once the CTO is in place, initially an individual can be discharged entirely at the discretion of specified professionals. Following a judicial process can protect service user rights and ensures treatment is 'proportionate', but it also places an extra administrative burden on the system (Dawson 2006).

Through comparing the CTO as it has been defined in England with other countries, the nature of what has been implemented in England becomes clearer. It is evident that if CTOs were placed on a spectrum from those that contain a higher legislative threshold for use (USA, Canada, Scotland) to those where the threshold is low and clinician discretion plays a large part (majority of Australasia), the English CTO would be included in the latter group. As has been noted (Dawson 2006; Lawton-Smith 2005), 'looser' CTO legislation is a key factor in enabling high levels of usage and therefore it is not altogether unexpected that CTOs have been implemented in relatively large numbers in England (Care Quality Commission 2012). The concluding section discusses what the other implications of such a broad framework might be.

CTOs in England: Some final remarks

CTOs characterised by wide-ranging features could encourage the continuing evolution of deinstitutionalisation, with it being reported that the implementation of CTOs in New Zealand has resulted in treatment shifting to a greater extent from the hospital to the community (Dawson 2006). Moreover, a more restrictive framework that limits discretion can bring its own risks especially if CTO policy is viewed as a devolutionary mechanism to pass responsibility to the practice level (Lawton-Smith et al. 2008). Conversely, an emphasis on clinical judgement might result in those made subject to a CTO being under compulsion for a longer period of time than if they were in hospital. The most recent figures on CTOs seem to bear this out to some extent. Not only are the number of CTOs far larger than expected, but the cumulative numbers suggest that once in place, CTOs might stay on for some time (Health and Social Care Information Centre 2012). Research on service user views suggests that CTOs can be viewed as the 'lesser of two evils' compared to hospitalisation (Gibbs et al. 2005; Swartz et al. 2003) but it should be questioned whether this view would still hold if compulsion in the community was extended indefinitely. By not limiting who CTOs may be applied to, they may also encompass a broader group than originally envisaged. The Care Quality Commission (2010) analysed 208 CTO cases and found 30% of them did not have a history of non-compliance or disengagement and therefore could be classed as having the potential to be treated voluntarily. Even for the typical 'revolving door' service user, CTOs might not entirely alleviate the issue of repeated admissions; the Health and Social Care Information Centre (2012: 5) states that a slight reduction in the use of Section 3 with a corresponding rise in CTO recalls and revocations, 'lend[s] weight to the suggestion ... that some patients who were recorded as having "repeated formal admissions" before the introduction of CTOs may now be showing as being subject to CTO recalls'. The inferences that can be drawn from this statistical analysis are supported by the findings of a large national randomised controlled trial (OCTET), which has examined the efficacy of CTOs in England, and concluded that they do not reduce the rate of hospital readmissions (Burns et al. 2013). Indeed, contrary to the experience of New Zealand, involuntary admissions in England have continued to rise, increasing by 10% over the past five years (Health and Social Care Information Centre 2012). It is also notable that the detailed data tables of CTO use show marked regional differences across England, which might be understood in terms of differential decision-making from area to area.

Such figures emphasise the need for more domestic research on how CTO policy is being translated into practice, taking country-specific disparities into account. While effectiveness studies like the OCTET trial are important, in a country where the use of CTOs depends so much on practitioner discretion, attention should also be paid to the process of CTO practice, which would involve 'on the ground' study of the perspectives and activities of actors and the ethical and experiential dimensions of CTOs, particularly with reference to how decisions are made, what dilemmas practitioners face and what different uses CTOs are being put to. The views and experiences of service users also have to be accounted for in terms of what changes they think being on a CTO has brought about, what the relationship between compulsion and coercion is and if CTOs have influenced in any way the relationship they have with the practitioners who work with them.

Moreover, most research on practitioner views and practice has focused mainly on psychiatrists, as the official 'decision-makers' with regard to CTOs (Manning et al. 2011; O'Reilly et al. 2000; Romans et al. 2004). The inclusion of other professional groups who work closely with people on CTOs and make the everyday informal decisions around their use, would bring an important insight into what the advent of CTOs might signify. Social workers in particular, do not just work as care coordinators, but also still retain the majority of Approved Mental Health Professional (AMHP) roles (Mackay 2012). As with other Mental Health Act assessments, AMHPs play an important part in deciding whether a CTO should be applied, and if it should be extended. On the face of it that means that AMHP social workers are in a good position to lessen the coercive impact of CTOs by advocating against their use when not appropriate, ensuring that the conditions attached to CTOs are absolutely necessary and emphasising that their consultation on CTOs is treated as a decision-making process rather than a 'rubber stamping' event. It is important to recognise that CTOs in certain circumstances are viewed as helpful both by social workers and the people they work with (Gibbs et al. 2006). However, preliminary findings from research the author is conducting also suggest that CTOs can involve a redrawing of ethical boundaries for mental health social workers, with compulsion within hospital deemed less morally problematic than the extension of that compulsion into daily community practice. In this sense, CTOs symbolise many of the issues present in wider social work practice; social workers often have to balance a commitment to rights and recovery with a consideration of risk and resources. It is important, therefore, for social workers to understand where polices like CTOs come from, and what shapes them, in order so that they can learn from international experiences, but also be able to practise within such a framework in a critically reflective way. An active research agenda on CTOs in this country would add to such a knowledge base for social workers.

Case study: When to discharge a CTO?

This chapter has explored how CTOs developed as a policy, and outlined what that might mean for practice. As has been indicated, practitioners may face ethical dilemmas when using CTOs. This case study will help you think through one of the main dilemmas you might experience, namely, when should a CTO be discharged?

Susan is in her early forties, and lives independently with her teenage son, although her parents are very much involved in her life. They provide a lot of support to Susan,

(Continued)

(Continued)

but there has been conflict between them over the years as well, particularly around how Susan manages her mental health and how she looks after her children.

Susan has been involved with mental health services for seven years, following what she describes as a 'breakdown', after her marriage ended. About four years ago, her parents began telling her care coordinator that her behaviour was becoming increasingly erratic and they were really worried that she was going to become unwell again. The consultant psychiatrist organised a review where an increase in medication was offered, which Susan refused, stating that she felt she was managing fine. Over the next six months, Susan was assessed twice under the Mental Health Act, but as it was judged that she posed little risk to herself or others, she was not detained. Susan's parents were very unhappy about this decision, feeling she was hiding the level of mental distress she was really experiencing. Susan was eventually brought into hospital for treatment, following a difficult late-night Mental Health Act assessment.

After an admission lasting six months, Susan was discharged onto a CTO as the consultant was concerned that she wouldn't take her medication without some compulsion. She has now been on a CTO for three years, with no recalls to hospital, and she feels she has made a good recovery. A tribunal was recently held to ascertain whether the CTO was legally appropriate. Susan's parents feel very strongly that, she needs to stay on the CTO for the foreseeable future and told the tribunal that, although they didn't feel the CTO was needed to ensure Susan complied with medication anymore, it gave them reassurance. Susan has not expressed a desire either way about the CTO and states that she is happy to go along with whatever the team thinks is best. The tribunal somewhat reluctantly upheld the CTO, but suggest that Susan's care team consider its necessity at her next review.

- If you were the care coordinator how would you prepare for the next review and the upcoming decision about whether to keep the CTO on or not?
- How would you involve Susan and her family in the decision-making?
- If you were the AMPH, and the consultant decided they were going to keep the CTO on at the review, would you challenge or agree with their decision?
- What factors would influence your thinking?

Key points

The key points to take away from this chapter are:

- Community Treatment Orders (CTOs) were introduced in England and Wales under the Mental Health Act 2007. They give mental health professionals the power to impose conditions on how service users live in the community, particularly in regard to medication. Their main feature is that they allow for service users to be recalled to hospital if they break conditions and/or if their mental health deteriorates.
- The use of CTOs has grown internationally in the last four decades and are now in place in around 70 different jurisdictions. Their popularity has been driven by

a number of factors, including deinstitutionalisation, the rise of a risk discourse, the dominance of a biomedical model of mental health, and a paternalistic concern with vulnerability and positive liberty.

- It is important for social workers to understand how and why policy mechanisms like CTOs are taken up by policy-makers, in order to think critically about what they might mean for practice. Policy transfer provides part of the picture, and in the case of CTOs, demonstrates that the use of evidence and knowledge from other countries was a highly political and selective strategy by key decision-makers.
- By comparing the characteristics of CTOs in England to other countries, we can see that they have a low threshold for use and consequently are largely reliant on practitioner discretion. Social workers play a significant role in the implementation of CTOs, as both care coordinators and AMHPs, and are in a good position to use their skills and knowledge to mitigate the potentially coercive effect of CTOs. Research on the everyday use of CTOs would highlight the practical and ethical challenges social workers face and provide a foundation for more informed practice.

Acknowledgements

I would like to thank Ian Shaw and Mark Hardy for their helpful comments on an earlier draft of this chapter.

Notes

1. References to England and English mental health law throughout this chapter also apply to Wales.
2. The most well-known and widely cited case was that of Jonathan Zito, a young man murdered in the London Underground in 1992 by Christopher Clunis, who had a diagnosis of schizophrenia. The subsequent inquiry highlighted a number of cumulative systemic failures in Clunis's management and care in the months prior to the murder. Zito's wife went on to set up the Zito Trust, which lobbied strongly for risk-related reforms in policy and practice, and specifically for the introduction of CTOs. The Zito Trust closed in 2009, stating that its objectives had been met with the introduction of the new Act.
3. CTO provisions are made at state level in Australia, Canada and the USA, and so there are a number of distinct CTO regimes within each country. As within-country jurisdictions tend to be similar, for the purpose of this analysis, CTOs will be referred to at a country level, unless there are specific differences worth noting.

References

Appelbaum, P.S. (1998) 'Missing the boat: Competence and consent in psychiatric research', *American Journal of Psychiatry*, 155: 1486–1488.
Appelbaum, P.S. and Gutheil, T.G. (1979) '"Rotting with their rights on": Constitutional theory and clinical reality in drug refusal by psychiatric patients', *Bulletin of the American Academy of Psychiatric Law*, 3: 306–315.

Bar El, Y.C., Durst, R., Rabinowitz, J., Kalian, M., Teitelbaum, A. and Shlafman, M. (1998) 'Implementation of order of compulsory ambulatory treatment in Jerusalem', *International Journal of Law & Psychiatry*, 21 (1): 65–71.

Bartlett, P. and Sandland, R. (2007) *Mental Health Law: Policy and Practice*, 3rd edn. Oxford: Oxford University Press.

Bennett, C. (1997) 'Understanding ripple effects: The cross-national adoption of policy instruments for bureaucratic accountability', *Governance*, 10 (3): 213–233.

Brophy, L. (2009) 'Using the Emancipatory Values of Social Work as a Guide to the Investigation: What Processes and Principles Represent Good Practice with People on Community Treatment Orders?', Unpublished thesis, University of Melbourne, School of Nursing and Social Work, Melbourne.

Brophy, L. and McDermott, F. (2003) 'What's driving involuntary treatment in the community? The social, policy, legal and ethical context', *Australasian Psychiatry*, 11 (1): 84–88.

Burns, T., Rugkasa, J., Molodynski, A., Dawson, J., Yeeles, K., Vazquez-Montes, M., Voysey, M., Sinclair, J. and Priebe, S. (2013) 'Community Treatment Orders for patients with psychosis (OCTET): A randomised controlled trial', *The Lancet*, 381: 1–7.

Cabinet Office (1999) *Modernising Government: White Paper 1999*. Available at: www.archive.official-documents.co.uk/document/cm43/4310/4310.htm (accessed 18 January 2012).

Cairney, P. (2009) '"The British policy style" and mental health: Beyond the headlines', *Journal of Social Policy*, 38 (4): 671–688.

Campbell, J., Brophy, L., Healy, B. and O'Brien, A.-M. (2006) 'International perspectives on the use of Community Treatment Orders: Implications for mental health social workers', *British Journal of Social Work*, 36 (7): 1101–1118.

Care Quality Commission (2010) *Monitoring the Use if the Mental Health Act in 2009/10*. London: Care Quality Commission.

Care Quality Commission (2012) *Monitoring the Use if the Mental Health Act in 2010/11*. London: Care Quality Commission.

Churchill, R., Owen, G., Singh, S. and Hotopf, M. (2007) *International Experiences of Using Community Treatment Orders*. London: Institute of Psychiatry, Kings College London.

Daw, R. (2007) 'The Mental Health Act 2007: The defeat of an ideal', *Journal of Mental Health Law*, November: 131–169.

Dawson, J. (2005) *Community Treatment Orders: International Comparisons*. Dunedin, New Zealand: Otago University Print.

Dawson, J. (2006) 'Fault-lines in community treatment order legislation', *International Journal of Law and Psychiatry*, 29: 482–494.

Dawson, J. (2009) 'Concepts of liberty in mental health law', *Otago Law Review*, 12 (1): 23–36.

Department of Health (DH) (2005) *Government Response to the Report of the Joint Committee on the Draft Mental Health Bill 2004*. London: The Stationery Office.

Dobson, F. (1998) *Frank Dobson Outlines Third Way for Mental Health*, Press Release. London: DH.

Dolowitz, D. (2009) 'Learning by observing: Surveying the international arena', *Policy and Politics*, 37 (3): 317–334.

Dolowitz, D.P. and Marsh, D. (1996) 'Who learns what from whom: a review of the policy transfer literature', *Political Studies*, 44: 343–357.

Dolowitz, D. and Marsh, D. (2000) 'Learning from abroad: The role of policy transfer in contemporary policy making', *Governance*, 13 (1): 5–24.

Evans, M. (2009) 'Policy transfer in critical practice', *Policy Studies*, 30 (3): 243–268.

Evans, M. and Davies, J. (1999) 'Understanding policy transfer: A multi-level, multi-disciplinary perspective', *Public Administration*, 77: 361–386.

Fennell, P. (2005) 'Convention compliance, public safety, and the social inclusion of mentally disordered people', *Journal of Law and Society*, 32 (1): 90–110.

Fistein, E.C., Holland, A.J., Clare, I.C.H. and Gunn, M.J. (2009) 'A comparison of mental health legislation from diverse Commonwealth jurisdictions', *International Journal of Law and Psychiatry*, 32: 147–155.

Geller, J., Fisher, W., Grudzinskas, A., Clayfield, J. and Lawlor, T. (2006) 'Involuntary outpatient treatment as "deinstitutionalised coercion": The net-widening concerns', *International Journal of Law and Psychiatry*, 29 (6): 551–562.

Gibbs, A., Dawson, J. and Mullen, R. (2006) 'Community Treatment Orders for people with serious mental illness: A New Zealand study', *British Journal of Social Work*, 36: 1085–1100.

Gibbs, A., Dawson, J., Ansley, C. and Mullen, R. (2005) 'How patients in New Zealand view community treatment orders', *Journal of Mental Health*, 14 (4): 357–368.

Goffman, E. (1961) *Asylums: Essays on the Social Situation of Mental Patients and Other Inmates*. Toronto: Anchor Books.

Haas, P. (1992) 'Epistemic communities and international policy coordination', *International Organization*, 46 (1): 1–35.

Hall, P. (1993) 'Policy paradigms, social learning and the state: The case of economic policy-making in Britain', *Comparative Politics*, 25: 275–296.

HC Hansard, Vol 461, col 1189, June 18, 2007.

HC Hansard, Vol 461, col 1190, June 18, 2007.

HC Hansard, Vol 461, col 1193, June 18, 2007.

Health and Social Care Information Centre (HSCIC) (October, 2012) *Inpatients Formally Detained in Hospitals under the Mental Health Act 1983, and Patients Subject to Supervised Community Treatment, Annual Figures, England, 2011/12*. Leeds: HSCIC.

Hiday, V. (2003) 'Outpatient commitment: The state of empirical research on its outcomes', *Psychology, Public Policy and Law*, 9 (1): 8–32.

HL Hansard, Vol 688, cols 702–703, January 17, 2007.

HL Hansard, Vol 693, col 843, July 2, 2007.

Holloway, F. (1996) 'Supervised discharge – paper tiger?', *Psychiatric Bulletin*, 20: 193–194.

House of Commons Library, Research Paper 07/33 (30 March 2007).

House of Lords, Paper 79–I (23 March 2005a).

House of Lords, Paper 79–II (23 March 2005b).

Hudson, J. and Lowe, S. (2009) *Understanding the Policy Process: Analysing Welfare Policy and Practice* (2nd edition). Bristol: Policy Press.

Jones, T. (2006) *Policy Transfer and Criminal Justice*. Maidenhead: Open University Press.

Kemshall, H.J. (2002) *Risk, Social Policy and Welfare*. Buckingham: Open University Press.

Kortrijk, H.E., Staring, A.B.P., van Baars, A.W.B. and Mulder, C.L. (2010) 'Involuntary admission may support treatment outcome and motivation in patients receiving assertive community treatment', *Social Psychiatry and Epidemiology*, 45: 245–252.

Lawton-Smith, S. (2005) *A Question of Numbers: The Potential Impact of Community-Based Treatment Orders in England and Wales*, Working paper. London: The Kings Fund.

Lawton-Smith, S., Dawson, J. and Burns, T. (2008) 'Community Treatment Orders are not a good thing', *British Journal of Psychiatry*, 193: 96–100.

Leff, J. (1997), *The Outcome for the Long-Stay Non-Demented Patients in Care in the Community: Illusion or Reality?* Chichester: Wiley.

Mackay, K. (2012) 'A parting of the ways? The diverging nature of mental health social work in the lights of the new Acts in Scotland, and in England and Wales', *Journal of Social Work*, 12: 179–193.

Manning, C., Molodynski, A., Rugkasa, J., Dawson, J. and Burns, T. (2011) 'Community Treatment Orders in England and Wales: National survey of clinicians' views and use', *The Psychiatrist*, 35: 328–333.

May, R., Hartley, J. and Knight, T. (2003) 'Making the personal political', *The Psychologist*, 16 (4): 182–183.

Mental Health Alliance (2007) *The Mental Health Act 2007: The Final Report*. Available at: www.mentalhealthalliance.org.uk/news/prfinalreport.html (accessed 22 July 2015)

Monahan, J., Bonnie, R.J., Appelbaum, P.S., Hyde, P.S., Steadman, H.J. and Swartz, M. (2001) 'Mandated community treatment: Beyond outpatient commitment', *Psychiatric Services*, 52 (9): 1198–1205.

Munetz, M.R. and Frese, F.J. (2001) 'Getting ready for recovery: Reconciling mandatory treatment with the recovery vision', *Psychiatric Rehabilitation Journal*, 25 (1): 35–42.

Novella, E.J. (2010) 'Mental health care in the aftermath of deinstitutionalization: A retrospective and prospective view', *Health Care Analysis*, 18 (3): 222–238.

O'Reilly, R. (2006) 'Community Treatment Orders: An essential therapeutic tool in the face of continuing deinstitutionalization', *Canadian Journal of Psychiatry*, 51: 686–688.

O'Reilly, R.L., Keegan, D.L. and Elias, J.W. (2000) 'A survey of the use of Community Treatment Orders by psychiatrists in Saskatchewan', *Canadian Journal of Psychiatry*, 45 (1): 79–81.

Peay, J. (2003) *Decisions and Dilemmas: Working with Mental Health Law*. Oxford: Hart Publishing.

Peck, J. and Theodore, N. (2010) 'Mobilizing policy: Models, methods and mutations', *Geoforum*, 41: 169–174.

Pilgrim, D. (2007) 'New "mental health" legislation for England and Wales: Some aspects of consensus and conflict', *Journal of Social Policy*, 36 (1): 79–95.

Pilgrim, D. and Ramon, S. (2009) 'English mental health policy under New Labour', *Policy and Politics*, 37 (2): 273–288.

Power, P. (1999) 'Community treatment orders: The Australian experience', *Journal of Forensic Psychiatry*, 10 (1): 9–15.

Prins, H. (2008) 'Counterblast: The Mental Health Act 2007 (a hard act to follow)', *Howard Journal*, 47 (1): 81–85.

Robertson, D.B. (1991) 'Political conflict and lesson drawing', *Journal of Public Policy*, 11 (1): 55–78.

Romans, S., Dawson, J., Mullen, R. and Gibbs, A. (2004) 'How mental health clinicians view community treatment orders: A national New Zealand study', *Australian and New Zealand Journal of Psychiatry*, 38: 836–841.

Rose, R. (1993) *Lesson Drawing in Public Policy: A Guide to Learning Across Time and Space*. Chatham, NJ: Chatham House.

Rose, N. (1996) 'Psychiatry as a political science: Advanced liberalism and the administration of risk', *History of the Human Sciences*, 2: 1–23.

Rose, N. (1999) *Powers of Freedom: Reframing Political Thought*. Cambridge: Cambridge University Press.

Rose, N. (2002a) 'At risk of madness', in T. Baker and J. Simon (eds), *Embracing Risk: The Changing Culture of Insurance and Responsibility*. Chicago, IL: University of Chicago Press.

Rose, N. (2002b) 'Society, madness and control', in A. Buchanan (ed.), *Care of the Mentally Disorder Offender in the Community*. Oxford: Oxford University Press.

Royal College of Psychiatrists (2009) *Recorded Matters Working Group*. London: Royal College of Psychiatrists.

Sjostrom, S., Zetterberg, L. and Markstrom, U. (2011) 'Why community compulsion became the solution: Reforming mental health law in Sweden', *International Journal of Law and Psychiatry*, 34: 419–428.

Smith, A. (2004) 'Policy transfer in the development of UK climate policy', *Policy and Politics*, 32 (1): 79–93.

Stone, D. (1999) 'Learning lessons and transferring policy across time, space and disciplines', *Politics*, 19: 51–59.

Swartz, M.S., Swanson, J.F., Wagner, R.H., Hannon, M.J., Burns, B.J. and Shumway, M. (2003) '"Assessment of four stakeholder group" preferences concerning outpatient commitment for persons with schizophrenia', *American Journal of Psychiatry*, 160: 1139–1146.

Torrey, E. and Kaplan, R. (1995) 'A national survey of the use of outpatient commitment', *Psychiatric Services*, 46: 778–784.

Wagner, H.R., Swartz, M.S., Swanson, J.W. and Burns, B.J. (2003) 'Does involuntary outpatient commitment lead to more intensive treatment?', *Psychology, Public Policy, and Law*, 9 (1–2): 145–158.

Wales, H.W. and Hiday, V.A. (2006) 'PLC or TLC: Is outpatient commitment the/an answer?', *International Journal of Law and Psychiatry*, 29: 451–468.

Wolff, N. (2002) 'Risk, response, and mental health policy: Learning from the experience of the United Kingdom', *Journal of Health Politics, Policy and Law*, 27 (5): 801–832.

Concluding Thoughts: The Interface between Social Policy and Social Work

Frank Keating

This book aimed to explore the relationship between social policy and social work, and proposed that social policy and social work are interconnected and as such it is argued that this relationship should be construed as dualistic. Policy is central to defining and shaping the nature of social work at both professional and practice levels. Likewise, social work practice can inform social policy development, but it has to be acknowledged that there is more limited scope for this to happen in the UK context. Social policy sets the priorities for action in the prevailing ideological context, whereas social work can be construed as 'policy in action' (Denney 1998). The concerns of social policy and social work fit into the same conceptual framework: to achieve social change with some overlaps and differences in their paradigmatic approaches (Denney 1998; Ramon 1998). A further aim of the book was to consider to what extent a critical perspective can help social workers to unravel the complexities surrounding policy and practice. It is inevitable that an edited book cannot be inclusive of all the concerns of social policy and social work. For example, a significant development in the welfare landscape is the Social Care Act 2014 that come into force in April 2015 and therefore fell outside the scope and time frame of this book.

Writing a concluding chapter that attempts to bring a neat 'pulling together' of the themes captured in this book is not easy, given the different epistemological and political stances and the nuanced differences across national and international contexts. A range of ideas and perspectives have been put forward in this book and these clearly point to the tensions between policy, welfare and politics in general and social work in particular. Social policy should take account of the broader social trends such as changing family structures, people moving across frontiers (legitimately and illegitimately), reduction in state involvement in welfare and a greater role for the private sector in providing welfare services. The last few years have seen a significant shift away from a broader understanding of welfare that emphasised collective wellbeing towards a more narrowed focus on individualism and social responsibility. Moves to privatise child protection services and to use social firms or enterprises to provide child and family welfare support are some recent examples. Developments such as these go against the principles of citizenship, social justice and rights-based approaches to welfare (Fraser 2005) and should be challenged.

Interface between social policy and social work

Social policy and social work are mutually interlinked. Policy can inform practice and similarly practice can inform policy although there are limited examples of the latter. The link between social policy and social work is multi-faceted, which stems from some differences and overlaps between the two disciplines. These pertain to values, scientific paradigms and characterisations (Ramon 1998). Social work places a value on supporting individuals and a focus on process, whereas social policy emphasises outcomes and collectives such as groups and communities or society as a whole. Policy adopts a more positivistic methodological stance in its focus on defining and meeting need whereas social work adopts a methodological stance along a continuum from positivism to heuristics (Ramon 1998). Social work premises its knowledge base on co-construction of knowledge between practitioners and service users, families and carers. Policy developments, on the other hand, are mainly informed by what is sometimes called 'hard' evidence. In terms of how the two disciplines are characterised, social policy is a discipline while social work is both a discipline and a profession. This duality is probably the most significant tension for social work: it is responsible to the state, service users, organisational contexts and must meet professional standards set by the regulating body (Dickens 2010).

Tensions for social workers are, for example, evident in that they are expected or required to implement policy through applying their authority as gatekeepers to valuable resources and fulfilling their powers and duties as enshrined in legislation, which often runs against the value base of the profession that promotes a commitment to anti-oppressive practice and social justice. The struggle for race equality as outlined by Frank Keating in Chapter 7 demonstrates this and also points to the ways in which policy and market principles can undermine the ideals of social work.

Key role of social policy in relation to social work

Social policy operates at two levels, that is to say professional layers and at practice level. The way in which policy shapes professional identity is evident in developments in relation to social work education. Alix Walton in Chapter 2 highlighted the sea changes in policy over the last 40 years and the centrality of policy in shaping ideas about the profession, and how we define the role of social workers and the implications of this for social work education and training. Hence the ensuing debates about whether preparing social workers for practice should be cast as education or training. The latter idea is gaining prominence in the UK espoused by views that practice can be improved by recruiting and fast-tracking high academic achievers who receive an intensive burst of training and are then placed in a practice context where the 'on the job' training continues. Examples of this are the Department for Education's 'Frontline' initiative for child and family social work (Clifton 2012) and the Department of Health's 'Think Ahead' initiative for mental health social work (Clifton and Thorley 2014). On the surface, it seems that these developments aim to improve the intellectual standing of social work, but on closer analysis it is deeply anti-intellectual in advocating or suggesting that social workers can mainly acquire competence through 'on the job' learning. Experiential learning is of great value, but the demands of practice require social workers to also be able to apply critical thinking to decisions that cannot be developed in the turbulence of everyday practice.

At practice level, policy informs social work's aims to promote positive wellbeing, reduce risk (e.g. safeguarding, protection), support and promote prevention. However, it seems that the risk agenda enshrined in current policy is a key force in practice decisions. Hannah Jobling in Chapter 10 illustrated how community treatment orders have developed to advance service users' rights, but when this is explored in greater depth it becomes clear that the policy is effectively aimed at addressing growing concerns about risk and safety. Jobling suggested that there needs to be a balance between managing risk and enhancing the ability of service users to make informed decisions about treatment. Risk aversiveness and how to manage it is nowhere as evident as in the discourse about safeguarding and protection. Rick Hood in Chapter 3, for example, showed how policy has shifted from a narrow focus on safeguarding and protection of children to a more rights-based focus as contained in *Every Child Matters* and how it has returned to a focus on protection and targeting high risk families. Anna Gupta in Chapter 4 has demonstrated how policy in relation to looked after children can limit and constrain professional practice to a narrow focus on meeting targets such as reduced times for adoption approvals. However, we should bear in mind that social work does not take a subordinate role to policy and therefore should not characterise social workers as bereft of agency. This book pointed to the fact that discretion (discussed in Chapter 1) is widespread. Gupta in Chapter 4, for example, explored how professionals have discretion in defining thresholds for intervention, but also argued that it is vulnerable to organisational and other external factors.

Maria Brent in Chapter 5 demonstrated how personalisation shows promise for promoting wellbeing based on the principles of empowerment, choice and control. She goes on to explore how the policy affects and shapes practice and suggests that this policy cast service users as consumers to fit the neoliberal agenda and that practice is therefore informed by market principles and not the ideals of empowerment that are central to social work.

The role of social work in relation to social policy

Social work straddles the demands of the state to bring discipline and order to society and its own value base and imperatives to strive for social justice (Denney 1998). It plays a vital role in how the principles enshrined in policy are translated into practice, as illustrated in this book. Social workers therefore have to balance competing demands such as responsibility to the state, service users (and families and carers), their organisational contexts and professional standards (Dickens 2010). Three key roles have been suggested in this book: implementation, advocacy, and challenge and change. Tony Evans and Fabian Kessl in Chapter 8 outlined how social workers can use policy to assist individuals and also how they can challenge and critique the shortcomings of policy. Donna Chung in Chapter 9 also demonstrated how activism can influence and change policy on the one hand, and inform practice on the other. These are good examples of critical social work practice.

Towards transformative practice

How do we overcome or at least manage these tensions in practice? Denney's (1998) suggestion that we need new forms of analysis for the advancement and development of social work and social policy is still relevant in the current context. Social workers need to develop critical thinking skills to embrace both 'downstream' theoretical standpoints (meeting the imperatives to fulfil our duties and powers as social workers) and 'upstream' stances (those that challenge the status quo). In this way social workers can analyse the scope for building resilience, social capital and supporting those who are in greatest need, which require an analysis that throws light on the impact of social policy and social structures on the lives of service users (Weiss et al. 2006). If social work is to be able to inform policy and policy development, it should shift focus from developing competencies or capabilities to a more pluralistic ideal: meeting human need and raising consciousness about the ways in which structural arrangements exacerbate human suffering.

The interconnections between social policy and social work can be strengthened through a closer alignment between the aims of social policy and the value base of social work by refocusing on human rights and social justice. Fraser (2005) argues that social justice requires arrangements that make it possible for all to participate fully in social life. This demands an emphasis on social relationships, a focus on those who 'lose out' or are invisible and to intervene where required. In this way we should be able to support those in greatest need, redress social inequality and promote social justice.

References

Clifton, J. (2012) (ed.) *Frontline: Improving the Children's Social Work Profession*. London: Institute for Public Research.

Clifton, J. and Thorley, C. (2014) *Think Ahead: Meeting the Workforce Challenges in Mental Health Social Work*. London: Institute for Public Research.

Denney, D. (1998) *Social Policy and Social Work*. Oxford: Clarendon Press.

Dickens, J. (2010) *Social Work and Social Policy: An Introduction*. London: Routledge.

Fraser, N. (2005) 'Reframing justice in a social world', *New Left Review*, 36: 69–88.

Ramon, S. (1998) *Interface between Social Policy and Social Work*. Birmingham: Venture Press.

Weiss, I., Gal, J. and Katan , J. (2006) 'Social policy for social work', *British Journal of Social Work*, 36: 789–806.

Index